First World War
and Army of Occupation
War Diary
France, Belgium and Germany

20 DIVISION
Divisional Troops
Royal Army Service Corps
Divisional Train (158, 159, 160, 161 Companies A.S.C.)
28 July 1915 - 30 April 1919

WO95/2110/5

The Naval & Military Press Ltd
www.nmarchive.com
Published in association with The National Archives

Published by

The Naval & Military Press Ltd

Unit 10 Ridgewood Industrial Park,

Uckfield, East Sussex,

TN22 5QE England

Tel: +44 (0) 1825 749494

www.naval-military-press.com

www.nmarchive.com

This diary has been reprinted in facsimile from the original. Any imperfections are inevitably reproduced and the quality may fall short of modern type and cartographic standards.

© Crown Copyright
Images reproduced by permission of The National Archives, London, England, 2015.

Contents

Document type	Place/Title	Date From	Date To
Heading	2110/5		
Heading	20th Division 20th Divl Train A.S.C. Jly 1915 Apr 1919 (158,159,160,161, Coys ASC)		
Miscellaneous	Army Book, 136a.		
Miscellaneous	Notes In The History of The 20th Train		
Miscellaneous	20th Div Train.		
Heading	War Diary 158-61 Extracted from HQ 20 DT. Army Book 136. 30/5/20		
Miscellaneous	March 1918p		
War Diary	Co To D.D.T		
Heading	1st Co to DHQ.		
Miscellaneous	Co To pain in have		
Miscellaneous			
Heading	20th Division. 20th Div. Train Vol I. Jly To Sept 15		
Miscellaneous	War Diary of O.C. 20th Divisional Train A.S.C From 28/7/15 To 30/9/15 The Officer i/c Adjutant General office at the Base		
War Diary	Lumbres	28/07/1915	28/07/1915
War Diary	Merris	29/07/1915	28/08/1915
War Diary	Estaires	30/08/1915	30/08/1915
War Diary	Estaires	03/09/1915	30/09/1915
Heading	War Diary Of O.C 20th Divisional Train A.S.C. From 1st-31st October 1915		
War Diary	Estaires	01/10/1915	31/10/1915
Heading	20th Divl Train Vol 3 Nov 15.		
Heading	War Diary Of O.C 20th Divisional Train A.S.C. From 1st November 1915-30th November 1915		
War Diary	Estaires	01/11/1915	30/11/1915
Heading	20th Div. Train Vol 4, 121/7935		
Heading	War Diary Of O.C 20th Divisional Train ASC From 1st December 1915 To 31 December 1915 Volume 4		
War Diary	Estaires	01/12/1915	31/12/1915
Heading	20th Divn. Train Vol 5 January 1916		
Heading	War Diary Of O.C. 20th Divisional Train. From 1st January 1916-31 January 1916		
War Diary	Estaires	01/01/1916	12/01/1916
War Diary	Blaringhem	12/01/1916	22/01/1916
War Diary	Oxelaere	23/01/1916	31/01/1916
Heading	War Diary Of O.C. 20th Divisional Train ASC From 1st To 29th February 1916		
War Diary	Oxelaere	01/02/1916	03/02/1916
War Diary	Esquelbec	04/02/1916	12/02/1916
War Diary	Poperinghe	13/02/1916	29/02/1916
Heading	War Diary Of O.C. 20th Divisional Train ASC From 1st-31st March 1916		
War Diary	Poperinghe	01/03/1916	31/03/1916
Heading	War Diary Of O.C. 20th Divisional Train From 1st To 30th April 1916. Vol 8		
War Diary	Poperinghe	01/04/1916	17/04/1916
War Diary	Esquelbec	18/04/1916	30/04/1916

Heading	D.A.G. 3rd Echelon. Herewith Please Find My Diary For May. The oversight in Not Forwarding it is Requested.		
War Diary	Esquelbec	01/05/1916	20/05/1916
War Diary	Poperinghe	20/05/1916	31/05/1916
Heading	D.A.G. 3rd Echelon, Base, Herewith Please Find War Diary For June.		
War Diary	Poperinghe	01/06/1916	30/06/1916
War Diary	War Diary Of O.C. 20th Divisional Train ASC From 1st to 31st July 1916		
War Diary	Poperinghe	01/07/1916	17/07/1916
War Diary	Esquelbec	18/07/1916	19/07/1916
War Diary	Bailleul	20/07/1916	25/07/1916
War Diary	Doullens	26/07/1916	26/07/1916
War Diary	Bus-Les-Artois.	27/07/1916	29/07/1916
War Diary	Couin	30/07/1916	31/07/1916
Heading	War Diary Of O.C. 20th Divisional Train ASC. From 1st To 31st August 1916. Vol 11		
Heading	Headquarters 20th Division. Herewith Diary for Current Month.		
War Diary	Couin	01/08/1916	16/08/1916
War Diary	Beauval	17/08/1916	18/08/1916
War Diary	Villers Bocage	19/08/1916	19/08/1916
War Diary	Treux	20/08/1916	20/08/1916
War Diary	F.26.d.1.3. Albert.	21/08/1916	21/08/1916
War Diary	Near Albert.	22/08/1916	22/08/1916
War Diary	Grove Town	23/08/1916	31/08/1916
Heading	War Diary Of O.C. 20th Divisional Train, ASC From 1st to 30th September 1916		
Heading	Headquarters, 20. Division. J Beg to forward War Diary For Period Month Herewith 30/9/16		
War Diary	Grovetown	01/09/1916	08/09/1916
War Diary	Corbie	09/09/1916	10/09/1916
War Diary	Forked Tree	11/09/1916	13/09/1916
War Diary	Grove Town.	14/09/1916	30/09/1916
Heading	20th Division Train. October 1916 Vol 13		
Heading	Headquarters 20th Division. Herewith My Diary For October 31/10/16		
Heading	War Diary of O.C. 20th Divisional Train ASC From 1st to 31st October 1916		
War Diary	Grove Town	01/10/1916	01/10/1916
War Diary	T 27.b Central	02/10/1916	07/10/1916
War Diary	Map 6 2 D	08/10/1916	12/10/1916
War Diary	F 27.C. Central (Map 62 Corbie)	13/10/1916	18/10/1916
War Diary	Vignacourt	19/10/1916	20/10/1916
War Diary	Belloy. Sur Somme	21/10/1916	31/10/1916
Heading	War Diary of O.C 20th Divisional Train ASC. From 1st to 30th November 1916		
War Diary	Oissy.	01/11/1916	15/11/1916
War Diary	Corbie	16/11/1916	11/12/1916
War Diary	F 27.a	12/12/1916	17/12/1916
War Diary	A 14d	18/12/1916	24/12/1916
War Diary	Corbie	25/12/1916	31/12/1916
Heading	War Diary of the No. 20 Divisional Supply Column January 1917 Vol 18		
Heading	War Diary of the 20th Divisional Train January 1917		

War Diary	Corbie	01/01/1917	01/01/1917
War Diary	F 17d.8.8.	04/01/1917	18/01/1917
War Diary	Minden	18/01/1917	23/01/1917
War Diary	Plateau	24/01/1917	28/01/1917
War Diary	Heilly	29/01/1917	31/01/1917
Heading	War Diary of 20th Divisional Train A.S.C. February 1917 Vol 17		
War Diary	Heilly	01/02/1917	08/02/1917
War Diary	Plateau A21.a.2.9	08/02/1917	08/02/1917
War Diary	Plateau	10/02/1917	27/02/1917
Heading	War Diary of 20th Divisional Train. March 1917 Vol 18		
War Diary	Plateau	02/03/1917	31/03/1917
Heading	War Diary 20th Divisional Train April 1917 Vol 19		
War Diary	Maricourt Bois A 16 C 9.7	01/04/1917	04/04/1917
War Diary	Maricourt Bois	05/04/1917	25/04/1917
War Diary	Lechelle	26/04/1917	30/04/1917
Heading	War Diary 20th Divisional Train May 1917 Vol 20		
War Diary	Lechelle	01/05/1917	23/05/1917
War Diary	Bapaume	25/05/1917	31/05/1917
Heading	War Diary of 20th Divnl From June 1917 Vol 21		
War Diary	Bapaume	01/06/1917	30/06/1917
Heading	War Diary 20th Divisional Train July 1917		
War Diary	Bernaville	01/07/1917	21/07/1917
War Diary	Proven	21/07/1917	31/07/1917
Heading	War Diary 20th Divisional Train Vol 23		
War Diary	Proven	01/08/1917	05/08/1917
War Diary	Peselhoek	06/08/1917	19/08/1917
War Diary	Proven	20/08/1917	31/08/1917
Heading	War Diary Divisional Train Vol 24		
War Diary	Proven	01/09/1917	11/09/1917
War Diary	Dragon Camp.	12/09/1917	29/09/1917
War Diary	Proven	30/09/1917	01/10/1917
War Diary	Rocquigny	02/10/1917	05/10/1917
War Diary	Nurlu	06/10/1917	31/10/1917
Heading	Herewith War Diary For Month November 1917		
War Diary	Nurlu	01/11/1917	30/11/1917
Miscellaneous	HQ. Qrs G 20th Divn Herewith War Diary For The Month Of December 1917		
War Diary	Nurlu	01/12/1917	05/12/1917
War Diary	Albert	06/12/1917	06/12/1917
War Diary	Fruges	07/12/1917	12/12/1917
War Diary	Blaringhem	13/12/1917	06/01/1918
War Diary	Heksken	07/01/1918	16/02/1918
War Diary	Blaringhem	17/02/1918	23/02/1918
War Diary	Ercheu	24/02/1918	28/02/1918
Miscellaneous	20th Division G. Herewith War Diary For The Month Of March. Lieut Colonel Comdg 20th Div Train		
War Diary	Ercheu	01/03/1918	22/03/1918
War Diary	Beaulieu	23/03/1918	23/03/1918
War Diary	Roye	23/03/1918	24/03/1918
War Diary	Gooyen Court	25/03/1918	25/03/1918
War Diary	Le Quesnel	26/03/1918	26/03/1918
War Diary	Mezieres	27/03/1918	27/03/1918
War Diary	Fossemanent	28/03/1918	28/03/1918
War Diary	Molliens-Vidame	29/03/1918	29/03/1918
War Diary	Fossemanent	28/03/1918	28/03/1918

War Diary	Molliens-Vidame	29/03/1918	29/03/1918
War Diary	Huchenneville	30/03/1918	30/03/1918
War Diary	Cahon	31/03/1918	31/03/1918
Heading	20th Div. G. Herewith War Diary For Month Of April 1918		
War Diary	Cahon	01/04/1918	06/04/1918
War Diary	Allery	07/04/1918	10/04/1918
War Diary	Grebault Mesnil	11/04/1918	11/04/1918
War Diary	Gamaches	12/04/1918	17/04/1918
War Diary	Frohen-Le Grand	18/04/1918	19/04/1918
War Diary	Herlin-Le-Sec	19/04/1918	20/04/1918
War Diary	Mingoval	21/04/1918	30/04/1918
War Diary	Chateau De La Haie	30/04/1918	30/04/1918
War Diary	Mingoval	01/05/1918	02/05/1918
War Diary	Villers Au Bois	02/05/1918	07/05/1918
War Diary	Chateau De La Haie	08/05/1918	06/10/1918
War Diary	Mingoval	07/10/1918	31/10/1918
War Diary	Cambrai	01/10/1918	02/10/1918
War Diary	Avesnes Lez-Aubert	02/11/1918	05/11/1918
War Diary	Vendigies	06/11/1918	08/11/1918
War Diary	Le-Grand.	08/11/1918	08/11/1918
War Diary	Bavoi	09/11/1918	11/11/1918
War Diary	Feignies	12/11/1918	22/11/1918
War Diary	Jenlain	23/11/1918	24/11/1918
War Diary	Bermerain	25/11/1918	26/11/1918
War Diary	Rieux.	26/11/1918	27/11/1918
War Diary	Cambrai	28/11/1918	30/11/1918
War Diary	Pas.	01/12/1918	28/02/1919
War Diary	Pas-En-Artois	01/03/1919	30/04/1919

2110/5

20TH DIVISION

20TH DIVL TRAIN A.S.C.

JLY 1915-APR 1919

(158, 159, 160, 161 Coys ASC)

Army Book, 136a.

4U

SUPPLIED
FOR THE
PUBLIC SERVICE

(5813) Wt.7537-M2975. 400M. Books 136A. 9-17. B. & S.

Notes on the History of the 20th Div. Train

Marched from Training Establishment Aldershot on 11th Nov. 1914 under command of ~~Major~~ Major Capt. Hardy ~~then Captain~~ then Captain, to Churchill School House, Crondall, the following officers then being with the Train

~~Captain~~ Major Clegg

" Clapper M.C.

" Cadbury-Brown

" (Scaines)

(Captain Hathaway)

" Meade

On 13th Nov 1914 Lt Col. E.W.S. Scott then Major joined the Train and

Major Hardy assumed the duties of Adjutant. The Train remained at Crondall until the commencement of March 1915, Lt Col E.W.W. Scott, leaving the Train about Feb. 1915 & handed over to Lieut Col Hamilton DSO then Major. During Lt Col E.W.W. Scott's period of command he strongly supported sport & he organised several Paper chases, the Train sending a team in several Cross Country races, one of which terminated at Farnham & the Train team being second & were congratulated in the A.S.C. magazine published from A'shot. The Brain also sent a team to compete in the Southern Counties Amateur Cross Country Championship held at A'shot in season 1914-15 competing against over one thousand competitors, thousands of spectators assembling to witness the finish of the race which was over a course of about 7½ miles, this being a military gathering the G.O.C. of the A'shot Command was present & gave the winners the medals.

About the commencement of March 1915 the Train proceeded to Stratfield Saye, & ~~took~~ taking up quarters at the Duke of Wellington's residence, whilst there, the supply details were re-organised, the Training establishment Aldershot with-drawing all the Privates in the two trades, bakers & butchers to form Field Bakeries & Field Butcheries respectively & replacing these men with clerks. On Easter Monday at Stratfield-Saye, Train held a sports meeting, Lieut DE KOCK winning the Officers race, Sergt

Hayes winning the N.C.O's race, Dr Pearman winning the 100 yds & 440 yds. Cmdt Lamb winning the mile & 1st Company winning the relay race. Mrs Hardy (Major Hardy's wife) presenting the prizes to the winners. On the 14th or 15th April the Divl. Train entrained at Mortimer for Salisbury Plain detraining at Amesbury & proceeded to occupy the Camp allotted for the Train known as Rollestone Camp. Here the supply Details were re-organised & were responsible for the feeding of the Division at Lark-hill-camps & were attending lectures held by Major N. L. Craig then S.S.O. of Division. About the 18th of April 1915 Lt Colonel Conway-Gordon arrived and assumed Command of the Divisional Train, vice Lieut. Col. Hamilton D.S.O. who remained as supernumary. The Transport details were then occupied in distributing supplies & also equipping, the stores being drawn from Tidworth, also training in Wagon Drill & Riding School. S.S.M. Butt taking the Riding school & Wagon

Drill assisted by Rough Riding Sergt. Madley. S.S.M. Ritchie was performing the duties of R.S.M. & Captain W.C. Biggs the duties of Adjutant. (~~to whom much credit was due for the efficiency of the Train on embarkation~~). Whilst at Rolleston Camp the Train competed in the Divisional Sports held at Larkhill but failed to attain any successes. Also about the end of June the Divisional Train together with the remainder of the Division was inspected by His Majesty the King ~~at home~~.

~~placed with the parade.~~

The transport at war be also inspected in marching order by the G.O.C. Division Major Genl Davies whilst on Salisbury Plain. During the month of June the details for the respective Field Ambulances & the 1st Line Transport personnel were despatched to their various Units. Two days before date of embarkation which was on 21st July 1915 the 4 Motor Cars then on the establishment of the Train arrived and also the Field Post Office details. The Train embark-

ed at Southampton and
dis-embarked at Le Havre
marching to a camp in the
town preparatory to entrain-
ing at the Gare Maritime
in the evening, arriving
at Lumbres about 2 am
on morning of 23rd July 1915
On or about the 26 July 1915
Lieut Col Conway Gordon
proceeded to take of ~~the~~
an M.T. Command ~~of CCR Corps Troops~~, Major
Hamilton then assuming
Command of the Train.
On the 27 July, the Train
proceeded by road to
MERRIS halting for the night
of 27 at LYNDE ~~&~~ ~~29~~ 28th
~~at RENESCURE~~. arriving at
MERRIS on 29th. While the
Train at MERRIS the No 2

Coy of the Train joined
the Eighth Division for
instructional purposes
along with the 59th Brigade
On 27th Aug Train moved
to ESTAIRES. During stay
at ESTAIRES nothing ex-
traordinary occurred.
Major F.B. Hardy being
transferred to Home
Establishment from Co
No 160. being succeeded
by Major Cadbury Brown
On 10 Jan 1916 Train
proceeded to rest area
in vicinity of BLARINGHEM
from there to area of CASSEL
Train HQ Qrs being at
Chateau in OXELAERE. on the
24th Jan 1916. moving from
there to ESQUELBECQ [illegible]

to ST JANS TER BIEZEN
on 11th Feb 1916, nothing
worthy of note occurred the
Train being ~~107~~ 6 Company
moving out in rest area
to ESQUELBECQ on 17 Apl. 1918.
being relieved at ST JANS
TER BIEZEN by the 6 Div.
Train. Whilst in this area
the 3 Brigade Co's with
their respective Brigades
proceeded to rest camp
at CALAIS. 61st Bde going
first for 10 days followed
by 60 Bde for 10 days
who were relieved by
59th Bde who were with-
drawn on 12th May at a
few hours notice receiv-
ing the order at 4.30 pm
& being on the road in.

marching order by 7pm the No 2 Coy along with their Brigade was complimented by the Brig Genl. on March discipline maintained & the way in which the forced marches were carried out. The Train moved up to POPERINGHE taking over camps vacated by the Guards Divn Train on 20 May (situated on the PROVEN road.) Moving from there less No 1 Co on 16 July 1916 for the ESQUELBECQ road area two or three days afterwards the No 3 Co along with the 60 Bde proceeded to the vicinity of NIEPPE

& No. 2 Co along with the 59th Bde of Infantry moved on the 20th July 1916 to LE LEUTHE S.E. of BAILLEUL in relief of the Australians. The Train afterwards moving by train to FREVENT detraining there about the 25th July, the Bde Coys being with their respective Bdes, (& the Head qrs Coy No 1, still being with the Artillery in the PROVEN RD camp.) halting at BOUQUEMAISON on 25th and AUTHIE on 26th arriving at COUIN on or about 28th July 1916. The three Bde Companies were encamped together the Headquarters Train being in the village.

Nothing worthy of note occurred during the the stay there. The Train the less HdQrs Company then proceeded on the 18th Aug to the Somme battle stay in the following areas en route 18th BEAUVAL 19th VILLERS BOCAGE 20 MEAULTE 21st HAPPY VALLEY, & then back to GROVE TOWN the Railhead on 23rd. There was a great demand for Transport for both water carrying, supplies & R.E. work, some of the horses & wagons being employed until early hours of the morning after being out on duty all day. We were then ordered to make improvised pack saddles which were very urgently required to carry rations and water up to the forward dump. Whilst here the HQ Coy company joined the Train having marched from the POPERINGHE area, about the 2nd week in September 1916. After the battle of Guillemont & Guinchy the Division ~~less Artillery~~ was moved to CORBIE area as also the Div Train, on the 8th Sept, but were forced to come back on the 11th Sept in relieved of either 6 Div or Guards Div who were held up in front of MORVAL. The Div Train arrived back at Grove Town on that Date. On the 1st October the Train Hd Coy & also the 4 Companies moved to HAPPY VALLEY the railhead was also moved there. The 9th Oct saw the three Bde Coy's along with the Inf Bdes & Train Hd Coy move back to the MEAULTE area & from there proceeded to the rest area in & around PICQUIGNY arriving in that area about the 21st October 1916. Whilst in this area the 60th Inf Bde held a Flat race meeting the Train horses figuring

About this period Capt Napper MS. was gazetted Major & was transferred to 61st Divn Train.

rather prominently.
About the 2nd Nov. 1916 the ~~Train~~ Bde Coy together with the other Units of the Division out at rest were moved into the MOLLIENS VIDAME area the 61st Bde held a Race Meeting & the Train horses were again prominent. Moving from that area to the Corbie area about the 16 Nov 1916. Whilst in this area ~~a~~ the ~~[illegible]~~ baggage of ~~Wagons~~ Sections from the 3 Bde Companies were detached ~~under Lt [illegible]~~ & were detailed for duty by the 29 Division & were attached to the 29th Div Train for accommodation

& rations at the PLATEAU. (nr MARICOURT) The remainder of the Train moved up to the PLATEAU & took over the Camps from 29 Div Train excepting no 1 Coy who were still in the HAPPY VALLEY.

The camps at the PLATEAU were in a dreadful state in fact the conditions at this period were probably the worst experienced by the Train both for personnel & animals. There was also a great demand for transport. The supply wagons being often having to turn

out for fatigues after delivering suplies & the whole of the baggage Wagons were in use daily on fatigues & in the ~~evening~~ night were used to bring back French feet cases from Guinchy corner getting back sometimes between 2 & 4 oclock in the morning. About the 23rd December the Train less No 1 Co commenced to move to the CORBIE area again completing the move by the 24 December. Nothing of importance during rest.
Moved up to PLATEAU

~~to~~ on 2 January & taking over camp vacated by 17th Div. Train.
About this period Lt Col Hamilton proceeded on leave to U.K. & did not return. Lt Col Standen arrived & took command. The Train transport was performing the duties as on previous occasion in that area.
On the 27 Jan. the Train less 4th Co moved to CORBIE area & on ~~a~~ 6 Feb ~~we~~ moved to MARICOURT. Whilst here the Decauville system was utilized by the Division for

the first time to convey rations to the Units, also No 1 Company moved from HAPPY VALLEY to the PLATEAU.

About this time Capt Adj Bigg was transferred to 35 Div. Train & Capt C.S. Evans (then OC No 2 Coy.) assumed the duties of Adjutant. On the 27th March the 3 Bde Coy. moved to LEUZE WOOD & on the 6th April to ROCQUIGNY area also Train Hd Qrs & No 1 Co. arrived in that area about that date. The Supplies at this period were conveyed by Decauville up to

Bapaume road having been split up at the Railhead at MARICOURT & were delivered from the Decauville to the Units by the Supply Wagons providing the ~~[illegible]~~ the Train arrived at its destination as frequently it was necessary for the Wagons to proceed to COMBLES owing to breakdowns on the line.

On & about the 28th the Train moved to BAPAUME taking over camp on the BAPAUME–ARRAS road vacated by the 5 Australian Divisional Train.

Sports held in conjunction with 14 Reserve Park at this Camp (May)

Beginning of September found the Train occupying camps outside PROVEN & moving up to PESELHOEK area on the 11 September refilling from PESELHOEK railhead

About the beginning of October the Train moved to NURLU occupying camps on the PERONNE – FINS road. & on the 30? November was forced to make a hurried departure owing to the Enemy advance, but this

was for one day only ~~the~~ as we moved back to the camp the next morning.
Prior to the enemy advance the ~~Tra~~ ration dumps were in HEUDICOURT, the supply section was also detached & were located in HEUDICOURT.
On the 4th December the Train commenced to move by road to the BLARINGHEM area (less No 1 Company) arriving in that area about the 12th December 1917.
On the 6th Jan 1918 commenced to move to WESTOUTRE area the

Companies occupying camps just outside RENINGHELST. vacated by the 34th Div. Train. On 13th Feb. commenced to move to BLARINGHEM area & on or about the 20th entrained at MORBECQUE & detrained at NESLE station moving up to ERCHEU ~~area~~, whilst here the supplies were drawn in bulk from NESLE by supply wagons & ~~the~~ delivered to the respective dumps & were picked up the following morning by the Unit Trans. post. ~~[illegible]~~ whilst

here the Division
had a race meeting
at ERCHU.
On the 21st March the
Train moved up to the
east of HAM. then ~~[illegible]~~ the CO's
~~[illegible]~~ moved back
along with the respective
Brigades.

Div. Train

50th Div. Train

~~17. Oct 1914~~

1 N.C.O. & 30 men reported to "C" Square Aldershot from Thornhill Camp (Mr. Seabome – Sgt. the N.C.O.) from 130 Coy Drill. 13 Oct 1914. No officer at all. Two days later Lieut. Hardy arrived – say 17th Oct. Formed a H.Q. Coy. Went on route marches. No horses. All in civvy clothes. 27 Oct. 3 Companies of train formed, 159, 160 & 161. 11th Nov. moved to ~~Cro~~ Crondall. ~~Div~~ Training. No horses. Winter & Xmas. 1st March to Strathfieldsaye for training. Supply work. Dummy dumps. 15th March left Strathfieldsaye & went to Salisbury Plain for Div. Training. First met the Div. ~~at~~ Left July 21st. 22nd Div. Train (161 Coy) left Southampton in S.S. Maidan. Arrived Havre 23rd. July 25 Arrived St Omer.

1st Commanding Offr. Major McKenzie a few weeks ~~Major~~ Lt. Col. C. Conway-Gordon for training

Then Capt. White. A few weeks.

10th Nov. Major E.W.W. Scott, till Feb 1915. Major Haughton D.S.O. who brought Train out. Left in Jan ~~18~~ 17. Then Lt. Col. Standen 4 Jan. 1917.

Easter Sunday. '15 Div. first formed.

S.S.O. Capt. N.L. Craig. ? One other | The Major Dawes.

WAR DIARY
158-61

Extracted from
H.Q. 20 D.T.

ARMY BOOK 136.

30/8/20

(1034) Wt 15512/M1397. 450M. Bks. 4/17. B. M. & S.

1918

March, 8

March 9

March 10

March 11
C.O. visits No. 4 Coy & No. 1. Coy. with Adjutant.

March 12th.
C.O. inspects wagons with A.A.&Q.M.G. re alteration of head ropes.
C.O. to No. 3. Coy.

March 13.
C.O. inspects Field Amb.
Lieut to Train H.Q. as Remaining officer.
2/Lieut Barnes to No 4 Coy. as S.O. 61st Bde.

March 14
C.O. inspects No. 2 Coy on parade.

March 15.
C.O. to D.D.S.&T. re. cars.

March 16.

March 17.
C.O. to G. re claims officers' appointment
One N.C.O. from each coy.
to Hotchkiss gun course at Estouilly

March 18.
C.O. to inspect transport at B.A. native troops.

March 19

C.O. inspects W. & G. with adjutant.

March 20.

Capt Moseley Adjt goes on leave - Lieut [illegible] assumes [illegible] duty

C O to D D S & T re car.

March 21

C O to No 1 Coy re move.

also visited No 3 Coy.

C O to Div [illegible] at HAM

No 2 Coy moved to Villers-St Christophe

3 " " " "

4 " " " TUGNY

22nd No 2 Coy. moved to TOULLE at 12 noon.

Train Hdqrs moved to [illegible]

23 Train Hdqrs moved to ROIGLISE then on to near ROYE, on AMIENS road. N 2 a 15 Sheet 66 D [illegible] for Coy Hdqrs.

No 1 Coy at RETHONVILLERS

" 2 " "

3 " Nr CHAMPIEN N 29 a 25 Sheet 66 D.

4 Coy at W 9 a 4 4 with 36 DIV.

24/ Col to SMTO, [illegible] Hdqrs.

No 1 Coy moved to CARREPUITS

Orders received at 2 pm for Train Hdqrs & No 1 Coy to move to GOYENCOURT.

4 GS wagons of No 1 Coy sent back to help move [illegible] Hdqrs

24 (cont)

No 2 Coy to CREMERY, [illegible]
to FRESNOY
No 3 Coy at [illegible]
No 4 Coy under orders of 30th Div.

25/ Refilling [illegible]
North of [illegible]
No 2 Coy moved to [illegible]
No 4 Coy [illegible]
camped [illegible] of FRESNOY
Enemy commenced shelling [illegible]
village of [illegible] at 9 [illegible]
Orders received at 10 pm [illegible]
to move at once to LE QUESNEL

26/

CO to Div Hdqs 12 p
Orders received [illegible]
[illegible] to MEZIERES [illegible]
for the night
CO back to [illegible] Coy to arrange about
refilling

31/. CO to DDT Southern additional supplies transport moved under C.H.T. Station of 59th Brig & 61st Brig

---

1/. CO to DDT Southern, also to AHTD to arrange for all surplus transport of 20th Div to report to Train Hdqrs CAHON.

8 G S wagons drew supplies from ABBEVILLE depot.

2/. additional surplus transport of 60th Brigade reported

Supplies drawn from ABBEVILLE by HT.

ADT visited Train Hdqrs

Detail for 70 G S wagons to clear ammunition from MARTENVILLE & convey to SAIGNEVILLE on the 3/4/18.

3/ 70 G S wagons paraded under Capt
May at 10 A M with orders to report to the
C O O MARTENVILLE at 2 pm.
Wagons parked in the depot for the
night.

4/ C O to Div Hdqs.
Wagons arrived at [illegible] at 3·30

5/ C O to A H T D. ABBEVILLE.
In communication with [illegible] R A
[illegible]

6/

Train Hdqrs & 4 Companies & surplus regimental transport marched at 8AM to ALLERY arriving at 2.30 pm.
Col to Div Hdqs
Rain

7/

Col rode to Camps-en-Amienois.
received orders from Div to remain at ALLERY
Surplus regimental transport rejoined their units, as baggage wagons.

8/

Refitting of Train Companies at HORNOY
Col to Div Hdqs. Sent to ABBEVILLE for remounts.
No 1 Coy to SENARPONT.
2 H [illegible] [illegible] [illegible]
61st Brigade.

9/ Supply wagons rejoined their units

(10/. Train Hdqs moved to CRIQ [illegible]
MESNIL.
Brigade companies rejoined their
Brigade areas.
CO to DIV Hdqs HUPPY

11/ Train Hdqrs moved at 10.30 AM to GAMACHES arriving at 11.30.
No 2 Coy to BOUVAINCOURT
No 3 " to HOCQUELUS.
4 " to ST QUENTIN.

12/ Orders to find an officer to be Adjutant HT Corps. Capt Lowe name submitted
No 1 Coy to GOUBERT

(13). Surplus 2nd LINE transport of 6" ox 2 Bns of 10 RB's & 7 KOYLI ordered to report to No 2 Sect DAC en route for ABBEVILLE

14/ C O visited the Brigade companies.

15/

16/ 550 evacuated sick to the Base Havre.

17/

Orders received at 4 pm for Div Train to move. Brigade companies concentrated at GAMACHES at 11.30 moved off 12 mn under Capt Lowe.

18/

Train Hdqs & 3 Brigade
Companies arrived at

19/

Train Hdqs & 3 Companies
moved at 3 p.m.

20/

Train Hdqs moved to MINGOVAL

No 2 Cy to TINGUETTE

No 3 Cy to CROCOURT.

No 4 Cy to TINGUETTE.

arriving 3 pm

CO to Div Hdqs.

21/ CO to Div Hdqs.

22/ OC visited [illegible] [illegible]

23/. A.Q.M.G. inspected Brigade Coy.

CO to Div Hdqs.

—

24/ 12 G.S. wagons on stone fatigue
from LIGNY St-FLOCHEL station
to roads.
CO to railhead
1 N.C.O. & 3 men per Coy sent on
M.G. course at CARENCY

— . —

25/ CO inspected transport of the
60th Field Ambulance.

26/ CO with D.A.D.V.S. inspected
1st Line transport of 59th Inf Brigade

~~At [illegible]~~
~~course [illegible]~~

26/. CO with DADVS inspected Transport of 61st FA.
aft. Inspection of 60th Brigade 1st Line Transport.
Lt Finlay joined Train Hdqrs for a course of instruction.

27/. Inspection of 62 FA by CO & DADVS
aft/ Inspection of 1st Line Transport of 61st Inf Brigade by CO & DADVS.

28th. Capt C.S. Evans returned from BGHTD
2nd Lt Barnes admitted to 12 ~~CCS~~ Stationary Hospital

29th CO inspected transport of M.G. Batt.
To DHQ with S.S.O in afternoon ~~[illegible]~~ to attend conference

30th 61st Bde moved forward. No 4 Coy to Camblain l'Abbé S.S.O to forward area with D~~A~~QMG. CO inspected transport of 61st F.A.

May

1st CO to DHQ in am re move of Train HQrs 3 & 4 Coys moved forward to CARENCY S.S.O with AA QMG to see Canadian Rly Coys in afternoon. CO to forward area in pm to see about billets for Train HQrs

2 CO to DHQ & to forward area in morning No 2 Coy moved to forward area from HQrs to billets au Bois. No 1 Coy arrived at Mazière

3. CO to see O.C. No 1 Coy 3rd Canadian Div Train To Canadian Corps after tea

4. CO to 3 Coy in morning to D.D.S.T & on also to ~~[illegible]~~ MT Coy. No 1 Coy moved to Ablain St Nazaire To Canadian Corps re agricultural land to be taken over from 4th Canadian Bn

5. CO with Capt Lowe to see land to be taken over from 4th Canadian Div also to Hallen. To DGRA in morning re this. To Vimy Ridge in afternoon.

6. CO with Capt Lowe to farm. To 2 Coy also to 1 Coy re painting of wagons.

7. Train HQ moved to Chateau de la Haie. CO to AHQ in afternoon.

8. To DADOS Canadian Corps & Noeux aux Mines re coal.

9. To AHQ in p.m. Capt RS Fisher ASC reported from Base as posted to HQ & Coy.

10. To DDS&T re coal also to Canadian Light Rlys.

11. To see Corps Q in am & pm re coal. To [illegible] to inspect transport.

12. With Col Lee Jones in morning to [illegible] with 2nd Lt Bentley then pm to forward coal dump.

13 2nd Lt Barnes reported from 12 Stationary Hospital

14. O.C. Train went on 3 days special leave to U.K.
Lt Ammon transferred to No 1 Coy Capt [illegible] [illegible]
[illegible] of [illegible] [illegible]

15 AA & QMG to Webb Siding in morning & saw
train units of No 3 Coy 59th & 60th Bde refilling &
[illegible] in afternoon S.S.O. to No 1 Coy re
[illegible] by 9th Bde of [illegible] of [illegible]

16 AA & QMG to Webb Siding & [illegible] [illegible] of
[illegible] & saw of No 1 Coy [illegible] [illegible]
58th Bde H.Q. also [illegible] 2nd Lt [illegible] [illegible]
To Ferguson [illegible] in afternoon

17. S.S.O. with AA & QMG to G.H.Q. re [illegible] of
[illegible] [illegible] while [illegible] [illegible] [illegible]

18 O.C. Train returned from special leave [illegible]
Lt [illegible] reported from Hospital

19. O.C. Train to [illegible] in morning to see [illegible]
of [illegible] [illegible] [illegible] by [illegible] [illegible]
area to Barber also to see D.O.S.T. [illegible]
afternoon 2nd Lt [illegible] transferred from No 1
Coy to No 3 Coy. AA & QMG inspected train units
of No 3 Coy at 10 am in morning

20 Both motor cars out of Commission. CO spoke to S.M.T.O Corps re loan of one of M.T. Coy's cars.

21st O.C. Train to ~~Aubrun~~ M.T. Coy & Corps HQrs in morning. S.S.O to Pernes Doullens & Hervent with Claims Officer. O.C. to see coal Dump at Dieval, & afterwards to Corps HQ re car & to see C.R.O.

22. CO inspected Transport of 59th Bde.

23 CO inspected Transport of 60th Field Amb^ce in morning. To 17 G.H.Q in afternoon

24. C.O inspected Transport of 60th Bde in afternoon

25 CO inspected Transport of 61st F.A^ce in morning also the parade of No 2 Coy

26 CO inspected Transport of 61st Bde in morning. Rivers Bout Farm in afternoon

27th CO inspected Transport of 62nd Fld Amb & DLI in morning. CO with DDS&T 1st Army to CALONNE Amn dump. 2nd Lt C F Barnes proceeded to UK on special leave.

28th CO inspected Transport of [illegible] Battn

29th

30 CO to No 2 Coy in morning & to AHQ in afternoon to [illegible] [illegible] out of No 2 & 4 Coys. Major J. H. [illegible] DSO reported from [illegible] [illegible] [illegible]

31 CO to Barlin R'head in morning

June 1st

1. CO to AHQ in morning also to coal dump at Webb Siding & to see Col Ryan Jones re coal

2. CO to AHQ in morning

3. Train HQ mess destroyed by fire at 3. am SSO to new Rhead Savy Berlette. CO to DDS&T in afternoon.

4. Court of Enquiry held on fire at Train HQrs. CO with Major Arnold to [illegible] in afternoon SSO to CALONNE to see Bowling

5. CO with AA&QMG & Major Arnold to see coal.

6. 2nd Lt J J Bowling returned from CALONNE coal dump & posted to OC No 4 Coy

7. 2nd Lt W Mead ASC left to report to OC 46th Div Train

8 CO spoke to all OC Coys & Subaltern Officers
re [illegible] of rations. SSO [illegible] to
Webb Siding. Experiments with motor [illegible]
started.

9 CO to Webb Siding in morning.

10 CO to [illegible] in morning with Brigadier [illegible] to
his 2 Coys. Met General Abbott & Col Stuart here. To
Boulogne in afternoon to fetch [illegible]

11 CO returned from Boulogne.

12 SSO to Camp [illegible] of the Coys [illegible]
in afternoon & evening.

13.

14 OC [illegible] at 1st Bde. then SSO returned
from Paris.

15. CO visited 1 & 3 Coys re bridge matters, then went
to Bde Farm.

16 CO to 3 Coy to meet ADMG Corps also RE Staff officer re briquetting

17

18 CO to Corps Q in car to obtain scythes & rakes for cutting hay behind No 1 Coy G.O.C. inspected No 1 & 3 Coy on parade

19 Adjt to 2 & 4 Coys re making of ~~briquettes~~ coal cakes

20 CO to Corps HQrs in car re coal cakes to 5th Army HQ Coy & 3rd Army re same in afternoon

21 CO with Capt Gray to Corps HQrs re coal cakes.

22 CO with AA & QMG to No 3 Coy for demonstration of coal cake making & burning. CO & ADMG inspected DHQ transport in afternoon, then went to AHQ.

23. 1 Officer & 2 OR to No 3 Coy to learn about the making of N.S. coal cakes. C.O. to Corps re same.

24. CO inspected Transport of 60th Bde in am. Also to 4, 2, 3 & 1 Coys re making of coal cakes. CO to A/HQ re same in afternoon. – ~~Plans~~ Drawings despatched to DQMGs of 1st & 13th Corps.

25. CO inspected 60th Bde Transport to 12th RB. 3 Coy & 5th Argyll & Sutherlands re coal cakes. To tank demonstration in afternoon.

26 CO inspected 59th Bde Transport. To No 2 [?] & met there C.T.O. & Major O'Flynn re coal cakes. To 3rd Army in pm. O.C. 1st Div Train called to see CO. 2nd Lt. D.C.W. Thomas ASC reported from BHTD & was posted to No 1 Coy of the Train as Transport Subaltern.

27th CO inspected 20th M.G. [?] Battn & 11th DLI on parade. Also to all Coys of the Train re coal cakes.

28 CO to Paris on leave

29

30 Moulds for making coal cakes sent to 20th Div[l] Train. 50 to [illegible] a special line for [illegible] return

July

1st —

2nd Bn race meeting

3rd.

4th Adjt round all Coys re coal cutter, also to Bde farm CO returned from leave to CMN

5 2nd Lt Dowling to Offa dump re DGO Co sent particulars of Allison coal [illegible] 6th Div. CO to AHQ after tea

6. CO with C.T.O to see dump of pitch. CO with SMTO 1st Corps to be 3 Coys in pm re coal cutter. CO to all Coys of the Train in evening re coal cutters [illegible] Officer promoted [illegible]

7. CO to No 3 Coy in morning, also saw DAAG 52nd Div & OC Corps MT Column. Interviewed [illegible] (20th Div) re making of coal cakes for the whole of the Div.

8. Arrangements made by SSO for Train War Savings Certificate Lottery. CO to [illegible] Siding in evening to choose site for coal cake factory. Lt Col [illegible] to Train HQ in pm.

9. CO to Corps Q in evening. Capt [illegible] ASC came to live at Train HQs.

10. CO to ? in am. OC 24th Train to see CO re coal cakes.

11. ~~[illegible]~~ 60 NCOs & men attached from Corps for coal cake making. 2nd Lt [illegible] from OFFA Dump to coal cake factory. CO with DADOS & [illegible] to AMBINCOURT.

12. CO to Corps Q in am also to Coal Cake factory. To latter & to DDS&T in pm. 2nd Lt [illegible] admitted to [illegible] F Amb

13th C.O. to CALONNE re pitch in morning. To pitch dump near BETHUNE in p.m., also to A.H.Q.

14th C.O. rode to Coal Cake Factory in a.m. C.O to M.T. Coy in p.m. 2nd Lt. G.C. Cooke A.S.C. retd from leave & was attached to No 2 Coy

15th C.O to M.T. Coy in afternoon re motors. To SAILLY at night to solve pitch. Issue of coal cake to units commenced

16. C.O to A.H.Q in p.m. with samples of coal cakes

17th C.O to meet D.A. & Q.M.G.

18th C.O to coal cake factory in a.m. & to A.H.Q. in p.m. Lt [illegible] assumed duties of O.C. 6th [illegible]

19th C.O to 1st Cy Divl Train [illegible] coal cake factory in a.m. & to [illegible] [illegible]

20th CO to C.C. Factory in am

21st —

22nd CO. to Corps HQ re trench boards for C.C. Factory. Capt [illegible], Divl [illegible] Officer returned from leave in U.K. 1 NCO & 15 OR recalled from CC Factory by 53rd [illegible] Coy.

23rd CO to [illegible] in am. To coal cake factory & [illegible] to [illegible] in afternoon.

24th CO. to Coal C. Factory & took 1 pack of CCs to DDS&T. Capt [illegible] of [illegible] Coy proceeded on leave. DDS&T [illegible] visit CC Factory in am. 2nd Lt [illegible] returned to [illegible] Coy & [illegible] took his place.

25th CO to [illegible] brick farm & to AGHQ in am. DDQMG [illegible] visited CC factory.

26 CO to CC Factory in am also to see Col [illegible]. To AGHQ in pm. 1 Sergt & 15 OR from 8th Divn arrived at CC Factory.

27th CO inspected 59th Bde Transport also that of 60th FA in am.

28th ~~CO inspected Transport of 60th~~ CO to CC Factory in am & to meet Corps Commander there in pm. Capt Mary ASC proceeded on 6 days leave to UK

29th CO inspected transport of 60th Bde & 61st FA in pm. To CC factory in evening to make further experiments re waste [illegible]

30th CO inspected transport of 61st Bde & 62nd FA

31st CO to Penne to preside over Court of Enquiry held on [illegible] [illegible] column.

August

1 CO inspected Transport of M.G. Batt. & DLI in am also to CC Factory to see Camp Commandant VIII Corps with programme of Horse Race Meeting to Div Farm & Race Course in evening Capt [illegible] proceeded to UK on 5 days Special Leave & Lieut [illegible] to UK on 14 days ordinary leave

2. CO to Corps HQrs in am SSO to Paris on duty. CO to M.T. Coy & ASHQ in pm.

3 CO to [illegible] as President of Board assembling [illegible]

4th CO returned from Boulogne

5th CO to Corps HQrs in am [illegible] Judge [illegible] in pm. SSO returned from Paris.

6th CO to Corps HQrs in am [illegible] 24th & 8th Trains to ASHQ in pm.

7th —

8th CO to Corps HQ. Train inspected by His Majesty the King. CO to AG&Q in pm.

9th CO to Boulogne for Race preliminaries.

10th Divl Train Race Meeting

11th Lt Sykes returned from leave in UK. CO to MT Coy in am. 2 bombs dropped in 2 Co lines & 2 casualties caused.

12th CO to [illegible] in am. [illegible]

13th ~~[illegible]~~ CO to [illegible] and to AG&Q in pm.

14th SSO to Paris on duty. CO to French museum at

Corps HQrs. 3 bombs dropped on No 1 Coy camp & 5 casualties caused to OR & 1 to animals.

15th. CO to No 1 Coy in am & to Salvage Dump.

16th CO to CALONNE in am re stay. To see Capt. Forsyth [illegible] in pm

17th CO to CC factory in am also to 2 & 4 Coy which Corps Commander was to inspect. Major Rashleigh ADC of C in C inspected HD horses (Shire) of Farm & [illegible] Lt Webb of No 3 Coy returned from leave

18 CO to NOEUX LES MINES in am to fetch mine managers & take them to CC Factory. To No 1 Coy in evening re changing of [illegible]

19th CO to 16 MAC in am.

20th CO to Corps HQ & 1st A HQ in am. To 1st Corps Horse Show in pm.

21st SSO to conference at Army. CO to Corps HQs in am. 12 men at C.C. Factory 9 men sent there from Div Co to Factory with Major OC 30th Labour Co. To Noeux les Mines in evening

22nd 20th M T Coy men returned to their unit from C.C Factory. CO to Corps in am. To AHQ in pm. Corps Commander gave lecture in afternoon

23rd C.O interviewed miners for return to UK. To AHQ in pm

24th Lt Cameron proceeded on 14 days special leave to UK. Corps Horse Show

25th ———

26th CO to AHQ in afternoon with SSO. To [illegible] in evening.

27th CO with SSO to Arras Railhead. To tea with Corps Commander.

28th. CO to CC Factory in am. To Boulogne in pm.

29th. [illegible] CO returned from Boulogne

30th CO to AGHQ in am.

31st. CO to 3rd [illegible] after lunch to AGHQ in pm.

August

1 CO to C.C. Factory & to NOEUX-LES-MINES for lunch. To former again in evening.

2. CO to AGHQ Capt. W.F. Wilson reported from BHTD & was posted to No 1 Coy of the Train

3. CO went on Paris leave. 2nd Lt Le Grove returned from hospital & assumed duties of S.O. 60th Bde

4 Major Arnold DSO came to Train HQrs

4&5 Major Arnold to C.C. Factory

6 —"—

7 —"—

8 —"— Sports at DHQ in p.m.

9 2nd Lt. W. S. Robertson proceeded on 10 day leave to UK

10th Lt Arunson returned from 14 days special leave in UK & relieved Capt Hanson as S.O. Corps Troops. 10 ORs, 2 saddlers & 2 [illegible] arrived from BH&TD

11th Capt [illegible] [illegible] [illegible] [illegible] [illegible]

12th SSO & Capt to Boulogne

13th SSO to Paris

14th Major Bell to Paris on 10 days leave. Capt with DAQMG to pick refilling points, billets & horses lines in case of move

15th CO ~~[illegible]~~ returned from leave in France

16th CO to CC [illegible] [illegible] to RSHQ. Capt [illegible] took over charge of Rest Farm vice Capt [illegible]

17th Capt Hutchins proceeded on 14 day leave to UK. CO to [illegible] [illegible] in [illegible] to CC [illegible] in [illegible]. WO [illegible] from BH&TD

18th. CO to A.H.Q in p.m. & to St Pol. Lt Col Hutchens ASC & Staff Captain from 6.0 visited Train H.Q.s & C.C. Factory.

19th CO to Factory in a.m. To 11th KRR Transport lines in p.m. for lecture.

20th 2nd Lt J.A. Archer to 6th [illegible]

21. C.O. to Boulogne. Adj. proceeded on 14 days leave to U.K. Capt Norman took over duties of adjutant.
A/adj to refilling with S.S.O.

22/

Div. Sports

23/ Lt [illegible] returned from Corps Troops S.C. & assumed duties of S.O. 2nd
2 Lt Chapman commenced a course of supply officers work
pm C O walked down to the [illegible] with S.S.O.

24/

CO out riding
Army Field Artillery Brigade No 242
question whether they were to be with Train for
administration &c.

25/ CO to Lens dinner at DDS&T
Major Bell returned from Paris leave
Lt Robertson returned from leave to UK

26/

27/ CO to DDS&T. & to VIII Corps
re coal cakes

28/ Lt Wilson left for 14 days special leave to U K.
Col to coal coke factory.
Capt Sykes took over duties of Div agricultural officer vice Lt Wilson.

29/ C O & 2 Lt Dowling left for U K on 14 days leave.
Div Sports
Major Arnold DSO took over command of the Train

30/ Capt Fabes returned from leave

Oct/

1/ a/OC [illegible] to companies [illegible]
re Bosch retirement
a/OC & SSO round the companies & to coal
coke factory.

2/. a/OC to MT Coy & to 58th MT Coy re
coal-cokes
SO conference at Q. Stn to coal coke
factory & companies.

3/. a/OC & a/adjt to Villers Chatel to see
12 [illegible] re [illegible].
a/OC to coal coke factory & companies.
Capt Hutchens returned from leave.

4/. a/OC to [illegible] to see OC 12 [illegible] Train
[illegible] round through the companies [illegible]
MT Coy re [illegible]

5/ A/OC Train & SSO to [illegible] conference
& new area
OC 13 [illegible] Train comm on, [illegible] to [illegible]
cont. [illegible] & conference with OC

6/ [illegible] Hqrs [illegible] & SSO left to report to
2nd American Corps
Train Hqrs moved to Mingoval
No. 2 Coy [illegible]
" 3 [illegible]
4 [illegible]

7/ Capt [illegible] returned from leave [illegible] Coy
moved to Achicourt

8. SSO & Capt [illegible] Refilling Points – Coys.
To Q in am. PO to BARLIN in pm re
coal.

9. SSO to Paris in am. 4SSO to Corps Fuel Officer & AGHQ in am. to re coal supply of same drawn from ARRAS Railhead. To conference at Corps HQs in pm. 1st Coy to CHERISY (Canadian Corps).

10. O.C. 63rd Train called at Train HQs re taking over billets.

11. —

12. Adjt visited 2 & 3 Coys of the Train

13. Adjt visited 3 & 4.

14. Adjt to see 1st Coy at CHERISY. Lt A.J. Wilson returned from 14 days leave in U.K.

15. O.C. Train returned from 14 days in U.K.

16. ~~[illegible]~~ CO to AHQ in pm.

17. CO to Corps HQrs & Chateau de la Haie in pm

18. CO to Corps HQrs & No 2 Coy in am To Coal Cake Factory in pm.

19. CO with [illegible] 2 Coy in am To ? in pm

20th —

21st CO to DHQ in am Inspected 59th Bde 1st Line Transport in pm

22nd CO went to [illegible] in am Inspected 60th Bde Transport in pm.

23rd CO to see MT Coy SO in am Inspected DHQ Transport in pm

24th CO inspected Transport of 14th Bde less DCLI in pm. 2/i/c returned from Paris leave.

25th CO to RDC in am. Inspected Transport of DCLI, 63rd FA & 14 Bde in pm.

26 CO inspected Transport of 64th FA - DCLI in am. To 63rd [illegible] Res FA Tracking in pm.

27 CO walked to DITO in am. Inspected Transport of 61st FA in pm also went to 3 Co To Hount to Mines in evening.

November

1 Train HQrs & Bde Coy of the Train arrived at CAMBRAI

2. 1 Coy moved with artillery to SAULZOIR

3rd Train HQrs moved to AVESNES LEZ AUBERT, 2 Coy to CAUROIR, 3 Coy to RIEUX & 4 Coy to CAGNONCLES.

4th Co to CAMBRAI Railhead [illegible] [illegible] [illegible] No 1 Coy [illegible] [illegible] 2 & 4 Coys moved to ST AUBERT 3 Coy to VENDEGIES

5th Co to [illegible] [illegible] [illegible] [illegible] 1 Co moved to [illegible] [illegible] [illegible]

6. Train HQrs moved to VENDIGIES, 1 Coy to JENLAIN, 3 Coy to SEMPERIES, 4 Coy to VENDIGIES

1918

7th No 2 Coy moved to VENDEGIES, 3 Coy to JENLAIN & 4 Coy to SEMPERIES

8 Train HQrs moved to MARGNIES-LE-GRAND 2 Coy to JENLAIN, 3 Coy to ST WAAST 4 Coy to

9 Train HQrs moved to I 31 b 5 2 (Sheet 51) 1 Coy to I 17 c 0 3 (Sheet 51)

10 3 Coy moved to FRIGNIES 4 Coy to ST WAAST

11 Hostilities ceased at 11 a.m. No 4 Coy moved to FRIGNIES & No 2 Coy to ST WAAST

12 Train HQrs moved to FRIGNIES 2 Coy to TASNIERES 3 Coy to J 17 d 9 0

13 Major [illegible] returned from leave in UK 2nd Lt [illegible] proceeded on leave in UK C.O. proceeded to Paris

14. —

15. 3 Coy moved to BETTICHIES [illegible] cleared from [illegible]

16/21. nil

22nd No 1 Coy moved to Wargnies le ~~[illegible]~~ Petit area

23rd Train HQrs moved to [illegible] [illegible] Coy to Vendegies area 2 Coy to Wargnies le Petit area, 3 Coy to [illegible] area & 4 to St Waast [illegible] Vendegies

24th 1 Coy to Cambrai 2 Coy to [illegible] [illegible] to Vendegies area & [illegible] Coy to Wargnies le Petit

25th Train HQrs to [illegible] [illegible] St Aubert 3 Coy to [illegible] [illegible] & 4 Coy to Vendegies

26th Train HQs. 1 Coy to Beugnatre

27th Train HQs to RIEUX 2 Coy to CAMBRAI
3 Coy to AVESNES & 4 Coy to Capinchies
1 Coy to Humbercamp

28 Train HQs to Cambrai also 3 Coy

29. Train HQs & 3 Coy on line of march to
Marieux area stopped at Beugnatre 2 Coy
stopped at Hapliñcourt 4 Coy to
Cambrai

30th Train HQs & 3 Coy stopped at BIENVILLERS
on line of march 2 Coy to
4 Coy to Beugnatre

December

1st Train HQrs to Pas 2 Coy to Acquierres
3 Coy to Authie St Leger.

2nd CO left on 5 days special leave to UK
2nd Lt Thomas returned off leave in UK
4 Coy to ACHEUX

3 Supplies drawn from Doullens R'head by
Bn Transport ~~Adjt on 5 days special
leave~~

4 Adjt to Doullens R'head Pack train drawn by
HT.

5 SSO & Adjt to R'head

6 Adjt to 2 & 3 Coys [illegible] [illegible]

7

8 Conference of Coy Education Officers with
Divl E.O.

9th O.C. Train retd from 5 days special leave in U.K

10th S.S.O. & Adjt to R'head in am to R.A. H.Q.s & 1 Coy in evening

11th R'head changed to Acheux

12. Capt C S Evans proceeded to U K on 14 days special leave.
Capt Whitty proceeded on 5 days leave to PARIS

13/ a/adj to No 3 Coy

14/ a/adj to railhead. No 4 Coy
Lt Robertson to Train Hdqs for [illegible] duty.

15/ a/adj to No 1 Coy
No [illegible] to PARIS to purchase [illegible] Stores for Xmas.

16/ CO out riding to 11 DLI.

17/. 61st Brigade refilling point changed from ACHEUX to VAUCHELLES
Baggage & supply wagons of C 91 & D 91 detached from Division to proceed with their batteries to artillery school

18/ a/adj to Nos 2 3 Coy

19/. a/adj to [illegible]
CO 18 [illegible] to [illegible]

20/. 18 O.R. [illegible] from [illegible] collecting station CAMBRAI for [illegible]
2 Lt Chapman proceeded on 14 days leave to the U.K.

21/. a/adj to No 3 Coy

22/. C O to Army Hdqrs.
SSO returned from PARIS
Lt Robertson assumed duties of
No 59.

23/. 2 Lt J J Dowling detailed to
report to Base Supply Depot Boulogne
[illegible] authority STP/353
C O to No 3 Coy on [illegible]
SSO - a/adj to No 3 Coy [illegible]
car

26/. C O proceeded to Paris on 10 days leave.

25/ a/OC Train round the companies.

26/. a/adj to No 1 Coy.

27/. Lt Aronson proceeded on 1 days leave to PARIS.
SSO to PARIS with empties
a/adj to column & No 3 Coy.

28/ a/adj to railhead & No 4 Coy.

29 Capt C S Rowan returns from special leave in UK

30/31. —

January 1919

1/3 —

4th CO returned from leave in Paris

5th Lt Aronson retd from leave in Paris

6th —

7th Capt J H D Norman proceeded on leave to UK. CO to A.H.Q's

8th CO to Grincourt on [illegible]

9th CO to No [illegible] Coy to Sqdn Saddler S.S. McDonald

10th CO with SSO round all Coys for the Train

11th Capt H [illegible] [illegible] UK. H.G.O.C. Div [illegible] Coys

12th 19th Divl Race Meeting

13th —

14th Capt F B Sykes proceeded on leave — to U.K. Lt A C Webb took over temp command of No 2 Coy

15th

16th SSO to Paris on duty. CO to Army HQ

17th —

18th CO inspected transport of 9th Bde

19th SSO returned from Paris. CO to Amiens to meet him

20th CO inspected 60th Bde Transport.

21st — — 61st — —

22nd C.O inspected 1st G Battn Transport

23 Field Ambce

24 D.L.I.

25
26 } —
27
28

29. G.O.C. visited 2, 3 & 4 Coys in am

30. Pepan [?] Thrown [?] precautions received
Whitty & Cook returned

February

4. C.O. retd from 3 days special leave in Paris.

7. C.O. with SSO to LUCHEUX to see wood Dumps there.

9. C.O. to AUTHIE to see wood dump. Arranged for 3 Coys to draw wood & take same to 60th Bde Refilling Point.

14. Capt Norman took over 5000 tons wood Lucheux Forest

15. Thaw precautions came into force. Coys drew supplies from ACHEUX R'head 2nd Lt D.W.C. Thomas reposted to 13th Div. Aux Hse Coy

16 Lt A.E. Webb returned from leave in U.K.

17th Lt Col H.E. Grove returned from leave in U.K. C.O. to A.H.Q.

21st 1 Coy moved to Mondicourt 2 & 4 Coys to AUTHIEULE supplies drawn from Doullens Railhead

22nd action commodities drawn from ACHEUX R'head in order to permit RSO's store to take remainder of rations from [illegible] R'head

25th Capt F H Hutchinson went on leave to UK ~~[illegible]~~

26 CO. [illegible] to Abbeville

27 CO. retd from Abbeville

March

2nd C.O. proceeded to UK on 14 days special leave.

3rd —

4th 5.50 to Paris on duty

5th 6th —

7th 5.50 retd from Paris. Major Bell proceeded to Corps Demobilization Camp.

8th Lt Le Grove proceeded on 7 days special leave in UK

9th 10th 11th 12th —

13th Capt & Adjt C.S. Evans proceeded on 14 days special leave in UK.

14 52 O.R.s ~~Corps~~ proceeded for demobilization
Capt Hutchings returned from leave

15/

16/ Lt Robertson returned from leave in the U K. Capt Hutchings took over command of No 1 Coy from Capt H.H. Whitty.

17.

18/

19/ Lt Le Gros returned from 7 days special leave to U K.

20. Lt Col Standen returned from leave to U K.

21/. Lt Armson & 500 OR's left for concentration camp at CANDAS for demobilization

22/ Lt Col Standen left for U K authority third army S T P/825
Capt C J Messenger took over command

of 20 ~~Div~~ Train. vice Lt Col R H F Stenders.
Car No [broad arrow] 24004 transferred to Train

23/. OC Train to railhead

24/

25/

26/

27/ OC Train to railhead, conferences & dumps
Capt Mettry & Lt le Gros moved to DOULLENS
under orders of SSO.
73 x Horses (HD) left for BEUVAL en
route for DIEPPE
Capt CF Colley returned to the Train

28/. OC & adjt round the companies in car
Capt Tolon left for concentration camp CANDAS
for demobilization

29 OC Train to railhead

30/ O.C. Trans [illegible]
Capt C S Evans returned from [illegible] days
Special Leave Lt W S Robertson &
Lt W Le Grow proceeded to report to O.C.
62nd Bde Train.

31. Lt G C Coombe proceeded to report to
41st Bde Train.

April.

2 Capt. H.W.D. [illegible] & Lt. A.C. Webb proceeded on route to report respectively to O.C. 41st & 62nd Bn. Trains

4 Capt. C.K. Colbourne left for demobilisation

10th Capt. L.A. Hayman reported from 62nd Train

11 " G.H. Colgrave left for demobilization

12th Capt. Hutchinson & Sykes left for 62nd Train

14 Lt. Young

17 All X animals exchanged for Z Animals.

23rd Capt. F.V. Ward [illegible] Train

24 1 Company handed over to Capt. F.V. Ward.

25 Adjutant for leave.
Capt J A Musgrave to Cap
Demobilisation camp. 3 O.Rs Demobbed.
26 C.O. to railhead & Dump

27 C.O. to railhead & Dump.

28 C.O. to railhead & Dump
in morning, in afternoon
to LUCHEUX. Forest.
2/Lt Chapman to DOULLENS to report
for duty under R.S.O.
Lt Young took over command
of 2nd Coy from 2/Lt Chapman.
29 CO. to railhead & Dump.

30 C.O. to railhead & Dump.
to 1 & 3 Coy

1 C.O. to railhead & Dump
2 ditto
3 ditto
to 1 & 3 Coy in afternoon

20th Division

121/7517

20th Divl: Train

Vol I

Jly to Sept 15

Jly 15
Apl 19

Confidential

War Diary

of

O.C. 20th Divisional Train. A.S.C.

from 28 7/15 to 30 9/15.

The Officer,

i/c Adjutant General's Office

at the Base.

Instructions regarding War Diaries and Intelligence Summaries are contained in F. S. Regs., Part II. and the Staff Manual respectively. Title pages will be prepared in manuscript.

WAR DIARY
or
~~INTELLIGENCE SUMMARY.~~

(*Erase heading not required.*)

Army Form C. 2118.

Place	Date	Hour	Summary of Events and Information	Remarks and references to Appendices
LUMBRES	28 7/15		Took over command of 20th Divisional Train from Lieut Colonel Conway Gordon ASC. Marched to LYNDE. Train Headquarters LE NOIR TROU. Bivouac.	
MERRIS	29 7/15		Marched to MERRIS – Division billetted over large area necessitating companies of Train remaining in brigade areas, likewise 5 refilling points viz Divisional Headquarters group MERRIS, 59th Brigade group VIEUX BERQUIN, 60th Brigade OUTERSTEEN, 61st Brigade LA COURONNE – RA group VERTE RUE, with railhead at LA GORGUE.	
do.	2 8/15		159 Company left for attachment to 8th Divisional Train and details 160 Company for attachment to 27th Division. Arranged camping ground for supply section on MERRIS – VIEUX BERQUIN road & with CRE for a well to be sunk for drinking water for men. Attending AA + QMG daily in connection with all ASC questions, & visiting ASC companies in their brigade areas, also refilling points.	

Instructions regarding War Diaries and Intelligence Summaries are contained in F. S. Regs., Part II. and the Staff Manual respectively. Title pages will be prepared in manuscript.

Army Form C. 2118.

WAR DIARY
or
~~INTELLIGENCE SUMMARY.~~
(Erase heading not required.)

Place	Date	Hour	Summary of Events and Information	Remarks and references to Appendices
MERRIS	9/8/15		159 Company A.S.C. returned from attachment to 8th Division	
do	12/8/15		Visited railhead at LA GORGUE, inspected refilling of 60th group attached to 8th Division	
do	16/8/15		First portions 60 & 61st Brigades return from attachment from 8th & 27th Divisions respectively	
			Inspected 1st Line transport of 7th K.O.Y.L.I. Satisfactory.	
do	18th		do. do 11th Durhams do	
do	22nd		Inspected transport of 12th KRR and 12th RB. Report in separate book.	
do	23rd		do. 6th Oxf Bucks L.I. and 6th K. Shropshire L.I.	
	24th		Went ESTAIRES with DAA & QMG, selected site for camp & arranged billets.	
do	27th		Marched to ESTAIRES. Train [struck out] companies now concentrated –	
do	28		Raised question as to return to Train of baggage wagons – was informed by AA & QMG that the matter was being referred to G.O.C.	

Instructions regarding War Diaries and Intelligence Summaries are contained in F. S. Regs., Part II. and the Staff Manual respectively. Title pages will be prepared in manuscript.

WAR DIARY
or
~~INTELLIGENCE SUMMARY.~~
(*Erase heading not required.*)

Army Form C. 2118.

Place	Date	Hour	Summary of Events and Information	Remarks and references to Appendices
ESTAIRES	30/8/15		Informed by A.A. & Q.M.G. that G.O.C. had decided that baggage wagons were to remain with their units	
do	3/9/15		New system of Supply Arrangements adopted.	
do.	4/9/15		Inspected transport of 7th S.L.I. & 7th D.C.L.I. – See separate book.	
do.	5/9/15		do do 12th Liverpool Regt do	
do	6.		do do 10th KRR. 11th KRR. 10th RB. 11th RB. do.	
do.	6		Refilling point shelled at 10.30 am – changed hour of refilling to 9 a.m.	
do.	7-23		Situation unchanged.	
do.	24		Baggage wagons returned to Train: Supply section delivering supplies straight to trenches in case of 61st Brigade, as far as railheads of tramways in case of 59th & 60th Brigades – Procedure as follows:- A. After refilling at 9 am supply waggons will be taken to transport lines of battalions and handed over to charge of Quartermasters where they will be parked until evening. B. The horses will return to A.S.C. lines until the evening, when they will return to take the waggons forward.	

Instructions regarding War Diaries and Intelligence Summaries are contained in F. S. Regs., Part II. and the Staff Manual respectively. Title pages will be prepared in manuscript.

WAR DIARY
or
~~INTELLIGENCE~~ SUMMARY.
(Erase heading not required.)

Army Form C. 2118.

Place	Date	Hour	Summary of Events and Information	Remarks and references to Appendices
ESTAIRES	24/2/15		(c) Guides from battalions will conduct supply waggons, and give instructions as regards necessary precautions	
			(d) After delivering rations the supply sections of Train will return to their own lines	
			The baggage waggons of R.A. Units - D.M.T. and Divisional Headquarters to remain with their units until orders for a move are issued. - They will be parked in field now used for watering horses at the junction of the LA BASSEE and SAILLY Roads where they will await the arrival of the H.Q Company of the Train which they will join.	
	25/2/15		Situation unchanged.	
	26/2/15		do. Report to Headquarters of Division that supply waggons came under direct rifle and machine gun fire when nearing dump.	

Army Form C. 2118.

Instructions regarding War Diaries and Intelligence Summaries are contained in F. S. Regs., Part II. and the Staff Manual respectively. Title pages will be prepared in manuscript.

WAR DIARY
or
INTELLIGENCE SUMMARY.
(Erase heading not required.)

Place	Date	Hour	Summary of Events and Information	Remarks and references to Appendices
ESTAIRES	27/9/15		Situation unchanged.	
"	28/9/15		Usual method of supply, ration handing over rations in battalion transport lines reverted to.	
			Baggage waggons returned to units by order of A.A & Q.M.G. –	
	29/9/15		Situation unchanged.	
	30.		do.	

1577 Wt. W10791/1773 500,000 1/15 D. D. & L. A.D.S.S./Forms/C. 2118.

Confidential

War Diary

of

V.C. 20th Divisional Train. A.S.C.

from 1st – 31st October 1915.

Instructions regarding War Diaries and Intelligence Summaries are contained in F. S. Regs., Part II. and the Staff Manual respectively. Title pages will be prepared in manuscript.

WAR DIARY
or
~~INTELLIGENCE~~ SUMMARY.
(Erase heading not required.)

20th Divisional Train Army Form C. 2118.

Place	Date	Hour	Summary of Events and Information	Remarks and references to Appendices
ESTAIRES	1 10/15		Situation unchanged.	
	2 "		Landings for use at refilling points constructed.	
	3 "		Captain Evans A.S.C. placed under instruction for S.S.O. Orders given for all cars to be paraded daily under a requisitioning officer & cleaned under his supervision.	
	4 "		Represented to Headquarters that as the G.O.C. had decided that baggage wagons were to remain with units, that greater efficiency & economy in working would be secured, if some central authority in each brigade controlled the working of regimental transport & A.S.C baggage wagons when attached to regiments.	
			Ordered by Headquarters to furnish a clerk for duty in Forest control office at LA MOTTE.	
			Requisitioned for rifle muzzle protectors for Train.	
			Received notification that Lieut T.R.G. Marshall was invalided to ENGLAND on 25 9/15, & struck off strength accordingly.	

Instructions regarding War Diaries and Intelligence Summaries are contained in F. S. Regs., Part II. and the Staff Manual respectively. Title pages will be prepared in manuscript.

WAR DIARY

or

~~INTELLIGENCE SUMMARY.~~

(*Erase heading not required.*)

Army Form C. 2118.

Place	Date	Hour	Summary of Events and Information	Remarks and references to Appendices
ESTAIRES	5.10.15		Requisitioned for 80 loads of bricks for horse lines.	
	6.		Instructions given to O.C. companies to so arrange their companies that the supply & baggage sections are kept separate & distinct. The Supply section subalterns to keep separate roll of N.C.Os, artificers, men & horses.	
			1st Line transport of the 59 Brigade inspected. Report in separate book.	
	7"		Hauling coal for Divisional baths &c.	
	8.		1st Line transport of the 60th Brigade inspected.	
			Applied for F. G. C. M. for the trial of Driver J. Cullen. 158 Company A.S.C.	
	9		1st Line transport of the 61st Brigade inspected.	
			Applied for supply section wagon for Veterinary Mobile Section under new War Establishments (August 1915)	
	10		Distributed remounts to various units of the Division.	
	11.		Trial by F.G.C.M. of Dr J. Cullen. A.S.C.	
			Requisitioned for 40,000 more bricks for horse lines &c.	

1577 Wt. W10791/1773 500,000 1/15 D. D. & L. A.D.S.S./Forms/C. 2118.

Instructions regarding War Diaries and Intelligence Summaries are contained in F. S. Regs., Part II. and the Staff Manual respectively. Title pages will be prepared in manuscript.

WAR DIARY
or
~~INTELLIGENCE SUMMARY.~~
(Erase heading not required.)

Army Form C. 2118.

Place	Date	Hour	Summary of Events and Information	Remarks and references to Appendices
ESTAIRES	12/10/15		Instructions given to S.S.O. to get into touch with O.C. Reserve Park and arrange loading of vehicles to suit the divisions requirements in case of necessity.	
	13.		Received instructions to appoint an officer to act as Divisional Claims Officer. – 2nd Lieut Hartridge name submitted –	
	14.		Proceedings of F.G.C.M. in the case of Dr Collen promulgated –	
	15.		Situation unchanged.	
	16.		do.	
	17.		do. New instructions received as to marking of wagons –	
	18.		Following order published. No wagons are to move south of the line ROUGE DE BOUT – Road junction M.14.d.8.8. on the LA BASSEE Road during daylight, unless specially ordered by an Officer, in which case single wagons may be permitted to move as far south as the following points but no further:– (1.) WINDY CORNER cross roads H.21.c.8.1. (11.) TRAM RAIL HEAD M.12.a.6.2. – (3) Eastern end of FORT D'ESQUIN. (4) Just short	MAP 36.

Army Form C. 2118.

WAR DIARY
or
~~INTELLIGENCE SUMMARY.~~

(*Erase heading not required.*)

Instructions regarding War Diaries and Intelligence Summaries are contained in F. S. Regs., Part II. and the Staff Manual respectively. Title pages will be prepared in manuscript.

Place	Date	Hour	Summary of Events and Information	Remarks and references to Appendices
ESTAIRES	18 10/15		to the North or West of LA FLINQUE cross roads, except for wagons going to L'EPINETTE Farm. (5) L'EPINETTE Farm. (6) House at M.21. b.6.7. (7) PONT DU HEM on the LA BASSEE Road.	
	19.		Situation unchanged.	
	20.		do.	
	21.		Report to Headquarters, that the 59th Infantry Bde were unduly favoring their 1st line transport at the expense of the A.S.C. baggage wagons attached to them, and asking if orders could be issued to this brigade on the subject.	
			3 Wagons sent to NIEPPE FOREST for duty under Forest Control Officer.	
			Remounts collected and distributed to units of Division.	
	22.		Report to O.C. 91st Brigade R.F.A. as to general treatment of baggage wagons, & requesting greater care in their employment.	
	23.		Recommendation forwarded for transfer of 2nd Lieut H. J. Carpenter to permanent regular army.	

1577 Wt. W10791/1773 500,000 1/15 D. D. & L. A.D.S.S./Forms/C. 2118.

Army Form C. 2118.

WAR DIARY
or
~~INTELLIGENCE SUMMARY.~~
(Erase heading not required.)

Instructions regarding War Diaries and Intelligence Summaries are contained in F. S. Regs., Part II. and the Staff Manual respectively. Title pages will be prepared in manuscript.

Place	Date	Hour	Summary of Events and Information	Remarks and references to Appendices
ESTAIRES	24.10.15		Report to Headquarters as to unsatisfactory drainage system of billets occupied by 156 + 159 Companies A.S.C.	
	25		Application made for 10 loads of cinders for use on lines	
	26		Complaint made to Headquarters as to delay in loading + unloading wagons by R.E. at LA GORGUE and LAVENTIE, pointing out the deterioration ~~[illegible]~~ in horses condition caused by these delays in very inclement weather.	
	27		Situation unchanged	
	28		do	
	29		do	
	30		do. Forwarded application for transfer to R. Flying Corps of 2nd Lieut Hartridge.	
	31		Marking of wagons with new signs completed throughout the division	

1577 Wt. W10791/1773 500,000 1/15 D. D. & L. A.D.S.S./Forms/C. 2118.

20th Distr. Train
Vol 3

121
7724

Nov. 15

Omgs
1-6

Confidential

War Diary

of

O.C. 20th Divisional Train. A.S.C.

from 1st November 1915 – 30th November 1915.

Army Form C. 2118.

Instructions regarding War Diaries and Intelligence Summaries are contained in F. S. Regs., Part II. and the Staff Manual respectively. Title pages will be prepared in manuscript.

WAR DIARY
or
~~INTELLIGENCE SUMMARY.~~

(Erase heading not required.)

20th Divisional Train.

Place	Date	Hour	Summary of Events and Information	Remarks and references to Appendices
ESTAIRES	1/11/15		Instructions received that application for transport of blankets should be made when necessary to 3rd Corps, giving when possible 12 hours notice.	
	2.		Situation unchanged.	
	3.		Issue of fuel wood to troops not in the trenches reduced to 1½ lbs per man per day. Allowance of coal increased to 2 lbs per man per day	
	4.		84 heavy draught remounts arrived. Wire to D.A.G base for men to complete establishment	
	5.		Notification received that 6 lbs per man per week of straw for paillasses will be issued when available	
	6.		Situation unchanged.	
	7.		Received notification from D.A.G Base that no A.S.C drivers were available to complete new establishment.	
			Issues of fuel for Field Forges withdrawn.	
	8.		Approval given by Army Hd Qrs for issue of Traces, wire, short, to each company of Train (4 pairs each) equipped with harness. P.D. G.S.	

Army Form C. 2118.

Instructions regarding War Diaries and Intelligence Summaries are contained in F. S. Regs., Part II. and the Staff Manual respectively. Title pages will be prepared in manuscript.

WAR DIARY
or
INTELLIGENCE SUMMARY.

(Erase heading not required.)

Place	Date	Hour	Summary of Events and Information	Remarks and references to Appendices
ESTAIRES	9/11/15.		Situation unchanged.	
	10		do.	
	11.		Instructions received from Hd Qrs that headcollars arriving with remounts are to be returned on such horses as may be evacuated to Mobile Veterinary Section.	
	12.		Directions given that as many oat sacks as possible are to be returned to the base, where they are required for sacking etc.	
	13.		Situation unchanged.	
	14.		Refilling point for 60th Brigade group changed to Map 36A L22 D.4.2. on ESTAIRES - NEUF BERQUIN road.	
	15.		Report to Headquarters stating that proposed A.B. 405 + 405A were considered suitable.	
	16.		The following re-arrangement of duties made. Major Craig to HAVRE, Capt Swanne(?) to S.S.O. Capt Clegg to S.O. Divisional troops. Capt Whyte to S.O. 60th Brigade. Lieut Openshaw to R.O. Divisional Troops	

1577 Wt. W10791/1773 500,000 1/15 D. D. & L. A.D.S.S./Forms/C. 2118.

Instructions regarding War Diaries and Intelligence Summaries are contained in F. S. Regs., Part II. and the Staff Manual respectively. Title pages will be prepared in manuscript.

WAR DIARY
or
~~INTELLIGENCE SUMMARY.~~
(Erase heading not required.)

Army Form C. 2118.

Place	Date	Hour	Summary of Events and Information	Remarks and references to Appendices
ESTAIRES	17/11/15		Furnished 1 G.S. wagon for transport of 197 Land drainage company, their own having broken down (authority A.A.&Q.M.G. 20th Division).	
"	18.		Following maps returned in accordance with instructions from III rd Corps. (3). ANTWERP = do (5). NAMUR " do. (6). BRUSSELS = do. (1). OSTEND - do. (2) GHENT. " do.	
"	19		Letter to A.G. office Base explaining that deficit of 48 H.T. A.S.C drivers is due to differences in new war establishments dated 1st August, recently come to hand.	
"	20.		On receipt of enquiry from Divisional Headquarters as to no transport officer being present at 60th Bde Refilling Point, replied that a W.O. was sent, the officer in question being ill. Explained that this was done to preserve organization of Train, as the W.O. would perform this duty if the division was on the march, and that I was endeavouring to avoid any change from normal procedure when the division was halted, as far as possible. Received instructions from	

1577 Wt. W10791/1773 500,000 1/15 D. D. & L. A.D.S.S./Forms/C. 2118.

Instructions regarding War Diaries and Intelligence Summaries are contained in F. S. Regs., Part II. and the Staff Manual respectively. Title pages will be prepared in manuscript.

WAR DIARY
or
~~INTELLIGENCE SUMMARY.~~
(Erase heading not required.)

Army Form C. 2118.

Place	Date	Hour	Summary of Events and Information	Remarks and references to Appendices
ESTAIRES	20/11/15		Div^l Headquarters to send an officer from some other company if necessary, & not to send W. Officer alone – Requested reconsideration of G.O.C. without result.	
"	21/11/15		Orders received from 1st Army to return as many bread sacks as possible. Issue of 2nd blanket approved.	
"	22/11/15		Detailed Captain E. A. K. MEADE, to prepare & deliver a lecture on the general system of Supply & correct methods and channels of Requisitioning, at the Infantry school of instruction –	
"	23/11/15		Report to Headquarters that the withdrawal of fuel for forge purposes, leaves insufficient coal for cooking & billets.	
"	24/11/15		Following changes in R.P. made. 60th Bde group. SAILLY-ESTAIRES road. 8.30 am G.27 B, east of 500 yards clear of 61st group.	
"	25/11/15		59 Brigade group R.P changed to G.15.D.9.8.	

1577 Wt. W10791/1773 500,000 1/15 D. D. & L. A.D.S.S./Forms/C. 2118.

Instructions regarding War Diaries and Intelligence Summaries are contained in F. S. Regs., Part II. and the Staff Manual respectively. Title pages will be prepared in manuscript.

Army Form C. 2118.

WAR DIARY
or
~~INTELLIGENCE~~ SUMMARY.

(Erase heading not required.)

Place	Date	Hour	Summary of Events and Information	Remarks and references to Appendices
ESTAIRES	27/11/15		Requested Headquarters to expedite posting of supply man, urgently required.	
"	28/11/15		Received instructions that lights were to be carried on vehicles.	
"	29/11/15		Fuel allowance changed as follows:-	
			Men out of trenches, 1½ lbs coal, ¼ lb coke, 2½ lbs wood.	
			" in " 2 lbs coke, ½ lb charcoal, ½ lb wood.	
"	30/11/15		Orders given that no vehicles should pass the following points during daylight. CHARRED POST. N.1.A.0.3.	
			TWO TREE FARM. N.2.C.2.8.	
			CROIX BLANCHE X roads H.32 A.5.1.	
			CROIX MARECHAL X roads H.34 A.9.7.	
			ELBOW FARM. H.29. C.0.3.	
			SMITHS VILLA. H.29. C.9.9.	
			Only single vehicles should proceed to Road junction M.5.D.8.3, ROUGE de BOUT along RUE de BIACHE - LA CROIX LESCORNEX - FLEURBAIX - RUE DE DELETTREE.	

1577 Wt. W10791/1773 500,000 1/15 D. D. & L. A.D.S.S./Forms/C. 2118.

20th Div: Train
Vol: 4

121
7935

Confidential

War Diary

of

O.C. 20th Divisional Train. A.S.C.

from 1st December 1915 to 31st December 1915

Volume 4.

Instructions regarding War Diaries and Intelligence Summaries are contained in F. S. Regs., Part II. and the Staff Manual respectively. Title pages will be prepared in manuscript.

WAR DIARY
or
~~INTELLIGENCE SUMMARY.~~
(Erase heading not required.)

Army Form C. 2118.

20th Divisional Train. A.S.C.

Place	Date	Hour	Summary of Events and Information	Remarks and references to Appendices
ESTAIRES	1 12/15		12 NCOs & men of F.P.Os billets attached to Train transferred for pay, rations to Divisional Headquarters. Instructions received that any German rations found are to be handed to the Supply Officer for transmission to nearest Field Supply Depot.	
"	2 12/15		Instructions given that Draught horses are to be rugged when waiting for lengthy periods.	
"	3 "		Notification received that 2nd Lieut E. S. O'KELLY was invalided to England on 24/11/15, and is now struck off strength.	
			A.F. M.T./B93 forwarded, recommending ~~S~~ Staff Sergeant Crampton for a commission	
"	4.		Remounts for the Division detrained & distributed. 2nd Lieut R.W. H. MASTERS reported for duty & posted to 159 Coy.	
"	5 "		System started whereby each company of the Train in turn is relieved from extra duties for 3 days, the horses & harness, vehicles &c being inspected at the end of each period.	

Instructions regarding War Diaries and Intelligence Summaries are contained in F. S. Regs., Part II. and the Staff Manual respectively. Title pages will be prepared in manuscript.

WAR DIARY
or
~~INTELLIGENCE SUMMARY.~~

(Erase heading not required.)

Army Form C. 2118.

Place	Date	Hour	Summary of Events and Information	Remarks and references to Appendices
ESTAIRES	6 12/15		Inspection of 1st Line Transport, Divisional Troops – Report in separate book.	
"	7 "		Inspection of 1st Line Transport, 61st Brigade.	
"	8 "		1st Army authority received to use N.C.Os., horses, men, & vehicles to assist farmers and civil inhabitants –	
"	9 "		Inspection of 1st Line Transport, 59th Brigade.	
"	10 "		Do. do. 60th Brigade.	
"	11 "		Capt E.A.K. MEADE instructed to repeat his lecture on Supply system &c to class at Infantry school of Instruction.	
"	12 "		15 Heavy Draught horses from 46th Divl. Train drawn & distributed to various units of the Division	
"	13 "		Instructions received from Divl. HdQrs to provide 4 wagons daily to transport clean linen from ESTAIRES Laundry to SAILLY Baths.	

1577 Wt. W10791/1773 500,000 1/15 D. D. & L. A.D.S.S./Forms/C. 2118.

Army Form C. 2118.

Instructions regarding War Diaries and Intelligence Summaries are contained in F. S. Regs., Part II. and the Staff Manual respectively. Title pages will be prepared in manuscript.

WAR DIARY
or
INTELLIGENCE SUMMARY.

(Erase heading not required.)

Place	Date	Hour	Summary of Events and Information	Remarks and references to Appendices
ESTAIRES	14/12/15		Temp Major F. B. HARDY proceeded to ENGLAND for duty with units serving at home, & is struck off strength accordingly (Authority D.D.of T. 1st Army).	
"	15/12/15		Instructions received to send S. Sgt CROMPTON to report to D.D.S&T. 1st Army, as to fitness for commission.	
"	16/12/15		Application made for return of Corporal Birch, on command with Forest Control Officer.	
			Captain H.D. Chaplin reported for duty from 25th Reserve Park.	
"	17/12/15		Report rendered on English H.D. horses to Divl Headquarters.	
			1. How do they do their work? Ans: Very well, being both fast walkers & true pullers.	
			2. Health? Ans. Good. The horses have been exposed to very bad weather, and to date are in good condition.	
			3. Any drawbacks to their use? Ans. Cannot be trotted in the way L.D. horses would be in case of necessity.	
	18/12/15		Instructions received from Divl Hd Qrs to render return of Supplies purchased on every Sunday, made up to Saturday evening.	

1577 Wt. W10791/1773 500,000 1/15 D. D. & L. A.D.S.S./Forms/C. 2118.

Army Form C. 2118.

Instructions regarding War Diaries and Intelligence Summaries are contained in F. S. Regs., Part II. and the Staff Manual respectively. Title pages will be prepared in manuscript.

WAR DIARY
or
~~INTELLIGENCE SUMMARY~~
(Erase heading not required.)

Place	Date	Hour	Summary of Events and Information	Remarks and references to Appendices
ESTAIRES	19/12/15		Attention of Col i/c A.S.C. Section posted called to the fact that T/2 20654 Dr. O'DONNELL posted to this Train on the 8th inst from B.H.T.D is due for discharge on 4/2/16	
"	20/12/15		Application made to O.C. Supply Column to furnish a relief for driver of 160 Company's car, the man being inefficient.	
"	21/12/15		Instructions given for all water carts to be filled & chlorinated under the supervision of the Orderly Officer.	
"	22 "		Instructions received to send S Sgt CROMPTON to D.A.D. of S&T. G.H.Q. Troops, for test as to fitness for commission.	
"	23 "		Information received from the R.P. No. 2. that the Headquarters of his Office & Cashier for payment of furlough advances are now situated at CAMBRIDGE BARRACKS, WOOLWICH.	

Instructions regarding War Diaries and Intelligence Summaries are contained in F. S. Regs., Part II. and the Staff Manual respectively. Title pages will be prepared in manuscript.

WAR DIARY
or
~~INTELLIGENCE SUMMARY.~~
(Erase heading not required.)

Army Form C. 2118.

Place	Date	Hour	Summary of Events and Information	Remarks and references to Appendices
ESTAIRES	24/12/15		Horses inspected by A.D.V.S. 20th Division.	
"	25/12/15		Bridges over River LYS are closed during the day as follows:-	
			PONT DE LA MEUSE (between ESTAIRES and LA GORGUE) 1 pm - 2.30 pm.	
			PONT D'ESTAIRES (East of ESTAIRES) Temporarily pending reconstruction. 12 noon - 3 pm.	
			SAILLY BRIDGE 10.30 am - 11 am, 11-15 am - 11.45 am	
"	26/12/15		All ranks warned as to German spies, and that failure to arrest a suspected person entails trial by Court-Martial.	
"	27/12/15.		Orders given for no man to pass SAILLY bridge after 8 pm. without a pass.	
	28/12/15.		Gas Helmets for drill purposes indented for.	
	29/12/15		Orders for Road Control at R.P. published	

1577 Wt. W10791/1773 500,000 1/15 D. D. & L. A.D.S.S./Forms/C. 2118.

Instructions regarding War Diaries and Intelligence Summaries are contained in F. S. Regs., Part II. and the Staff Manual respectively. Title pages will be prepared in manuscript.

WAR DIARY
or
INTELLIGENCE SUMMARY.
(Erase heading not required.)

Army Form C. 2118.

Place	Date	Hour	Summary of Events and Information	Remarks and references to Appendices
ESTAIRES	30/12/15.		One wagon (bond), horses and driver attached to Salvage Company by order of Divisional Headquarters.	
"	31/12/15		Special indent for H.D remounts forwarded to Headquarters, owing to large number of casualties since last fortnightly return.	
			[illegible] Lieut Col.	
			O.C. 20th Divisional Train ASC	

20th Divl: Train

Vol: 5

January 1916

Confidential

War Diary

of.

OC, 20th Divisional Train.

from 1st January 1916 – 31 January 1916

Instructions regarding War Diaries and Intelligence Summaries are contained in F. S. Regs., Part II. and the Staff Manual respectively. Title Pages will be prepared in manuscript.

WAR DIARY
or
INTELLIGENCE SUMMARY
(Erase heading not required.)

Army Form C. 2118

20th Divisional Train. A.S.C.

Place	Date	Hour	Summary of Events and Information	Remarks and references to Appendices
ESTAIRES	1/1/16		Report to 1st Army recommending the removal of the fitting under limbered wagons for carrying the leather bucket.	
"	2/1/16		Report to A.P.M. as to horses of the Guards division being exercised past refilling points.	
"	3/1/16		Attention of D.A.G. Base called to deficiencies in personnel, and requesting that they may be made good.	
"	4/1/16		Instructions received from Divl. HdQrs to hand over limbered wagon, with drivers & horses complete to O.C. 20th Signal Company R.E., and that it would afterwards be attached to Divl HdQrs.	
"	5/1/16		Horses of train malleined.	
"	6/1/16		do. Inspection of 1st line transport	
"	7		Inspection of 1st line transport.	
"	8.		Notification received that hay ration will be reduced temporarily from 10 to 6 lbs per horse.	

1875 Wt. W593/826 1,000,000 4/15 J.B.C. & A. A.D.S.S./Forms/C. 2118.

Instructions regarding War Diaries and Intelligence Summaries are contained in F. S. Regs., Part II. and the Staff Manual respectively. Title Pages will be prepared in manuscript.

WAR DIARY
or
INTELLIGENCE SUMMARY
(Erase heading not required.)

Army Form C. 2118

Place	Date	Hour	Summary of Events and Information	Remarks and references to Appendices
ESTAIRES	9/1/16		One blanket per man of 59th Brigade, carted to VIEUX BERQUIN & stored with D.C. Supply Column.	
"	10/1/16		59th Brigade, 96 Field Coy R.E. and 159 Company A.S.C. marched to VIEUX BERQUIN and billetted. One blanket per man 61st Brigade carted to VIEUX BERQUIN.	
"	11/1/16		62nd Field Ambulance marched to MORBECQUE. 83rd Field Company R.E. 61st Infantry Brigade, 161 Company A.S.C. to VIEUX BERQUIN. 59th Brigade, 96th Field Company R.E. and 159 Company A.S.C. marched to Reserve Area, 3rd Corps. ~~Supply~~ Refilling point, SEC BOIS Station, map 36 A, E.13. a. 0. 3 for last 3 units. All artillery (less D.A.C.) refilling point, North of R. L72, G. 21. a. to G. 15. D. One blanket per man 60th Brigade carted to VIEUX BERQUIN.	
"	12/1/16		61st Brigade marched to Reserve Area. 3rd Corps. likewise 83rd Field Company R.E. 161 Company A.S.C.:— To VIEUX BERQUIN, 60th Brigade, Pioneer Battalion, 160 Company A.S.C.— To BLARINGHEM, Divisional Headquarters & 158 Company A.S.C.	

1875 Wt. W593/826 1,000,000 4/15 J.B.C. & A. A.D.S.S./Forms/C. 2118.

Army Form C. 2118

Instructions regarding War Diaries and Intelligence Summaries are contained in F. S. Regs., Part II. and the Staff Manual respectively. Title Pages will be prepared in manuscript.

WAR DIARY
or
INTELLIGENCE SUMMARY
(Erase heading not required.)

Place	Date	Hour	Summary of Events and Information	Remarks and references to Appendices
BLARINGHEM	12/1/16		Refilling Points 59th Brigade, 96th Field Company R.E., 62. Field Ambulance, 159 Company A.S.C. } D. 25. B. Sheet 36 A. 61st Brigade, 83rd Field Co. R.E., 161 Company A.S.C. } See Bois Station Sheet 36 A. E.13. a. 0. 3 All Artillery (less D.A.C.) as for 11th inst.	
"	13/1/16		60th Brigade, Pioneer Battalion, 160 Company A.S.C. to Reserve Area, 3rd Corps. Refilling point, See Bois Station, E 13 a. 0. 3. Remaining units refill at D. 25. B. D.M.T., 60 & 61 F Ambulances. D.A.C. 20th F.A.W.V., 84th Field Coy R.E. transferred to 8th Division for supplies.	

1875 Wt. W593/826 1,000,000 4/15 J.B.C. & A. A.D.S.S./Forms/C. 2118.

Army Form C. 2118

Instructions regarding War Diaries and Intelligence Summaries are contained in F. S. Regs., Part II. and the Staff Manual respectively. Title Pages will be prepared in manuscript.

WAR DIARY
or
INTELLIGENCE SUMMARY
(Erase heading not required.)

Place	Date	Hour	Summary of Events and Information	Remarks and references to Appendices
BLARINGHAM	14/1/16		Blanket wagons supplied by 1st Army Auxiliary Transport Company carrying blankets from VIEUX BERQUIN to the various units of the Division in Reserve Area, 3rd Corps	
"	15/1/16		Blanket wagons returned to their company on completion of above duty.	
"	16/1/16		Situation unchanged.	
"	17/1/16		Report to Divl. Headquarters that men have been trained in the various A.S.C. Companies as cooks.	
"	18/1/16		Court of Inquiry appointed to investigate the circumstances by which a farm servant at La ferme de l'HOPITAL, where 158 Company A.S.C. was billetted, was injured.	
"	19/1/16		All motor cars ordered to be sent to O.C. Supply Column to have 1st Army mark painted on them.	

1875 Wt. W593/826 1,000,000 4/15 J.B.C. & A. A.D.S.S./Forms/C. 2118.

Instructions regarding War Diaries and Intelligence Summaries are contained in F. S. Regs., Part II. and the Staff Manual respectively. Title Pages will be prepared in manuscript.

WAR DIARY
or
INTELLIGENCE SUMMARY
(Erase heading not required.)

Army Form C. 2118

Place	Date	Hour	Summary of Events and Information	Remarks and references to Appendices
BLARINGHEM	20th		Application made to O i/c A.S.C. Records, recommending 4 S.S.M. Wells for promotion to Tempy Lieut & Qmr	
"	21st		Situation unchanged. Extra baggage of units stored in HAZEBROUCK.	
"	22nd		Division marched to join 6th Corps. 2nd Army. 41 Blanket wagons attached from 6th Reserve Park. Divl. H.Q. at OXELAERE. Train Headquarters & of Headquarter Company. Map 27 O 17 a. Remaining A.S.C. Companies in brigade areas in the rectangle WINNEZEELE — RUBROUCK — NIEURLET (3 miles N.N.E. of St. OMER) and EECKE. Blanket & baggage wagons accompanied their units — supply sections with their respective A.S.C. companies — after refilling.	
OXELAERE	23rd		Blanket wagons returned to O.C. 6th Reserve Park. Refilling points Div: H.Q. Group OXELAERE. Artillery and D.H.T. BALEMBERG — LE MENEGAT. 59th Brigade HARDIFORT. 60th Brigade Main road E of St. MARIE CAPPEL. 61st Brigade X roads E of WEMAERS - CAPPEL.	

1875 Wt. W593/826 1,000,000 4/15 J.B.C. & A. A.D.S.S./Forms/C. 2118.

Instructions regarding War Diaries and Intelligence Summaries are contained in F. S. Regs., Part II. and the Staff Manual respectively. Title Pages will be prepared in manuscript.

WAR DIARY
or
INTELLIGENCE SUMMARY
(Erase heading not required.)

Army Form C. 2118

Place	Date	Hour	Summary of Events and Information	Remarks and references to Appendices
OKELAERE	24 1/16		Application made for trial by F.G.C.M. of T/1795 Saddler Corporal Masterson.	
"	25 1/16		Attention of O.C. Sanitary Section drawn to the fact that underclothing received in exchange from him had so much vermin in it that it was necessary to destroy it.	
"	26 1/16		Further application made for return of L/Cpl Birch, employed in office of Forest Control, 3rd Corps.	
"	27 1/16		5 Reinforcements (drivers) arrived from Base.	
"	28 1/16		Instructions received from O i/c A.S.C. Section Base to send 2 Clerks to Base for re-posting – names sent & request for drivers to replace made.	
"	29 1/16		Report to Headquarters re capes mackintosh – not altogether waterproof, & were more satisfactory when worn inside out.	

1875 Wt. W593/826 1,000,000 4/15 J.B.C. & A. A.D.S.S./Forms/C. 2118.

Army Form C. 2118

Instructions regarding War Diaries and Intelligence Summaries are contained in F. S. Regs., Part II. and the Staff Manual respectively. Title Pages will be prepared in manuscript.

WAR DIARY
or
INTELLIGENCE SUMMARY
(Erase heading not required.)

Place	Date	Hour	Summary of Events and Information	Remarks and references to Appendices
OXELAERE	30/1/16		Situation unchanged.	
"	31/1/16		Visited railhead & refilling points –	
			J A Hamilton Lieut Col. O.C. 20th Divisional Train. ASC	

1875 Wt. W593/826 1,000,000 4/15 J.B.C. & A. A.D.S.S./Forms/C. 2118.

Confidential

War Diary

of

O.C. 20th Divisional Train ASC

From 1st To. 29th February 1916.

Army Form C. 2118

20th Divisional Train ASC

Instructions regarding War Diaries and Intelligence Summaries are contained in F. S. Regs., Part II. and the Staff Manual respectively. Title Pages will be prepared in manuscript.

WAR DIARY
or
INTELLIGENCE SUMMARY
(Erase heading not required.)

Place	Date	Hour	Summary of Events and Information	Remarks and references to Appendices
OXELAERE	1/7/16		Instructions received to render A.F. B. 212A to D.H.Q. not later than 9.0 pm. Thursday made up to noon Saturday.	
"	2 "		Situation unchanged. Billetting parties sent forward to 49th Divisional area.	
"	3 "		Following units, with their respective transport, moved as follows:-	
			H.Q. 20th Division to ESQUELBECQUE.	
			1 Platoon Cyclist Coy " "	
			H.Q. Signal Coy " "	
			H.Q. R.E. " "	
			Salvage Co. " "	
			H.Q. + H.Q. Co. Train " "	
			61st Brigade group " "	
			32nd Sanitary Section " "	
ESQUELBECQ.	4 "		59th Brigade group marched to HOUTKERQUE + HERZEEL area.	
			20th Div. R.A. " " ZEGGERS CAPPEL area.	
"	5 "		D.M.T. " " NAGTEGAEL FARM + vicinity C.14.	

1875 Wt. W593/826 1,000,000 4/15 J.B.C. & A. A.D.S.S./Forms/C. 2118.

Instructions regarding War Diaries and Intelligence Summaries are contained in F. S. Regs., Part II. and the Staff Manual respectively. Title Pages will be prepared in manuscript.

WAR DIARY
or
INTELLIGENCE SUMMARY
(Erase heading not required.)

Army Form C. 2118

Place	Date	Hour	Summary of Events and Information	Remarks and references to Appendices
ESQUELBEC	5/2/16		Motor M. Gun Battery marched to ESQUELBEC.	
			20th Divl Cyclists (less 1 platoon) " " "	
			11th D.L.I. " " WINNIZEELE + OUDEZEELE.	
			F.A.W.U. " " ESQUELBEC.	
			Mobile Vet. Section " " C. 27. a. 6. 4.	Map 36 A.
			60th Brigade group " " WATOU & vicinity.	
"	6/2/16		Supply & Transport arrangements in the event of order to "Move for Corps Reinforcement".	
			1 (a) 158 - 159 + 161 Companies supply sections will concentrate on the road WINNEZEELE — DROGLANDT. J. 11. d.	
			(b) 160 Company will remain at WATOU. To supply the O.C. Train and O.C. Supply Column will immediately arrange to refill at J. 11. d 160 Company at WATOU.	

1875 Wt. W593/826 1,000,000 4/15 J.B.C. & A. A.D.S.S./Forms/C. 2118.

Army Form C. 2118

Instructions regarding War Diaries and Intelligence Summaries are contained in F. S. Regs., Part II. and the Staff Manual respectively. Title Pages will be prepared in manuscript.

WAR DIARY
or
INTELLIGENCE SUMMARY
(Erase heading not required.)

Place	Date	Hour	Summary of Events and Information	Remarks and references to Appendices
ESQUELBEC	5/2/16		(c) After concentration (or refilling) the whole of the supply sections will move to the PROVEN – POPERINGHE road, square F. 28 & await further orders. The baggage section to be parked at WORMHOUDT.	
			3. After refilling (if required) the Supply Columns to return to railhead at ARNEKE. After reloading the Supply Columns will rendezvous at WINNEZEELE.	
"	6/2/16		Attention of Headquarters R.A. drawn to the necessity of sending guides to conduct transport into camp, & pointing out that considerable difficulty had been experienced during the last march owing to neglect to comply with orders issued on this subject.	
"	7/2/16		Decision received that no Tempy Qr Mrs were at present required in this Force.	
"	8/2/16		Attention of 60th Bde called to the fact that some of their 1st Line Transport is improperly marked.	

1875 Wt. W593/826 1,000,000 4/15 J.B.C. & A. A.D.S.S./Forms/C. 2118.

Army Form C. 2118

Instructions regarding War Diaries and Intelligence Summaries are contained in F. S. Regs., Part II. and the Staff Manual respectively. Title Pages will be prepared in manuscript.

WAR DIARY
or
INTELLIGENCE SUMMARY
(Erase heading not required.)

Place	Date	Hour	Summary of Events and Information	Remarks and references to Appendices
ESQUELBEC.	9 2/16		Situation unchanged.	
"	10 2/16		do.	
"	11 2/16		160 Company moved to lines vacated by 14th Divisional Train F.19.d.6.4.	Map 27.
"	12 2/16		Headquarters Train marched to St JAN DER BEEZEN. L.2.a.2.8.	
			Headquarter Company " " F.27.b.8.2.	Map 27.
			159 Company moved to lines vacated by No 3 Company, 14th Divisional Train at F.26.c.2.7.	
POPERINGHE	13 2/16		161 Company marched to lines vacated by No 4 Company, 14th Divisional Train at F.25.b.8.7.	
			Two private visitors arrived & posted to 159 & 160 Companies.	
"			Instructions received from AA & QMG to hire 30 civilian wagons.	
"	14 2/16		12 civilian wagons taken over from O.C. 14th Divisional Train, 9 hired from Maire of WATOU, 9 from Maire of PROVEN & all at 2 francs per diem from 15th inst, to be returned in good condition	

1875 Wt. W593/826 1,000,000 4/15 J.B.C. & A. A.D.S.S./Forms/C. 2118.

Army Form C. 2118

Instructions regarding War Diaries and Intelligence Summaries are contained in F. S. Regs., Part II. and the Staff Manual respectively. Title Pages will be prepared in manuscript.

WAR DIARY
or
INTELLIGENCE SUMMARY
(Erase heading not required.)

Place	Date	Hour	Summary of Events and Information	Remarks and references to Appendices
POPERINGHE	15/2/16		Application made to D.A.D.O.S. for wire extension traces for use with civilian wagons.	
"	16/2/16		16 Civilian wagons handed over to O.C. 92 Brigade R.F.A. for fatigues of Division, by order of A.A. & Q.M.G.	
"	17/2/16		Orders issued that M.T. vehicles proceeding on the roads east of POPERINGHE will not use headlights	
"	18/2/16		Orders issued that no transport is allowed East of the ELVERDINGHE-VLAMERTINGHE road between the hours of 5.45 am and 6.15 pm.	
"	19/2/16		Stocktaking of all mobilization stores.	
"	20/2/16		2 Civilian hired wagons handed over to O.C. 11th D.L.I. by order of A.A. & Q.M.G.	
	21/2/16.		Report to the effect that a strapping of bedford cord would be preferable to leather for pantaloons under existing conditions.	

Army Form C. 2118

Instructions regarding War Diaries and Intelligence Summaries are contained in F. S. Regs., Part II. and the Staff Manual respectively. Title Pages will be prepared in manuscript.

WAR DIARY
or
INTELLIGENCE SUMMARY
(Erase heading not required.)

Place	Date	Hour	Summary of Events and Information	Remarks and references to Appendices
POPERINGHE	22/2/16		Instructions ~~received~~ [issued, ADVC, 15E by] to detail 2 G.S. Wagons daily at 8.30 am to report at Divisional Baths for transporting washing.	
do	23/2/16		Attention of O.C. Companies again drawn to the necessity for strict supervision in the sterilizing of water obtained from the pumps in the district.	
do	24/2/16		Instructions received from D.D. S&T as to Supply Officers keeping in close touch with their formations, & that they should visit the Headquarters of their formations at least 3 times a week & every unit at least once a week. Orders for Requisitioning officers &c. as to methods of purchase.	
do	25/2/16		Situation unchanged.	
do	26/2/16		Application made to D.H.Q for French interpreters to be exchanged for Belgians in case of 160 Company. Application refused.	
	27/2/16		4 Wagons sent to 93rd Bde RFA at ELVERDINGHE to remove straw in dangerous ~~posi~~ proximity to gun positions.	

1875 Wt. W593/826 1,000,000 4/15 J.B.C. & A. A.D.S.S./Forms/C. 2118.

Instructions regarding War Diaries and Intelligence Summaries are contained in F. S. Regs., Part II. and the Staff Manual respectively. Title Pages will be prepared in manuscript.

WAR DIARY
or
INTELLIGENCE SUMMARY
(Erase heading not required.)

Army Form C. 2118

Place	Date	Hour	Summary of Events and Information	Remarks and references to Appendices
POPERINGHE	28/2/16		In response to enquiry from DHQ report made that wagons are not overloaded in the Train & no necessity for same.	
"	29/2/16		Instructions received from DHQ to remove post office to No 6 1 rue de Furnes POPERINGHE. Complied with.	
			J.A.S. [illegible] Lieut Col. OC 20th Divl Train ASC	

1875 Wt. W593/826 1,000,000 4/15 J.B.C. & A. A.D.S.S./Forms/C. 2118.

20 Div
Train

Vol 6

7

Confidential

War Diary

of

O.C. 20th Divisional Train ASC

From 1st – 31st March 1916.

Instructions regarding War Diaries and Intelligence Summaries are contained in F. S. Regs., Part II. and the Staff Manual respectively. Title Pages will be prepared in manuscript.

WAR DIARY
~~or~~ ~~INTELLIGENCE SUMMARY~~
(Erase heading not required.)

Army Form C. 2118

20th Divisional Train A.S.C.

Place	Date	Hour	Summary of Events and Information	Remarks and references to Appendices
POPERINGHE	1/3/16		Further instructions issued as to strict attention being paid to road discipline. All lights to be screened in POPERINGHE.	
"	2/3/16		2nd Army Traffic orders issued. Loads for R.E. stores on G.S. wagons published to avoid overloading.	
"	3/3/16		Instructions received that horse & wagon lines are hired & paid for by the rent officer of the Claims Commission.	
"	4/3/16		8 Drivers (re-inforcements) arrived from base & posted as follows One – 158 Company, Seven – 159 Company.	
"	5/3/16		Instructions received from Q.M.G. G.H.Q that no hay is henceforth to be purchased in the British Army Area.	
"	6/3/16		Instructions received from D.H.Q. that no French interpreters are to be granted permission to leave the area of ~~the~~ their formation.	

Instructions regarding War Diaries and Intelligence Summaries are contained in F. S. Regs., Part II. and the Staff Manual respectively. Title Pages will be prepared in manuscript.

WAR DIARY
or
INTELLIGENCE SUMMARY
(Erase heading not required.)

Army Form C. 2118

Place	Date	Hour	Summary of Events and Information	Remarks and references to Appendices
POPERINGHE	7/3/16		By order of D.A.Q. 3 sergeants attached to Brigade Machine Gun Companies to assist in their transport work.	
"	8/3/16		Approval given for the issue of two pairs of Trousers, wire, short, to each Infantry Battalion.	
			6 wagons from supply section detailed to carry coal at POPERINGHE Station, also 8 wagons to remove these to PESELHOEK.	
"	9/3/16		Enquiry received from D.A.Q. as to whether the Train saddlers could repair ye harness of Machine Gun Companies - Answer to the effect that in my opinion the suggestion was unsound owing to the distance separating the units.	
"	10/3/16		Instructions given that an officer of each company is to visit his billets once every evening between 6 pm & 9 pm to ensure that the precautions against fire are being observed.	

1875 Wt. W593/826 1,000,000 4/15 J.B.C. & A. A.D.S.S./Forms/C. 2118.

Instructions regarding War Diaries and Intelligence Summaries are contained in F. S. Regs., Part II. and the Staff Manual respectively. Title Pages will be prepared in manuscript.

WAR DIARY
or
INTELLIGENCE SUMMARY
(Erase heading not required.)

Army Form C. 2118

Place	Date	Hour	Summary of Events and Information	Remarks and references to Appendices
POPERINGHE	11/3/16		Instructions received from D.H.Q. that 1 wagon (complete turn out) was to be attached to Yeomanry on being attached to the 2nd Cavalry Division, and that the Bomb wagon was to be used for this purpose.	
"	12/3/16		Instructions received that all manure from horse lines is to be carted away at least 200 yards from billets.	
"	13/3/16		BRIELEN closed for collection of bricks, supply limited at ELVERDINGHE.	
			5 Supply wagons detailed to take emergency rations from PESELHOEK to 61st Brigade.	
"	14/3/16		On application from Mayor of PROVEN, 1 Civilian wagon returned to owner for farm work, and another hired in its place.	
"	15/3/16		3 Saddlers attached to Machine Gun Companies by order of DHQ	
"	16/3/16		5 re-inforcements arrived - Two posted to Hd Qrs Company + One to each brigade company.	

1875 Wt. W593/826 1,000,000 4/15 J.B.C. & A. A.D.S.S./Forms/C. 2118.

Instructions regarding War Diaries and Intelligence Summaries are contained in F. S. Regs., Part II. and the Staff Manual respectively. Title Pages will be prepared in manuscript.

WAR DIARY
or
INTELLIGENCE SUMMARY
(Erase heading not required.)

Army Form C. 2118

Place	Date	Hour	Summary of Events and Information	Remarks and references to Appendices
POPERINGHE	17 3/16		Application made for trial by F.G.C.M. of Corporal W. THORNLEY 158 Company A.S.C.	
	18 3/16		Reduction made in coal issue owing to shortage.	
			Dried vegetables issued twice a week in lieu of fresh.	
			Approval given for issue of hay nets in the proportion of one per animal.	
	19 3/16		Instructions issued re damage to crops, & various detailed orders as to sanitation of lines & billets	
	20 3/16		Lecture given by Captain Meade A.S.C to Officers Class on Supply duties.	
	21 3/16		Application made for increased allowance of field boots.	
	22 3/16		Report made to D.H.Q that partitions in limbered wagons are not required for A.S.C work.	

1875 Wt. W593/826 1,000,000 4/15 J.B.C. & A. A.D.S.S./Forms/C. 2118.

Instructions regarding War Diaries and Intelligence Summaries are contained in F. S. Regs., Part II. and the Staff Manual respectively. Title Pages will be prepared in manuscript.

WAR DIARY
or
INTELLIGENCE SUMMARY
(Erase heading not required.)

Army Form C. 2118

Place	Date	Hour	Summary of Events and Information	Remarks and references to Appendices
POPERINGHE	23/3/16		The attention of O.C. Units again drawn to Corps Memorandum No 13 dated 21st 7/15 and requesting that every effort be made to avoid waste & unnecessary expenditure.	
"	24/3/16		Lieut T. S. ALEXANDER. A.V.C. posted to the Train vice Lieut M. CARSON A.V.C. to ENGLAND.	
"	25/3/16		Instructions given that no transport is to proceed during daylight on the road McGINTY'S CORNER to I.1.d.0.9	
"	26/3/16		Orders given that all ponds used for watering horses are to be fenced.	
"	27/3/16		Instructions issued that every endeavour must be made to prevent noise by transport proceeding through ELVERDINGHE.	
"	28/3/16		The following roads may not be used by horse traffic in both directions (1). BRIELEN – VLAMERTINGHE. (2) HOSPITAL FARM – BRIDGE JUNCTION (3). SIEGE JUNCTION – PIONEER JUNCTION	

1875 Wt. W593/826 1,000,000 4/15 J.B.C. & A. A.D.S.S./Forms/C. 2118.

Instructions regarding War Diaries and Intelligence Summaries are contained in F. S. Regs., Part II. and the Staff Manual respectively. Title Pages will be prepared in manuscript.

WAR DIARY
or
INTELLIGENCE SUMMARY
(Erase heading not required.)

Army Form C. 2118

Place	Date	Hour	Summary of Events and Information	Remarks and references to Appendices
POPERINGHE	29/3/16		Instructions given that O.C. units must make every endeavour to have their men inoculated when the military situation permits.	
"	30/3/16		Revised Traffic Control issued for horse transport.	
"	31/3/16		Orders given that constant attention must be made to the cleanliness and sanitation of camps and their outskirts.	
			J. Somerville [?] Lieut Col.	
			O.C. 20th Div. Train. ASC	

1875 Wt. W593/826 1,000,000 4/15 J.B.C. & A. A.D.S.S./Forms/C. 2118.

20 Div Train vol 8

Confidential

War Diary

of

OC. 20th Divisional Train.

from 1st to 30th April 1916.

Instructions regarding War Diaries and Intelligence Summaries are contained in F. S. Regs., Part II. and the Staff Manual respectively. Title Pages will be prepared in manuscript.

WAR DIARY
or
~~INTELLIGENCE SUMMARY~~
(Erase heading not required.)

Army Form C. 2118

20th Divisional Train. ASC

Place	Date	Hour	Summary of Events and Information	Remarks and references to Appendices
POPERINGHE	1/4/16		Instructions received from D.H.Q. to permanently attach the Divisional Band wagon to the "Officers School" for duty –	
"	2/4/16		Captain Whitty instructed to relieve S.S.O. at PESELHOEK. (temp).	
"	3 "		O i/c ASC Records notified as to absence off leave of T/26455 Dr. E. Cole, full description forwarded.	
"	4.		Notification received that from 10th inst. jam ration is reduced from 4 oz to 3 oz; condensed milk increased from 1/16" tin – 1/12" tin.	
"	5.		Report made to A.P.M concerning drivers of motor lorries belonging to 14th Corps Troops cutting into convoys &c.	
"	6.		Instructions received that no vehicles of any description whether attended or unattended are to be left standing on the permanent way of the light railways running along streets and roads in the area.	
"	7		Instructions received to appoint an officer to conduct a convoy of 2 limbered G.S. wagons per battalion in the Division to THEROUANNE.	

1875 Wt. W593/826 1,000,000 4/15 J.B.C. & A. A.D.S.S./Forms/C. 2118.

Instructions regarding War Diaries and Intelligence Summaries are contained in F. S. Regs., Part II. and the Staff Manual respectively. Title Pages will be prepared in manuscript.

WAR DIARY
or
INTELLIGENCE SUMMARY
(Erase heading not required.)

Army Form C. 2118

Place	Date	Hour	Summary of Events and Information	Remarks and references to Appendices
			Contd	
POPERINGHE.	7 4/16		7th D.C.L.I. only to send one L.G.S. wagon, being at present one short.	
"	8 "		In reply to enquiry from 2nd Army as to amount of bran required, suggest 3 lbs per day when available for the division.	
"	9 "		In accordance with instructions from Divl Headquarters, inspected 25 limbered G.S. wagons being returned by battalions to ABBEVILLE, and found them fit for service.	
"	10 "		Report forwarded to Divl H.Q. as to state of rations stored at the defended posts.	
"	11 "		Instructions received to return 2 motor cars to 2nd Army Troops Supply Column.	
"	12 "		2 Austin cars returned in accordance with above. Sat as president of F.G.C.M. for the trial of 27710 Corpl. Tack, R.E.	
"	13 "		Notification received that T. Captain H.J. Whyte had been granted an extension of leave on medical certificate until 16 4/16.	
"	14 "		Application made for trial by F.G.C.M. of T/3/023999 Saddler Corporal Clements, and of T/2/018082 Farrier Corporal Thomas.	

1875 Wt. W593/826 1,000,000 4/15 J.B.C. & A. A.D.S.S./Forms/C. 2118.

Army Form C. 2118

Instructions regarding War Diaries and Intelligence Summaries are contained in F. S. Regs., Part II. and the Staff Manual respectively. Title Pages will be prepared in manuscript.

WAR DIARY
or
INTELLIGENCE SUMMARY
(Erase heading not required.)

Place	Date	Hour	Summary of Events and Information	Remarks and references to Appendices
POPERINGHE	15/4/16		Orders received to return all potato sacks to railhead	
"	15/4/16		Everyone granted ordinary leave beyond 18th inst recalled so as to be back with his unit by midnight 18/19th.	
			Refilling Points. 61st Bde group. Infantry Battalion at ELVERDINGHE and F camp refilled twice (for 16 & 17th) – Remainder as usual.	
"	16/4/16		Refilling Points – 61st Bde group. Two units, Infantry Battalion from STEENVOORDE HILL and Infantry Bn from G Camp refill twice.	
"	17/4/16		Units which arrived CALAIS on 16th April refill at Detail Store 2 pm. 11th Durham L.I. 20th KRR WINNEZEELE at 11.30 am.	
ESQUELBEC	18/4/16		Train Headquarters, & Headquarters Company marched to ESQUELBEC. Refilling points as on 17th.	
"	19/4/16		Railhead changed to ARNEKE.	

1875 Wt. W593/826 1,000,000 4/15 J.B.C. & A. A.D.S.S./Forms/C. 2118.

Instructions regarding War Diaries and Intelligence Summaries are contained in F. S. Regs., Part II. and the Staff Manual respectively. Title Pages will be prepared in manuscript.

WAR DIARY
or
INTELLIGENCE SUMMARY
(Erase heading not required.)

Army Form C. 2118

Place	Date	Hour	Summary of Events and Information	Remarks and references to Appendices
ESQUELBEC	19/4/16	(contd).	Refilling points.	
			61st Brigade group — CALAIS	
			R.A. — PROVEN ROAD.	
			60th Brigade group. — WATOU.	
			59th " " — WORMHOUDT.	
			11th D.L.I. — do.	
			20th KRRC. — do.	
			Divisional H.Q. & all Divisional Troops not included in Brigade groups — do	
"	20/4/16		Refilling points	
			R.A. — PROVEN ROAD. & LEGGERS - CAPPEL	
			Remainder as for 19th	
			Position of ASC Companies. 158. ESQUELBEC.	
			159. WORMHOUDT.	
			160 WATOU.	
			161. CALAIS.	

1875 Wt. W593/826 1,000,000 4/15 J.B.C. & A. A.D.S.S./Forms/C. 2118.

Instructions regarding War Diaries and Intelligence Summaries are contained in F. S. Regs., Part II. and the Staff Manual respectively. Title Pages will be prepared in manuscript.

WAR DIARY
or
INTELLIGENCE SUMMARY
(Erase heading not required.)

Army Form C. 2118

Place	Date	Hour	Summary of Events and Information	Remarks and references to Appendices
ESQUELBEC	21 X/16		Absence off leave of Captain F. J. Whyte reported to Divl. Hd. Qrs.	
"	22.		Particulars forwarded to O i/c A.S.C. Records of T/3/024261 Driver A. HAZELGROVE, absent off leave in U.K.	
"	23.		Question raised by D.D. of S.&T. as to number of forage wagons in train – Answer 20 made up as follows R.A. 12 D.A.C. 2 Infy Bdes 3 Yeomanry 1. A.S.C. 2.	
"	24.		By order of Divl Hd Qrs, one G.S. wagon (complete team out) sent to CLAIRMARAIS for wood cutting.	
"	25.		Instructions received that one of the spare wagons held by the Train to replace casualties is to be used to carry rations for examining guards & control posts, also for conveyance of prisoners to railheads & sometimes stragglers to their units – This wagon to be returned to Train when necessity for its use ceases.	

1875 Wt. W593/826 1,000,000 4/15 J.B.C. & A. A.D.S.S./Forms/C. 2118.

Instructions regarding War Diaries and Intelligence Summaries are contained in F. S. Regs., Part II. and the Staff Manual respectively. Title Pages will be prepared in manuscript.

WAR DIARY
or
INTELLIGENCE SUMMARY
(Erase heading not required.)

Army Form C. 2118

Place	Date	Hour	Summary of Events and Information	Remarks and references to Appendices
ESQUELBEC	26/7/16		Information received that Captain F.J. Whyte, reported absent, had been granted an extension of leave on medical certificate.	
"	27/7/16		Report to Divl. Hd Qrs that I am in favour of exchanging the limbered G.S. wagon held for supplies of the Signal Company with the G.S. wagon (supply) of the Cyclist Company.	
"	28/7/16		Instructions received that the D.M.T would take their wagons with them when proceeding to join the 2nd Cavalry Division. (AA & QMG.)	
"	29/7/16		In response to enquiry from Divl Headquarters, forwarded names of Lieuts Hartridge & Openshaw as likely to prove useful motor machine gun officers	
"	30/7/16		All T.C. Companies warned as to their responsibilities in the event of a fire occurring in their billets – Copies of fire orders to be submitted to this office J.A. Hamilton Lieut Col OC 20th Divl Train ASC	

1875 Wt. W593/826 1,000,000 4/15 J.B.C. & A. A.D.S.S./Forms/C. 2118.

HEADQUARTERS
Date 1.7/16.
No. HT/XX/1805
20TH DIVISIONAL TRAIN A.S.C.

Secret.

D.A.G. 3rd Echelon

Herewith please find my diary for May. The oversight in not forwarding it is regretted.

1 7/16.

J A Hamilton Lt Col.
OC 20th Divisional Train

20 Div Train
Vol 8
MAY

Army Form C. 2118

Instructions regarding War Diaries and Intelligence Summaries are contained in F. S. Regs., Part II. and the Staff Manual respectively. Title Pages will be prepared in manuscript.

WAR DIARY
or
INTELLIGENCE SUMMARY

(Erase heading not required.)

20th Divisional Train

Place	Date	Hour	Summary of Events and Information	Remarks and references to Appendices
ESQUELBEC	1 5/16		Reported to Divisional Headquarters that the billets allotted to the Train were in a bad sanitary condition when we took them over	
"	2 5/16		Notification received that an increase of bran to two tons a day for division would be made as soon as stocks are available	
"	3 5/16		Orders on prevention of fires again read on parade.	
"	4 5/16		Orders again published as to damage to trees.	
			Refilling points. Following orders published. Units of the 60th Brigade group will draw two days rations from detail store, CALAIS on 5th inst for 6th & 7th & will refill 1 mile E of WATTEN on 7th inst for consumption on 8th and at WORMHOUDT at end of march on 8th inst.	

1875 Wt. W593/826 1,000,000 4/15 J.B.C. & A. A.D.S.S./Forms/C. 2118.

Instructions regarding War Diaries and Intelligence Summaries are contained in F. S. Regs., Part II. and the Staff Manual respectively. Title Pages will be prepared in manuscript.

WAR DIARY
or
INTELLIGENCE SUMMARY
(Erase heading not required.)

Army Form C. 2118

Place	Date	Hour	Summary of Events and Information	Remarks and references to Appendices
ESQUELBEC	5/5/16		Orders received from AA & QMG. to send a farrier sergeant to 20th K.R.R.	
"	6/5/16		Orders again given that all bran sacks are to be returned to the base.	
"	7/5/16		Information requested from O i/c ASC Section - Base as to whether transfers from the Train to Infantry & Artillery units might be considered.	
"	8"		Instructions requested from Div Headquarters as to what powers we had to empty manure pits in farms - Reply received that unless owner is agreeable, nothing can be done in the matter.	
"	9"		Information received that Cpl WHYTE, F. J. had been found unfit by a medical board, & was to be struck off the strength	

Army Form C. 2118

Instructions regarding War Diaries and Intelligence Summaries are contained in F. S. Regs., Part II. and the Staff Manual respectively. Title Pages will be prepared in manuscript.

WAR DIARY
or
~~INTELLIGENCE SUMMARY~~
(Erase heading not required.)

Place	Date	Hour	Summary of Events and Information	Remarks and references to Appendices
ESQUELBEC	10 5/16		T. Capt C. S. NAPIER joined the Train from No 3. Base Supply Depot.	
"	11 "		Situation unchanged.	
"	12.		In answer to D.D.S.T. 2nd Army reported that no R.O.s were being employed on Claims work.	
"	13. "		Instructions received that no officer is to gain admission to No 3 A.S.C. Repair Shop ST OMER without previously obtaining authority to do so.	
	14 "		Instructions received that full advantage is not being made of the 19 wheelers in the Train and that they should be capable of repairing the 1st line vehicles	
	15.		Orders issued forbidding transport to travel East of the ELVERDINGHE—VLAMERTINGHE Road between 3 am and 8.30 pm	

1875 Wt. W593/826 1,000,000 4/15 J.B.C. & A. A.D.S.S./Forms/C. 2118.

Instructions regarding War Diaries and Intelligence Summaries are contained in F. S. Regs., Part II. and the Staff Manual respectively. Title Pages will be prepared in manuscript.

WAR DIARY
or
INTELLIGENCE SUMMARY
(Erase heading not required.)

Army Form C. 2118

Place	Date	Hour	Summary of Events and Information	Remarks and references to Appendices
ESQUELBEC	16 5/16		In response to instructions from Divl Headquarters, submitted names of two men as engineer and electrical engineer respectively.	
"	17 5/16		Application made for trial by F.G.C.M. of T/34574 Dr Hall	
"	"		Instructions given that 3 pairs of H.D. horses with harness + drivers should proceed to POPERINGHE + report to the Town Major for scavenging work.	
"	18		161 Company moved from WATOU to POPERINGHE.	
"	19		160 Company moved from WORMHOUDT to POPERINGHE	
"	20th		Headquarters of Train + 158 Coy marched from ESQUELBEC to POPERINGHE.	

1875 Wt. W593/826 1,000,000 4/15 J.B.C. & A. A.D.S.S./Forms/C. 2118.

Instructions regarding War Diaries and Intelligence Summaries are contained in F. S. Regs., Part II. and the Staff Manual respectively. Title Pages will be prepared in manuscript.

WAR DIARY
or
INTELLIGENCE SUMMARY
(Erase heading not required.)

Army Form C. 2118

Place	Date	Hour	Summary of Events and Information	Remarks and references to Appendices
POPERINGHE	20/5/16.		Refilling points — 61st Brigade, 62 F. Amb., 84 F. Coy. RE., 96 " ", 161 Coy. ASC, H.Q. RE., 60th Brigade, 83 F. Coy. RE., 160 Coy ASC — Brown Road. F. 27 b. to F. 28 a.	Map 27.
			59th Bde., 60th F. Amb., 159 Coy ASC. — WATOU. E 28. c.	
			Divisional Troops, 61st F. Amb. — WORMHOUDT.	
			Royal Artillery at LEGGERS CAPPEL.	

1875 Wt. W593/826 1,000,000 4/15 J.B.C. & A. A.D.S.S./Forms/C. 2118.

Army Form C. 2118

Instructions regarding War Diaries and Intelligence Summaries are contained in F. S. Regs., Part II. and the Staff Manual respectively. Title Pages will be prepared in manuscript.

WAR DIARY
or
INTELLIGENCE SUMMARY
(Erase heading not required.)

Place	Date	Hour	Summary of Events and Information	Remarks and references to Appendices
POPERINGHE	21		Refilling point for all troops EDEWAARTHOEK. G.S.6.	Map 27.
"	22		Instructions received to take action as to castor oil beans having been found in oats. Necessary orders issued.	
"	23		Orders received from AA & QMG, that the waggons of 160 Coy ASC attached to 6th O&B, 12th KRR & 12th RB will not proceed to refilling point: these battalions to draw rations under their own arrangements.	
"	24		Orders given to protect all spokes & naves against shrinkage	
"	25		Instructions issued that lights in buildings are to be properly screened after dark.	
"	26		Reported verbally to Div. Headquarters that the 20 Civilian waggons which they had ordered me to hire, were still doing nothing.	

1875 Wt. W593/826 1,000,000 4/15 J.B.C. & A. A.D.S.S./Forms/C. 2118.

Army Form C. 2118

Instructions regarding War Diaries and Intelligence Summaries are contained in F. S. Regs., Part II. and the Staff Manual respectively. Title Pages will be prepared in manuscript.

WAR DIARY
or
INTELLIGENCE SUMMARY
(Erase heading not required.)

Place	Date	Hour	Summary of Events and Information	Remarks and references to Appendices
POPERINGHE	27/5/16		Orders issued warning men against allowing led horses to graze on sown land	
"	28		Orders received that the withdrawal of the second blanket per man is held in abeyance.	
"	29		Instructions issued re unauthorised use of ambulances	
"	30		Instruction given that on and after 31st inst A/93 will refill as a whole at EDEWAARDHOEK with 61st Bde group	
"	31		No transport of any description permitted to pass East of VLAMERTINGHE by daylight unless in possession of pass signed & stamped by the APM XIVth Corps.	
			31/5/16	
			[illegible] Lt Col. OC 20th Div Train	

1875 Wt. W593/826 1,000,000 4/15 J.B.C. & A. A.D.S.S./Forms/C. 2118.

HEADQUARTERS
Date 3/7/16
No. HT/XX/808
20th DIVISIONAL TRAIN A.S.C.

D.A.G. 3rd Echelon, Base.

Herewith please find my diary for June.

J A Hamilton Lt Col.
O.C. 20th Divl Train

3/7/16.

20 Div Train
June
Vol 9

Instructions regarding War Diaries and Intelligence Summaries are contained in F. S. Regs., Part II. and the Staff Manual respectively. Title Pages will be prepared in manuscript.

WAR DIARY
or
~~INTELLIGENCE SUMMARY~~
(Erase heading not required.)

Army Form C. 2118

20th Divisional Train ASC.

Place	Date	Hour	Summary of Events and Information	Remarks and references to Appendices
POPERINGHE	1/6/16.		Parade service for 4th inst at 159 Coy ASC Headquarters.	
"	2/6/16		Instructions recd that all repairable and unserviceable service dress clothing was to be returned to D.A.D.O.S.	
"	3 "		Instructions given that the hour by which all W.Os. N.C.Os & men must be in their billets extended to 9 pm.	
"	4.		Order received from 2nd Army that no green forage is to be requisitioned in Belgian Territory and that purchases are only to be made from inhabitants willing to sell.	
"	5/6		Stone trough built G 2.A 8 4 (on POPERINGHE Switch Road)	
"	6		In answer to enquiry of DAA & QMG reported that I would be glad to receive Sergeant of A.V.C. to be attached to the Train but did not think that it was necessary.	

1875 Wt. W593/826 1,000,000 4/15 J.B.C. & A. A.D.S.S./Forms/C. 2118.

Army Form C. 2118

Instructions regarding War Diaries and Intelligence Summaries are contained in F. S. Regs., Part II. and the Staff Manual respectively. Title Pages will be prepared in manuscript.

WAR DIARY
or
~~INTELLIGENCE SUMMARY~~
(Erase heading not required.)

Place	Date	Hour	Summary of Events and Information	Remarks and references to Appendices
POPERINGHE	7 6/16		Orders again issued about disposal of manure.	
"	8 6/16.		Instructions received that all billets are to be limewashed	
"	9 6/16.		Orders again given about return of empty bran sacks.	
"	10 "		Information received that Tem. Capt C. J. NAPIER has been granted an extension of leave on medical certificate	
"	11 "		T/Major Cadbury Brown granted an extension of leave on medical certificate	
"	12 6/16.		Instructions received to return any leather jerkins or sheepskin lined coats in possession	
"	13 6/16		Orders again issued about nobody being allowed to have a camera in ~~the~~ his possession	
"	14 6/16.		In accordance with Divl Headquarters instructions hired one [illegible] pattern wagon + delivered it to 59th Brigade.	

1875 Wt. W593/826 1,000,000 4/15 J.B.C. & A. A.D.S.S./Forms/C. 2118.

Instructions regarding War Diaries and Intelligence Summaries are contained in F. S. Regs., Part II. and the Staff Manual respectively. Title Pages will be prepared in manuscript.

WAR DIARY
or
~~INTELLIGENCE SUMMARY~~
(Erase heading not required.)

Army Form C. 2118

Place	Date	Hour	Summary of Events and Information	Remarks and references to Appendices
POPERINGHE	15/6/16		Application of Daylight Saving Bill came in to force.	
"	16.		In consequence of above no transport allowed E. of the ELVERDINGHE – VLAMERTINGHE Road between 4 am & 9.30 pm.	
"	17 "		Orders given for blankets to be disinfected at LAITERIE, Proven Road. Map reference L 5 c 5.9, sheet 27.	
"	18 "		Notification received from A.D.M.S. that the Medical Officer, Capt O'CONNOR, was to be transferred to the 6th Oxford & Bucks. L.I. from 22nd inst. Lieut C.W. WALKER RAMC joining in his place.	
"	19 "		Orders received that in view of coming winter, all horse standings are to be repaired & where necessary new ones built.	
"	20.		Orders given for men to keep their hair closely cut.	

Army Form C. 2118

Instructions regarding War Diaries and Intelligence Summaries are contained in F. S. Regs., Part II. and the Staff Manual respectively. Title Pages will be prepared in manuscript.

WAR DIARY
or
INTELLIGENCE SUMMARY

(Erase heading not required.)

Place	Date	Hour	Summary of Events and Information	Remarks and references to Appendices
POPERINGHE	21 6/16		Orders given to officers as to necessity for secrecy being maintained also again cautioned about fires re	
"	22 "		Order received that no motor car is allowed to approach REIGERSBURG CHATEAU or allowed E. of X roads B29.D.7.5	
"	23 "		Orders given that when a motor car passes a horse vehicle or lorry on a pavé road on which men are walking, the driver invariably sounds his horn & slows down until well clear of the other vehicle'	
"	24 6/16.		Attention again drawn to orders as to disposal of manure.	
"	25 "		Orders given as to disinfection of blankets	
"	26 "		Instructions again received about units bringing to railhead service head collars for each animal arriving on remount trains	

1875 Wt. W593/826 1,000,000 4/15 J.B.C. & A. A.D.S.S./Forms/C. 2118.

Army Form C. 2118

Instructions regarding War Diaries and Intelligence Summaries are contained in F. S. Regs., Part II. and the Staff Manual respectively. Title Pages will be prepared in manuscript.

WAR DIARY
or
~~INTELLIGENCE SUMMARY~~
(Erase heading not required.)

Place	Date	Hour	Summary of Events and Information	Remarks and references to Appendices
POPERINGHE	27/6/16		Surprise parade for 158 Coy. Length of time to turn out 35 minutes.	
"	28/6/16		Orders received as to methods of dealing with unserviceable & reparable S.D. Clothing.	
"	29.		Situation unchanged.	
"	30.		Machines horse clipping Stewart pattern to be returned to Base for overhaul and repair, through D.A.D.O.S.	
			30/6/16. J A Hamilton Lieut Col. OC. 20th Div. Train	

1875 Wt. W593/826 1,000,000 4/15 J.B.C. & A. A.D.S.S./Forms/C. 2118.

20 Div Train July
Vol 10

Confidential

War Diary

of

O.C. 20th Divisional Train ASC

from 1st to 31st July 1916.

Instructions regarding War Diaries and Intelligence Summaries are contained in F. S. Regs., Part II. and the Staff Manual respectively. Title Pages will be prepared in manuscript.

WAR DIARY

~~or~~

~~INTELLIGENCE SUMMARY~~ T.C. 20th Divisional Train

(*Erase heading not required.*)

Army Form C. 2118

Place	Date	Hour	Summary of Events and Information	Remarks and references to Appendices
POPERINGHE	1 7/16		In answer to enquiry of AA & QMG reported that no second blankets were brought over-seas by the Train.	
"	2 "		Instructions received as to precautions to be taken in gas attacks	
"	3 "		Application made to Base for a Staff Sergeant Major to be posted to 61st Field Ambulance.	
"	4		Instructions given re care of bicycle tyres.	
"	5 "		Owing to inclement weather, return of gum boots suspended for the present.	
"	6 "		Orders received that when moving from one area to another no tents or huts are to be moved.	
"	7 "		40 Remounts taken over at railhead & distributed to various units	
"	8 "		Orders given that all horse transport returning from YPRES at night along the YPRES - VLAMERTINGHE Road, will proceed at a walk, whether wagons are empty or otherwise.	

1875 Wt. W593/826 1,000,000 4/15 J.B.C. & A. A.D.S.S./Forms/C. 2118.

Instructions regarding War Diaries and Intelligence Summaries are contained in F. S. Regs., Part II. and the Staff Manual respectively. Title Pages will be prepared in manuscript.

WAR DIARY
or
~~INTELLIGENCE SUMMARY~~
(Erase heading not required.)

Army Form C. 2118

Place	Date	Hour	Summary of Events and Information	Remarks and references to Appendices
POPERINGHE	9/7/16		Orders received that it may be necessary to issue Worcester or other sauce in lieu of pickles. Scale of issue, 1 oz of sauce = 3 oz pickles	
"	10.		Decision received from O i/c A.S.C. Section that the question being at present under consideration no ~~transfer of~~ A.S.C. personnel would be transferred to fighting units.	
"	11.		By instructions of A.A. & Q.M.G. 2 G.S. wagons furnished for work with the Divisional Laundry.	
"	12.		2nd Lieut MASTERS detailed for work with XIV Corps in the event of a move from present position; by order of 30th Division.	
"	13.		Notification received that Lieut G.O. OPENSHAW had been granted sick leave of absence until 23rd inst, when a further medical board would assemble.	
"	14.		Decision received from Div^l H^d Qrs that the proposal of A.D.P.S to attach men of the Post Office to the Train for transport was irregular.	

1875 Wt. W593/826 1,000,000 4/15 J.B.C. & A. A.D.S.S./Forms/C. 2118.

Instructions regarding War Diaries and Intelligence Summaries are contained in F. S. Regs., Part II. and the Staff Manual respectively. Title Pages will be prepared in manuscript.

WAR DIARY
or
~~INTELLIGENCE SUMMARY~~
(Erase heading not required.)

Army Form C. 2118

Place	Date	Hour	Summary of Events and Information	Remarks and references to Appendices
POPERINGHE	15 7/16		160 Coy marched to G.6.a.5.7. and joined up with their brigade (Map 36) was attached to IInd Anzac Corps	
"	16.		159 Coy & 161 Coy marched to C.10.b.5.2 & L.4.d.6.9. Map 27. respectively. HQ Coy Train marched to WORMHOUDT.	
"	17.		HQ Coy Train marched to E.7.b.4.4. sheet 27 – 158 Company remaining at F.28.d.9.2. Map 27.	
ESQUELBEC	18.		Orders received from AA & QMG that in the event of the division being concentrated in the area WATOU–PROVEN: POPERINGHE the baggage section is to be parked at DROULANDT. The supply section at WATOU. The R.A. portion of the HQ Coy to remain as at present at F.28 so long as the Artillery remains in the line.	
"	19.		Instructions received from DDST 2nd Army to exchange Sunbeam car No 17856 for a closed Wolseley car belonging to 14th Corps Heavy Artillery. The latter car required a thorough overhaul.	

1875 Wt. W593/826 1,000,000 4/15 J.B.C. & A. A.D.S.S./Forms/C. 2118.

Instructions regarding War Diaries and Intelligence Summaries are contained in F. S. Regs., Part II. and the Staff Manual respectively. Title Pages will be prepared in manuscript.

WAR DIARY
or
~~INTELLIGENCE SUMMARY~~
(Erase heading not required.)

Army Form C. 2118

Place	Date	Hour	Summary of Events and Information	Remarks and references to Appendices
BAILLEUL	20 7/16		Train Hdqrs moved to BAILLEUL. Orphan House on LOCRE Road.	
"	21 "		Instructions given to all O.C. Companies as to the importance of maintaining all water carts in thorough working order. Indent forwarded, by order of DAQMG, for 35 LD horses to replace similar number of HD	
"	22 "		1 NCO + wagon sent to ABEELE to draw 3 Handcarts + to deliver them at D.H.Q. Orders received from ADMS. for Lieut WALKER. RAMC. M.O. i/c Train to rejoin Hdqrs at once.	
"	23 "		Present map references 160 Coy ASC P.26 d.9.7. 161 Coy ASC P.20.c.7.7.	
"	24		Instructions given to OC. 158 Coy ASC. to show promotion of SSM Ritchie to A/i/c SSM in current AF.B 213 A. Colonel i/c ASC Section informed that ABs 64 of personnel of Field Ambulances have been verified + brought up to date.	

1875 Wt. W593/826 1,000,000 4/15 J.B.C. & A. A.D.S.S./Forms/C. 2118.

Instructions regarding War Diaries and Intelligence Summaries are contained in F. S. Regs., Part II. and the Staff Manual respectively. Title Pages will be prepared in manuscript.

WAR DIARY
or
~~INTELLIGENCE SUMMARY~~
(Erase heading not required.)

Army Form C. 2118

Place	Date	Hour	Summary of Events and Information	Remarks and references to Appendices
BAILLEUL	25/7/16		159 Coy A.S.C. entrained for FREVENT at HOPOUTRE	
			161 " " " DOULLENS at CASSEL.	
			HQrs Train " " " " .	
			Report to D.D.S.T. 2nd Army that 2 reinforcements had arrived considerably deficient in clothing & equipment.	
DOULLENS	26/7/16		Situation unchanged.	
BUS-les-ARTOIS.	27"		Situation of Train now as follows Sheet 11. LENS.	
			Headquarters of Train BUS-les-ARTOIS	
			158 Coy MAP 27 F 28. d. 9. 2.	
			159 " " LENS 11. 300x N. of E in HUTHIE.	
			160 " " " " VAUCHELLES-les-AUTHIE	
			161 " " " S in BUS-les-ARTOIS.	
"	28"		Companies marched to T. 8. a. & bivouacked.	
"	29"		Headqrs Train marched to COUIN.	
COUIN.	30"		Instructions given to Companies to comply with orders as to concealment from hostile aircraft. Examined road up to [illegible] les BOIS.	
"	31		Capt PAKENHAM detailed for duty as O i/c Reserve Lines at La BELLE EGLISE.	

J. Hamilton Lieut Col.
O.C. 20th Divl. Train A.S.C.

1875 Wt. W593/826 1,000,000 4/15 J.B.C. & A. A.D.S.S./Forms/C. 2118.

20
20 Div Train
Vol 11

Confidential

War Diary

of

O.C. 20th Divisional Train A.S.C.

June 1st to 31st August 1916.

Confidential

Headquarters, 20th Division.

Herewith diary for current month.

J. H. Hamilton Lt Col

31/8/16. O.C. 20th Divl. Train

Instructions regarding War Diaries and Intelligence Summaries are contained in F. S. Regs., Part II. and the Staff Manual respectively. Title Pages will be prepared in manuscript.

WAR DIARY
or
INTELLIGENCE SUMMARY
(Erase heading not required.)

Army Form C. 2118

20th Divisional Train A.S.C.

Place	Date	Hour	Summary of Events and Information	Remarks and references to Appendices
COUIN	1 8/16		Return of purchases forwarded to D.D. S&T. Reserve Army. Information received that T/Lieut Openshaw having been pronounced fit for duty is to rejoin this unit.	
"	2 8/16		Instructions received from Reserve Army that no unripe wheat & oats to supplement the forage ration is to be bought. (R.O. 69).	
"	3 8/16		C.S.M. Hardy posted to 61st Field Ambulance on probation for S.S. Major.	
"	4 "		Information received that Lieut Hartridge had been selected for training as a pilot in the R.F.C. & is to proceed to England	
"	5 8/16		Application from O.C. 320 Co. ASC for transfer of Capt Templeton to R.A. not recommended as this officer is under arrest.	
"	6 8/16		Sergt McPhail. ASC. recommended for a temporary commission in the RA.	

1875 Wt. W593/826 1,000,000 4/15 J.B.C. & A. A.D.S.S./Forms/C. 2118.

Instructions regarding War Diaries and Intelligence Summaries are contained in F. S. Regs., Part II. and the Staff Manual respectively. Title Pages will be prepared in manuscript.

WAR DIARY
or
~~INTELLIGENCE SUMMARY~~
(Erase heading not required.)

Army Form C. 2118

Place	Date	Hour	Summary of Events and Information	Remarks and references to Appendices
COLIN	7/8/16		Orders received that wagons are not to use either of the roads leading COLINCAMPS at its Eastern end i.e. to EUSTON or the SUCRERIE during daylight	
"	8 "		Instructions requested from D.A.D. as to replacement of Town Major at present found by [illegible] Coy 38th Div Train, ~~at~~ now attached to this unit.	
"	9 "		Orders issued as to prevention of wastage of water.	
"	10 "		Evacuation recommended of H.Q.s riders. chestnut gelding No. 20.	
"	11 "		Orders issued concerning men being conveyed in wagons to get out & walk when going up hill.	
"	12 "		Instructions given for all remounts to be kept separate from other horses for at least a week in order to prevent the introduction of infectious or contagious diseases.	

1875 Wt. W593/826 1,000,000 4/15 J.B.C. & A. A.D.S.S./Forms/C. 2118.

Army Form C. 2118

Instructions regarding War Diaries and Intelligence Summaries are contained in F. S. Regs., Part II. and the Staff Manual respectively. Title Pages will be prepared in manuscript.

WAR DIARY
or
~~INTELLIGENCE SUMMARY~~
(Erase heading not required.)

Place	Date	Hour	Summary of Events and Information	Remarks and references to Appendices
COUIN	13/8/16		Orders issued in connection with traffic regulations - wagons to keep as near as possible to right side of road, gaps to be left at frequent intervals, cross roads & junctions to be left clear. Transport not to halt in towns & villages.	
"	14"		Instructions given as to collection of stores	
"	15"		Orders received that transfers to other units must be submitted to ~~DAG~~ 3rd Echelon for final approval.	
"	16"		Orders given for all horses & mules to be branded with the broad arrow.	
"			160 Coy ASC marched to ORVILLE.	
BEAUVAL	17"		161 Coy marched to THIEVRES. Headquarters to BEAUVAL.	

1875 Wt. W593/826 1,000,000 4/15 J.B.C. & A. A.D.S.S./Forms/C. 2118.

Instructions regarding War Diaries and Intelligence Summaries are contained in F. S. Regs., Part II. and the Staff Manual respectively. Title Pages will be prepared in manuscript.

WAR DIARY
or
~~INTELLIGENCE SUMMARY~~
(Erase heading not required.)

Army Form C. 2118

Place	Date	Hour	Summary of Events and Information	Remarks and references to Appendices
BEAUVAL	18/8/16		160 Coy ASC marched to BERNEVIL.	
			161 " " " HEM.	
			159 " " " BEAUVAL.	
VILLERS BOCAGE	19/8/16		Div. H.Q. Transport etc + 59th Bde group marched to VILLERS BOCAGE	
			61st Bde group " " "	
			60th " " marched to NAOURS.	
TREUX	20/8/16		T/Lieut G.H. STUDDERT transferred to No I Forage Magazine ABANCOURT.	
			59th Bde Group marched to MEAULTE	
			61st " " " " MORLANCOURT.	
			60th " " " " VILLE SOUS CORBIE	
F.26.d.1.3. ALBERT.	21/8/16		Headquarters Train marched F.26.d.1.3. Application made to have for 1 CSM 1 Corporal H.T.	

1875 Wt. W593/826 1,000,000 4/15 J.B.C. & A. A.D.S.S./Forms/C. 2118.

Army Form C. 2118

WAR DIARY
or
INTELLIGENCE SUMMARY
(Erase heading not required.)

Instructions regarding War Diaries and Intelligence Summaries are contained in F. S. Regs., Part II. and the Staff Manual respectively. Title Pages will be prepared in manuscript.

Place	Date	Hour	Summary of Events and Information	Remarks and references to Appendices
near ALBERT.	22 8/16		Train collected at GROVE TOWN.	
GROVE TOWN	23 8/16		T/Lieutenant H. A. HENSON A.S.C. transferred from 158 Coy A.S.C. to 160 Coy from this date.	
"	24 8/16		Refilling point for the whole division at GROVE TOWN railhead L.1.c. Central. at 8.0 am	
"	25 8/16		S.T.A./130 Dr. Nock + T/24872 Dr. Nook having been sent to this Train in error, transferred this day to 24th Divisional Train.	
"	26 8/16		Instructions issued as to necessity of wearing regulation pattern identity discs.	
"	27 8/16		Attention drawn to necessity of carrying out in every detail the instructions contained in 4th Army Traffic orders.	
"	28 8/16		Major Soames – S.S.O. detailed by DHQ to act as Judge Advocate.	
"	29.		Instructions received as to disposal of shelters + tents when the Division moves	

1875 Wt. W593/826 1,000,000 4/15 J.B.C. & A. A.D.S.S./Forms/C. 2118.

Instructions regarding War Diaries and Intelligence Summaries are contained in F. S. Regs., Part II. and the Staff Manual respectively. Title Pages will be prepared in manuscript.

WAR DIARY
or
~~INTELLIGENCE SUMMARY~~
(Erase heading not required.)

Army Form C. 2118

Place	Date	Hour	Summary of Events and Information	Remarks and references to Appendices
GROVE TOWN	30 8/16		T/12917 S.S.M. Hinton promoted acting 1st Class. S.S.M.	
"	31 8/16		Instructions received from D.H.Q. as to evacuation of H.D. horses 147 & 111, attached to 11th D.L.I. reported by them as jibbers.	
			J.A. Hamilton Lt.Col.	
			31 8/16 O.C. 20th Div. Train ASC	

1875 Wt. W593/826 1,000,000 4/15 J.B.C. & A. A.D.S.S./Forms/C. 2118.

Confidential

War Diary

of

O.C. 20th Divisional Train. ASC

From 1st to 30th September 1916.

Vol 12

Confidential

Headquarters, 20th Division,

I beg to forward war diary for present month herewith.

J A Smith Lt Col
O.C. 20th Div Train ASC

30 9/16

Instructions regarding War Diaries and Intelligence Summaries are contained in F. S. Regs., Part II. and the Staff Manual respectively. Title Pages will be prepared in manuscript.

WAR DIARY
or
~~INTELLIGENCE~~ SUMMARY
(Erase heading not required.)

Army Form C. 2118.

20th Divisional Train. A.S.C

Place	Date	Hour	Summary of Events and Information	Remarks and references to Appendices
GROVETOWN	1 9/16		Position of Train as follows. HdQrs L 1 c 5.7 159 Coy. F 29. d.4.1. 160 " F 25. d. 8.2 161 " L 7 c. 3. 8.	
			Application made to A.D.V.S. to return saddlery & equipment of V.O. on Train charge.	
"	2 9/16		Orders given that wherever possible, horse transport & horses move by tracks, and roads left clear for Mechanical Transport.	
"	3 "		Capt G. N. W. BARNES invalided to England and struck off strength.	
"	4 "		Orders received from Divisional Headquarters to detail an officer to receive and distribute remounts arriving from DIEPPE.	
"	5 "		Instructions received to send a G.S. wagon to H.Qrs for the use of Divisional band.	
"	6 "		Refilling point GROVETOWN. Headquarters, Sanitary Section, Veterinary Section, SAA. Section at CORBIE. Time 10.30 am.	

2449 Wt. W14957/M90 750,000 1/16 J.B.C. & A. Forms/C.2118/12.

Instructions regarding War Diaries and Intelligence Summaries are contained in F. S. Regs., Part II. and the Staff Manual respectively. Title Pages will be prepared in manuscript.

WAR DIARY
or
~~INTELLIGENCE SUMMARY~~
(Erase heading not required.)

Army Form C. 2118.

Place	Date	Hour	Summary of Events and Information	Remarks and references to Appendices
GROVE TOWN	7 9/16		Instructions received to send a motor car for use of Capt Clegg, proceeding by road with R.A. to rejoin this Division.	
"	8 9/16		158 Company marched via ABEELE to HARDIFORT. 159 " " to CORBIE 160 " " " " 161 " " " MERICOURT.	
CORBIE	9 9/16		158 Company marched via CASSEL - AIRE to SERNY.	
"	10 9/16		158 Company refit at LILLERS and marched to WAVRANS - distance 28 miles.	
Forked Tree.	11 9/16		Train moved to following positions: Hd. Qrs F. 26. c.; 159 L.7. c.2.6.; 160 E.17. b.6.7.; 161 F. 21. b. 158 refit at St POL & proceed to Pt BOUBERS.	
"	12 9/16		158 Coy refit at FREVENT & march to OCCOCHES.	

2449 Wt. W14957/M90 750,000 1/16 J.B.C. & A. Forms/C.2118/12.

Instructions regarding War Diaries and Intelligence Summaries are contained in F. S. Regs., Part II. and the Staff Manual respectively. Title Pages will be prepared in manuscript.

WAR DIARY
or
INTELLIGENCE SUMMARY
(Erase heading not required.)

Army Form C. 2118.

Place	Date	Hour	Summary of Events and Information	Remarks and references to Appendices
FORKED TREE	15 9/16		158 Company refit at CANAPLES and marched to FLESSELLES.	
GROVE TOWN	14.		Present position of Train Wagons} 158. } F 30. c. 4. 4 159. L. 7. c. 2. 6. 160. K. 12. a. 9. 3. 161. K. 2. b. 8. 4.	
"	15.		Instructions received from AA & QMG. that if regimental transport is in difficulty, ~~that~~ the train wagons must proceed to Brigade H.Q. as near as possible before transferring rations - Orders given to all companies accordingly. 40 pack saddles for brigade made & handed over.	
"	16.		Orders given to O.C. 159 Company for baggage wagons to return to company lines - O.C. companies instructed to pay strict attention to smoke helmets, field dressings, and identity discs.	

2449 Wt. W14957/M90 750,000 1/16 J.B.C. & A. Forms/C.2118/12.

Instructions regarding War Diaries and Intelligence Summaries are contained in F. S. Regs., Part II. and the Staff Manual respectively. Title Pages will be prepared in manuscript.

WAR DIARY
or
INTELLIGENCE SUMMARY

(Erase heading not required.)

Army Form C. 2118.

Place	Date	Hour	Summary of Events and Information	Remarks and references to Appendices
GROVE TOWN	17 9/16		Instructions received from Div HQ to take 1000 petrol tins filled with water to the dump on the west edge of BERNAFAY WOOD daily until further orders	
"	18 9/16		Orders received from Div: HQ for baggage wagons of 59th Bde to return to their Transport Lines – Action taken accordingly	
"	19 "		Order received to send 500 full petrol tins to MINDEN POST on 20th inst & duly complied with	
"	20 "		Report forwarded to H Qrs that horse shoes supplied are of inferior quality but that our practice has been to calk the heels, thereby getting a shoe to last about 14 days.	
"	21 "		Orders received that the Train will remain in their present bivouacs with the exception of 160 Coy, who will proceed to VILLE-SUR-ANCRE.	
"	22 "		Refilling point for whole division – E.30.c.	
"	23 "		R.P. for Divisional H.Q. & 160th Bde group J.6.d. Central at 9 am. Divisional Commander publishes an order that all COs are to pay attention to the cleaning & renovating of all harness.	

2449 Wt. W14957/M90 750,000 1/16 J.B.C. & A. Forms/C.2118/12.

Instructions regarding War Diaries and Intelligence Summaries are contained in F. S. Regs., Part II. and the Staff Manual respectively. Title Pages will be prepared in manuscript.

WAR DIARY
or
INTELLIGENCE SUMMARY
(Erase heading not required.)

Army Form C. 2118.

Place	Date	Hour	Summary of Events and Information	Remarks and references to Appendices
GROVETOWN	24/9/16		Application made to O i/c A.S.C. Section for permission to promote S4/061018 Corporal Whyte, J. if no sergeant clerk was available at base.	
"	25 "		Instructions issued as to use of collar pads. – Reported to Div. H.Qrs that the Lewis Gun Handcart did not lend itself to adaptation to shaft draught – suggested traces & spreader, with handles in rear to steady loads.	
"	26 "		Division refilled twice at I 30 c. Div H.Qrs refilled at TREUX at 9 am and at GROVETOWN at 2 pm.	
"	27 "		R.P. for whole division – I. 30. c. 2 pm. 160 Coy reported Trans	
"	28		Reported to Divl. Headquarters that oat straw was being improperly taken from grounds near our camp by 126 Battery R.F.A.	
"	29 "		Proceedings of Court of Enquiry in case of injury to T4/073189 Dr. R. Lunt forwarded to Colonel i/c A.S.C. Section.	
"	30 "		Refilling changed to HAPPY VALLEY – F. 27. a. at 2 pm.	

J.A. Hamilton Lieut Col.
O.C. 20th Divl. Train A.S.C.

Vol 13

20th Divisional Train.

October 1916

Confidential

Headquarters 20th Division

Herewith my diary for October.

J A Hamilton Lt Col.
O.C. 20th Train

31/10/16.

Confidential

War Diary

of

O.C. 20th Divisional Train ASC

From 1st to 31st October 1916.

Army Form C. 2118.

Instructions regarding War Diaries and Intelligence Summaries are contained in F. S. Regs., Part II. and the Staff Manual respectively. Title Pages will be prepared in manuscript.

WAR DIARY
or
INTELLIGENCE SUMMARY
(Erase heading not required.)

O.C. 30th Divisional Train

Place	Date	Hour	Summary of Events and Information	Remarks and references to Appendices
GROVE TOWN	1/10/16	10.30 am	Struck camp at F. 30 c. 4.4 (Map 62D) and marched to F. 27 c Central.	
F. 27. c. Central	2/10/16		Two new sail covers handed over to the D.A.D.O.S. by order of A.A. & Q.M.G. All ranks warned concerning aerated waters of local manufacture.	
"	3 "		Report rendered to Div. H.Q. that, in my opinion, 2 H.D. horses would be better than a team of mules in a water cart, owing to lack of experienced drivers	
"	4.		Orders issued for all wagons to carry feeds for their horses when on any journey or fatigue	
"	5.		Instructions received no vehicles of any description to go east of BERNAFAY CROSS ROADS between 12 noon & 3 pm.	
"	6 "		Attention drawn in Administrative Orders to the importance of units sending their representatives at the hour ordered for distribution of remounts.	

2449 Wt. W14957/M90 750,000 1/16 J.B.C. & A. Forms/C.2118/12.

Instructions regarding War Diaries and Intelligence Summaries are contained in F. S. Regs., Part II. and the Staff Manual respectively. Title Pages will be prepared in manuscript.

WAR DIARY
or
INTELLIGENCE SUMMARY
(Erase heading not required.)

Army Form C. 2118.

Place	Date	Hour	Summary of Events and Information	Remarks and references to Appendices
F.27.c. Central (Map 62D)	7 10/16		Orders issued with regard to strict compliance with orders for chlorination of water, fly proofed latrines and general supervision of cooking arrangements.	
	8 10/16		Traffic orders of 4th Army published & attention drawn to the fact that owing to state of roads & congestion of the area, strict road discipline was to be maintained	
"	9 10/16		Position of Brigade Companies 159 Coy J. 6 d. 7.7 160 " I. 30. a. 6.4 161 " I. 30 a 6. 4	
"	10 "		Authority given for issue of horse rugs on a scale of one per horse	
"	11 "		Instructions received from DADPS, XIV Corps for the F.P.O to remain with 158 Coy in the event of Train H.Q. being separated from the company.	
"	12 "		Instructions received that all N.C.Os & men proceeding on leave must be medically inspected.	

2449 Wt. W14957/M90 750,000 1/16 J.B.C. & A. Forms/C.2118/12.

Instructions regarding War Diaries and Intelligence Summaries are contained in F. S. Regs., Part II. and the Staff Manual respectively. Title Pages will be prepared in manuscript.

WAR DIARY
or
INTELLIGENCE SUMMARY
(Erase heading not required.)

Army Form C. 2118.

Place	Date	Hour	Summary of Events and Information	Remarks and references to Appendices
F 27. c. Central (Map 62 d.)	13 10/16		A. F. M.T./3993 relating to T2/SR 01225 S.S.M. Montague Smith forwarded.	
	14 "		Situation unchanged.	
CORBIE	15		H'dqrs Train moved to CORBIE. Position of companies as follows.	
			158 (Albert) F. 27. c. Central.	
			159 " J. 6. d. 7 7.	
			160 (62nd) N. 12. d. 2. 3.	
			161 " O. 4. d 7 8.	
"	16 "		Instructions received for all ranks who have not been re-inoculated since 1-1-16 to be inoculated before the 28th inst.	
"	17 "		Time of refilling for 60th Bde group changed to 8.30 am.	
"	18 "		Situation unchanged.	
VIGNACOURT	19		Headquarters of Train marched to VIGNACOURT.	
"	20.		XIV Corps order received, again protesting against overloading of Vehicles.	

2449 Wt. W14957/M90 750,000 1/16 J.B.C. & A. Forms/C.2118/12.

Instructions regarding War Diaries and Intelligence Summaries are contained in F. S. Regs., Part II. and the Staff Manual respectively. Title Pages will be prepared in manuscript.

WAR DIARY
or
INTELLIGENCE SUMMARY

(Erase heading not required.)

Army Form C. 2118.

Place	Date	Hour	Summary of Events and Information	Remarks and references to Appendices
BELLOY sur SOMME	21 10/16		H.Q. of Train marched to BELLOY-sur-SOMME, position of companies	
			158 Coy (Albert) 7.27.c. (central)	
			159 " (Amiens 17) 150 yards of railway station PICQUIGNY.	
			160 " do. under the S in MONTONVILLERS.	
			161. do. S of the O in LA-CHAUSSEE-TIRANCOURT.	
"	22"		New location of 160 Coy (LENS 11) 500 yds W of V in VIGNACOURT.	
"	23		Attention of all concerned drawn to the danger of using braziers etc in places where there is no proper ventilation	
"	24		At request of Div. HQ. inspected personally the transport of the 59th Bde. M G Co. I found it in good condition & reported that the I.O.M. agreed.	
"	25		S4/072331 Pte Webb, 159 Co. + S4/070183 Pte Morton 161 Coy sent to Adv Base Depot for reporting	
"	26		Report as to exchange of remounts forwarded to AA&QMG.	
"	27		Instructions sent to O.C. 158 Coy to send Wolseley Car 15904 to workshops for repair/French [illegible]	
"	28		Information asked from [illegible] for painting of billeting boards for billets	
"	29		O.C. 159 Coy instructed to apply for material for above.	
"	30		Situation unchanged	
	31		T4/110877 Pte A. Lows sent to base by order of ADMS	

2449 Wt. W14957/M90 750,000 1/16 J.B.C. & A. Forms/C.2118/12.

Jas[illegible] Lt Col
OC 20th Div Train

31 10/16

Vol 14

Confidential

War Diary

of

O.C. 20th Divisional Train A.S.C.

From 1st to 30th November 1916

Army Form C. 2118.

WAR DIARY
or
INTELLIGENCE SUMMARY
(Erase heading not required.)

Instructions regarding War Diaries and Intelligence Summaries are contained in F. S. Regs., Part II. and the Staff Manual respectively. Title Pages will be prepared in manuscript.

T.C. 20th Divisional Train

Place	Date	Hour	Summary of Events and Information	Remarks and references to Appendices
OISSY.	1 My/16		Disposition of Train – Hd Qrs Train Chateau OISSY. 160 Company CROUY. 161 " MOLLIENS-VIDAME. 159 " PICQUIGNY.	
"	2 "		159 Company moved to FOURDRINOY – BREILLY Road due east of FOURDRINOY Church.	
"	3 "		Instructions received for Major NAPPER to report for duty with 61st Divisional Train.	
"	4 "		Orders issued as to billeting parties ascertaining the source of water supply.	
"	5 "		Instructions issued that no men are allowed to enter barns containing hay or straw or to be in the vicinity of ricks of hay or corn.	
"	6 "		Application to DD. of S.T. for forage bought by Army purchasing board –	

2449 Wt. W14957/M90 750,000 1/16 J.B.C. & A. Forms/C.2118/12.

Army Form C. 2118.

Instructions regarding War Diaries and Intelligence Summaries are contained in F. S. Regs., Part II. and the Staff Manual respectively. Title Pages will be prepared in manuscript.

WAR DIARY
or
INTELLIGENCE SUMMARY
(Erase heading not required.)

Place	Date	Hour	Summary of Events and Information	Remarks and references to Appendices
OISSY.	7 11/16		Orders received that if a unit is route marching, 1st Line Transport will accompany it	
"	8.		All ranks warned not to walk on ground which is cultivated.	
"	9.		Interpreter HONOREZ temporarily attached to S.O. 160th Brigade	
"	10.		Permission received to indent for bayonets	
"	11.		Attention again drawn to GRO. 1882 re picked up nails	
"	12.		Baggage wagon horses returned to 158 Coy from RA	
"	13.		Application forwarded for a regular commission for Lt Corker	
"	14.		Issue of waterproof ration bags on scale of 100 per Battalion in the front line approved.	
"	15.		Hd Qrs Train moved to AILLY-sur-SOMME	
CORBIE	16.		Map references of Train as follows 158 (Albert) F.27.c. Central 159 " J.6.a.6.4. 160 (62D) I.29.c.9.1. 161 (Dieppe 16) AVESNES [illegible]	

2449 Wt. W14957/M90 750,000 1/16 J.B.C. & A. Forms/C.2118/12.

Army Form C. 2118.

Instructions regarding War Diaries and Intelligence Summaries are contained in F. S. Regs., Part II. and the Staff Manual respectively. Title Pages will be prepared in manuscript.

WAR DIARY
or
INTELLIGENCE SUMMARY
(Erase heading not required.)

Place	Date	Hour	Summary of Events and Information	Remarks and references to Appendices
CORBIE.	17th		Orders issued as to Field Punishment – no man to be tied to a fixed object in view of civil population.	
"	18.		161 Company moved to AIRAINES.	
"	19.		Report on chaff cutter rendered	
"	20.		Chargers issued by remounts for 61st Bde Commander handed to V.O. 32nd Divl. Det. Sec.	
"	21.		2nd G.S. Wagons handed over to 29th Divl. Train by order of Divl. Headquarters.	
"	22.		Complaint made as to length of time required to obtain Ordnance Stores.	
"	23.		161 Coy moved to BOURDON (Amiens 17).	
"	24.		Orders received that all transport vehicles are not to be trotted, except Officers mess carts, & in cases of emergency.	

2449 Wt. W14957/M90 750,000 1/16 J.B.C. & A. Forms/C.2118/12.

Instructions regarding War Diaries and Intelligence Summaries are contained in F. S. Regs., Part II. and the Staff Manual respectively. Title Pages will be prepared in manuscript.

WAR DIARY

~~or~~

~~INTELLIGENCE SUMMARY~~

(Erase heading not required.)

Army Form C. 2118.

Place	Date	Hour	Summary of Events and Information	Remarks and references to Appendices
CORBIE	25 11/16		Orders given that horses and mules will not be tied to vehicles except in cases of emergency	
"	26 "		H.Q. Headquarters, 91st Bde R.F.A. and one section D.A.C. refilled at Rue DETRICHOIR - COURBIE at 10 am	
"	27 "		Orders again given that the practise of overloading vehicles must cease.	
"	28 "		Instructions received that wherever practicable all transport is to proceed by cross-country tracks.	
"	29 "		Instructions given to improve billets occupied by us as far as possible	
"	30 "		Inspection of 1st Line Transport completed.	
			J.A. Hamilton Lieut Col. O.C. 20th Divisional Train ASC	

2449 Wt. W14957/M90 750,000 1/16 J.B.C. & A. Forms/C.2118/12.

Instructions regarding War Diaries and Intelligence Summaries are contained in F. S. Regs., Part II. and the Staff Manual respectively. Title Pages will be prepared in manuscript.

WAR DIARY
~~or~~
~~INTELLIGENCE SUMMARY~~
(Erase heading not required.)

Army Form C. 2118.

O.C. 20th Divisional Train, A.S.C.

Vol 15

Place	Date	Hour	Summary of Events and Information	Remarks and references to Appendices
CORBIE	1st/16		Information received that the 14 Chaff cutters already authorised are to be regarded as Area stores, & not to be taken away by units on transfer	
"	2.		Capt Meade detailed to give lectures on supplies at 4th Army School of Instruction. 161 Company A.S.C. marched to BUSSY-LES-DAOURS.	
"	3.		Certificates of transfer of Nos 2 & 3 Co. forwarded.	
"	4.		Orders received that any dead animal which is destroyed is buried within 24 hours, and all equipment salved.	
"	5.		Information received no horses are now to be clipped except for veterinary reasons	
"	6.		Orders given that all oat sacks issued this day will be French and must be returned to Refilling points.	
"	7.		Information received that T/Major W.B. CLEGG had been granted 3 days extension of leave	
"	8.		Report forwarded on suggested contrivance for carrying water on wagons.	

2449 Wt. W14957/M90 750,000 1/16 J.B.C. & A. Forms/C.2118/12.

Army Form C. 2118.

WAR DIARY
or
INTELLIGENCE SUMMARY

(Erase heading not required.)

Instructions regarding War Diaries and Intelligence Summaries are contained in F. S. Regs., Part II. and the Staff Manual respectively. Title Pages will be prepared in manuscript.

Place	Date	Hour	Summary of Events and Information	Remarks and references to Appendices
CORBIE	9/12/16		161 Company marched to CHATEAU CORBIE.	
			160 " " " E. 11. d. 9. 1. (ALBERT)	
"	10.		Situation unchanged.	
"	11.		Present position of Train.	
			Hd Qrs F. 27. C. Central (Albert)	
			158. do.	
			159. A. 15. c. 4.4 "	
			160. E. 11. D. 9. 1. "	
			161. A. 14. D central "	
F. 27. c. Central	12.		Instructions received that recommendations for promotion of 2nd Lieutenants to Lieutenants are not to be forwarded except for very exceptional reasons.	
"	13.		Orders issued as to headlights of motor vehicles being painted black on the upper portion of the glass.	
"	14.		Urgent reminder sent to D.A.D.O.S. re issue of horse rugs.	

2449 Wt. W14957/M90 750,000 1/16 J.B.C. & A. Forms/C.2118/12.

Instructions regarding War Diaries and Intelligence Summaries are contained in F. S. Regs., Part II. and the Staff Manual respectively. Title Pages will be prepared in manuscript.

WAR DIARY
or
INTELLIGENCE SUMMARY

(Erase heading not required.)

Army Form C. 2118.

Place	Date	Hour	Summary of Events and Information	Remarks and references to Appendices
Fargo Camp.	15 12/16		Baggage wagons of units not returned to Train & pooled for work.	
"	16 "		Instructions received that during relief units are permitted to move their 1st Line transport over the roads which are closed to other traffic from 7.30 am to 11 am – Baggage wagons are not included in this concession.	
"	17 "		158 Company taken over by Capt HATHAWAY during absence on leave of Capt CHAPLIN.	

2449 Wt. W14957/M90 750,000 1/16 J.B.C. & A. Forms/C.2118/12.

O.C. 20th Div Train

Army Form C. 2118.

WAR DIARY
or
INTELLIGENCE SUMMARY.
(Erase heading not required.)

Instructions regarding War Diaries and Intelligence Summaries are contained in F. S. Regs., Part II. and the Staff Manual respectively. Title pages will be prepared in manuscript.

Place	Date	Hour	Summary of Events and Information — December 1916.	Remarks and references to Appendices
A 14d (ALBERT)	18th inst		O.C. Train went on leave. Visited 60th & 61st Bde HQs & arranged for ration dumps to be brought forward –	
			Inspected siding for refilling by Decauville system N. of Mancourt –	
	19th inst		Supply Train derailed – no orts in first meat on Train. park.	
	20th inst		Visited 59th Bde HQs	
			Arranged Refilling for move into reserve. Baggage wagons returned	
	21st inst		to units	
			59th Bde moved to TREUX area. 157 Coy to MEAULTE – 1st Line	
	22nd inst		Transport used for blankets.	
			61st Bde moved to MEAULTE. 59th Bde to CORBIE. 159 Coy to CORBIE	
	23rd inst		& 161 Coy took over from 158 Coy at MEAULTE – 9 Supply wagons	
			of 158 Coy attached to 17th Division – 23 wagons 28th Division transferred	
			to Guards Division – 3 baggage horses of 158 Coy lent to DHQ.	
			for the move – Railhead changed to CORBIE for 1 Brigade.	
			Railhead at CORBIE except for 93rd Bde & 2 secs DAC still at	
	24th inst		PLATEAU – 61st Bde moved to VILLE. also 160 Coy to TREUX.	
			Transport of DHQ group to CORBIE. also Div. Train HQs.	

1577 Wt. W10791/1773 500,000 1/15 D. D. & L. A.D.S.S./Forms/C. 2118.

Army Form C. 2118.

Instructions regarding War Diaries and Intelligence Summaries are contained in F. S. Regs., Part II. and the Staff Manual respectively. Title pages will be prepared in manuscript.

WAR DIARY
or
INTELLIGENCE SUMMARY.
(Erase heading not required.)

Place	Date	Hour	Summary of Events and Information	Remarks and references to Appendices
CORBIE			December 1916	
25th inst			Relief of Division by 17th Division complete. DHQ at CORBIE at 10 am. – as no oats for RA at PLATEAU borrowed from day in hand & replaced by oats drawn from VIGNACOURT MERICOURT & EDGEHILL.	
			Train HQs at CORBIE 158 Coy F 27 c central 159 Coy CORBIE 160 Coy J 5.6.8.6 161 Coy E 17 b 8.6. (Ref Map 62 D)	
26th inst			Baggage horses returned to No 2 sect. DAC before relief – DAC reorganised with No 4 sect for S.A.A. – 10 tons Anthracite Cake purchased for Division –	
27th inst			No 2 sec relieved by No 1 sec DAC from MORLANCOURT – Baggage horses returned to 93rd Bde before relief – visited 160 & 161 Coys. & arranged to draw 85 tons Coal from EDGEHILL.	
28th inst			Inspected 1st Line Transport 59th Bde – in fair condition if circumstances are considered –	
29th inst			Inspected 1st Line Transport of 60th & 61st Bdes. latter in excellent condition – visited friends Divisional Train to arrange for taking over.	

1577 Wt. W10791/1773 500,000 1/15 D. D. & L. A.D.S.S./Forms/C. 2118.

Instructions regarding War Diaries and Intelligence Summaries are contained in F. S. Regs., Part II. and the Staff Manual respectively. Title pages will be prepared in manuscript.

WAR DIARY
or
INTELLIGENCE SUMMARY.

(Erase heading not required.)

Army Form C. 2118.

Place	Date	Hour	Summary of Events and Information — December 1916.	Remarks and references to Appendices
30th inst			Judge Advocate at Courtmartial. Meeting at DDS+T Office to arrange for Artillery to draw from a separate park.	
31st inst			Visited DDS+T. & made final arrangements for relief of Guards Division & taking over of 29th Div. wagons.	
			[illegible] Major A.S.C.	
			31/12/16 for O.C. 20th Div Train	

1577 Wt. W10791/1773 500,000 1/15 D. D. & L. A.D.S.S./Forms/C. 2118.

Vol 18

WAR DIARY

of the

No 20 DIVISIONAL SUPPLY COLUMN

January 1917

WAR DIARY

Vol 16

of the

20th DIVISIONAL TRAIN

January 1917

Instructions regarding War Diaries and Intelligence Summaries are contained in F. S. Regs., Part II. and the Staff Manual respectively. Title pages will be prepared in manuscript.

WAR DIARY
or
INTELLIGENCE SUMMARY.

(Erase heading not required.)

Army Form C. 2118.

Place	Date	Hour	Summary of Events and Information	Remarks and references to Appendices
CORBIE	1/1/17		Relief of Guards Division begins – 2 Battalions to COMBLES area. – visited DDS. T + arranged re Grouping of Corps Artillery –	
	2		2 Battalions into the line – Railhead changed to PLATEAU – but refilling for units in forward area at FRICOURT Circus – 159 Coy ASC to A 19 b 2.9 – 160 Coy ASC to A 19 b 7.9. 161 Coy ASC to F 24 a 8.4 – 23 waggons 29th Divisional Train detailed by Guards Division to clear train park.	
	3		Move of Division complete except D.H.Q. Div Train HQs to F 17 d 8.8 – Waggons of 29th Div. Train returned to that unit – 8 Supply waggons of 92nd Bde RFA returned to units at MORLANCOURT as that Brigade in G.H.Q. Reserve.	
F 17 d.8.8.	4.		R.O. to MORLANCOURT to arrange for storage of THAW Rations – Landing [illegible] instructions received from 14th Corps as to their disposal.	
	5		– Received Supply of ingredients for anti-trench foot powder from	
			No 8. F.S.D.: but much fewer cases than when in line previously –	
	6		– Obtained material for sheds at Refilling Point	
	7		C. 91st Bde to forward area – refilling at GROVETOWN on the march – Supply waggons R.A. for general detail reduced to 4 – 2 days forage issued to all units to enable them to turn it over –	

1577 Wt. W10791/1773 500,000 1/15 D. D. & L. A.D.S.S./Forms/C. 2118.

Instructions regarding War Diaries and Intelligence Summaries are contained in F. S. Regs., Part II. and the Staff Manual respectively. Title pages will be prepared in manuscript.

WAR DIARY
or
INTELLIGENCE SUMMARY.

(Erase heading not required.)

Army Form C. 2118.

Place	Date	Hour	Summary of Events and Information	Remarks and references to Appendices
F17d8.8	8/1/17		92nd Bde move up from MORLANCOURT - B93 to DAOURS - 14 waggons Guards Divisional Train returned to them - THAW Ration (Oats) issued to units - Iron Rations retained on dump -	
	9/1/17		Visited MARICOURT Railhead with ADMT 14th Corps & chose site for new Train camp - Division took over part of 8th Division front -	
	10/1/17		Trench rations to be issued for day units leave trenches - went with O.C. 3 Bde Coy to new camp at MARICOURT - 6 men left to take over.	
	11/1/17		Pitprops & fascines drawn on authority of XV Corps to make new road to Camp.	
F17d8.8.	12/1/17		Transferred THAW rations for 92nd Bde to PLATEAU.	
	13/1/17		Issued THAW ration (Oats) to RA HQs & 92nd Bde RFA.	
	14/1/17		D.A.C reorganised Nos 1 & 2 secs to be Echelon A. 3 sec to become Ammunition Column to Army Brigade - 4 sec to be S.A.A. section - THAW ration issued to DAC withdrawn till changes complete. No 2 sec DAC to PLATEAU. No 3 sec DAC to MORLANCOURT.	
	15/1/17		B. Battery 166th Bde from 33rd Div arrives - with 1 baggage & 1 supply waggon from 33rd Div Train.	

Instructions regarding War Diaries and Intelligence Summaries are contained in F. S. Regs., Part II. and the Staff Manual respectively. Title pages will be prepared in manuscript.

WAR DIARY
or
INTELLIGENCE SUMMARY.
(*Erase heading not required.*)

Army Form C. 2118.

Place	Date	Hour	Summary of Events and Information	Remarks and references to Appendices
F17d 5.8	16/1/17		Informed by D.D.S.T. that anti-frostbite powder only experimental, & no more will be provided until reports are received as to its efficiency. Visited lines of 3 Bde Companies & found everything in good order. Entrance to camp completed.	
	17/1/17		THAW rations issued to D.A.C. – & dumps for them formed at TRONES Wood DAOURS & MORLANCOURT. – Oats received at Railhead only 13 lbs for HD. 9 for L.D with 2 lbs extra for R.A horses (L.D.). – Cart belonging to Senior Chaplain at CORBIE condemned. – 10 tons straw for billets & 3 tons oil-cake at MERICOURT.	
	~~[illegible]~~		Major (Temp. Lt. Col) J. A Hamilton struck off the strength with effect from 13th inst. – S/4/061268 L/Cpl Midgley & S/4/197345 Pte Kay sent to Base as intelligent clerks. – Limbers & G.S wagons returning empty from forward area are to be available for Salvage work – salved stores to be taken to XV Corps Salvage Dump at TRONES Wood.	
	18.		Lieut. Col. RHF Standen (RASC) took over command of Train.	

1577 Wt. W10791/1773 500,000 1/15 D. D. & L. A.D.S.S./Forms/C. 2118.

Army Form C. 2118.

Instructions regarding War Diaries and Intelligence Summaries are contained in F. S. Regs., Part II. and the Staff Manual respectively. Title Pages will be prepared in manuscript.

WAR DIARY
or
INTELLIGENCE SUMMARY
(Erase heading not required.)

Place	Date	Hour	Summary of Events and Information	Remarks and references to Appendices
MINDEN POST	18/1		Lieut. Col. R.H.F. STANDEN reported arrival 3.30 p.m. to assume command of Div. Train	
			See Administrative orders, para. 8 Reduction of oat ration	
			Collection + distribution of Remounts from EDGEHILL to units of Division	
			Ration of chestnuts issued	
	19		O.C Train reported arrival to D.H.Q.	
			Completed distribution of remounts	
	20th		O.C Train inspected no. 158 (Headquarter) Co.	
	21st		O.C. Train inspected nos. 159, 160 and 161 Coys.	
	22nd		Inspection of 59th Bde 1st Line Transport + M.G. Coy.	
	23rd		Inspection of 60th Bde 1st Line Transport + M.G. Coy.	

2449 Wt. W14957/M90 750,000 1/16 J.B.C. & A. Forms/C.2118/12.

Army Form C. 2118.

Instructions regarding War Diaries and Intelligence Summaries are contained in F. S. Regs., Part II. and the Staff Manual respectively. Title Pages will be prepared in manuscript.

WAR DIARY
or
INTELLIGENCE SUMMARY
(Erase heading not required.)

Place	Date	Hour	Summary of Events and Information	Remarks and references to Appendices
PLATEAU	January 24		O.C. Train visited new billeting ~~areas~~ with Officers Commanding Companies.	
			Reported re adjustment of wagons, H.Qr. Co. on reorganization of R.A.	
	25th		Capt. E.R.M. MORTON A.S.C. 8th Div. Train, reported for temporary duty, + attached to 181 company.	
	26th		2 Lieut. Harvey, 160 Co. reported at HEILLY for interview re transfer to R.F.C.	
			No. 161 Co. marched from PLATEAU, en route for FRANVILLERS at 8.0 a.m.	
	27th		Nos. 159 and 160 Co's marched from PLATEAU to FRANVILLERS and MEAULTE respectively. No. 161 Co. from FRANVILLERS to COISY.	
	28th		Train H.Qrs. marched from MINDEN POST to HEILLY	

2449 Wt. W14957/M90 750,000 1/16 J.B.C. & A. Forms/C.2118/12.

Instructions regarding War Diaries and Intelligence Summaries are contained in F. S. Regs., Part II. and the Staff Manual respectively. Title Pages will be prepared in manuscript.

WAR DIARY
or
INTELLIGENCE SUMMARY
(Erase heading not required.)

Army Form C. 2118.

Place	Date	Hour	Summary of Events and Information	Remarks and references to Appendices
HEILLY	29/1		O.C. Train inspected 1st line Tpt. of 61st Bde.	
	31.		Captain MEADE, 161 Co. delivered a lecture at Divisional School of Instruction, DAOURS, on Supplies in the Field.	

2449 Wt. W14957/M90 750,000 1/16 J.B.C. & A. Forms/C.2118/12.

Vol 17

WAR DIARY

of

20th DIVISIONAL TRAIN A.S.C.

FEBRUARY 1917

Army Form C. 2118.

Instructions regarding War Diaries and Intelligence Summaries are contained in F. S. Regs., Part II. and the Staff Manual respectively. Title Pages will be prepared in manuscript.

WAR DIARY
or
INTELLIGENCE SUMMARY
(Erase heading not required.)

Place	Date	Hour	Summary of Events and Information	Remarks and references to Appendices
HEILLY	FEB 1		O.C. Train visited 160 Co. at MEAULTE	
	2		O.C. Train visited 159 Co. at FRANVILLERS	
	3		O.C. Train visited new area to be taken over from 39th Divisional Train.	
	4.		Major Clegg assumed duties of S.S.O., during temporary absence of Major Soames	
	6		No. 159 Co. moved from LA HOUSSOYE to MARICOURT BOIS ~~PLATEAU~~	
			No. 161 Co. moved from COISY to HEILLY	
	7th		No. 161 Co. moved from HEILLY to PLATEAU	
			No. 160 Co. moved from MEAULTE to MARICOURT BOIS	
	8.		Train HEADQUARTERS moved from HEILLY to PLATEAU	
PLATEAU A21.a.2.9.				

2449 Wt. W14957/M90 750,000 1/16 J.B.C. & A. Forms/C.2118/12.

Instructions regarding War Diaries and Intelligence Summaries are contained in F. S. Regs., Part II. and the Staff Manual respectively. Title Pages will be prepared in manuscript.

WAR DIARY
or
INTELLIGENCE SUMMARY

(Erase heading not required.)

Army Form C. 2118.

Place	Date	Hour	Summary of Events and Information	Remarks and references to Appendices
PLATEAU	10th		O.C. Train inspected Companies at MARICOURT BOIS 2/Lieut C.W. Miles reported for duty with Train, & posted to 161 Company.	
			Major Soames returned from PARIS.	
	11th		O.C. Train conferred with "Q" Staff at Div. Hdqrs. re accommodation at MARICOURT BOIS for 3 Brigade Companies –	
	12th		O.C. Train visited RAILHEAD, and site of new lines for 158 Co.	
			MAJOR CLEGG reported sick in [illegible]	
	13th		161 Company marches from PLATEAU to MARICOURT BOIS	
			O.C. Train reported to G.O.C.	

2449 Wt. W14957/M90 750,000 1/16 J.B.C. & A. Forms/C.2118/12.

Instructions regarding War Diaries and Intelligence Summaries are contained in F. S. Regs., Part II. and the Staff Manual respectively. Title Pages will be prepared in manuscript.

WAR DIARY
or
INTELLIGENCE SUMMARY
(Erase heading not required.)

Army Form C. 2118.

Place	Date	Hour	Summary of Events and Information	Remarks and references to Appendices
PLATEAU	Feb 14		138 Company moved from HAPPY VALLEY to PLATEAU 2nd Lieut. E.S. HARVEY proceeded to Hdqrs. R.F.C. for duty.	
	16		Corps ammunition dump, PLATEAU, attacked by enemy bombs at 5.15; explosions throughout the day, no casualties to personnel or animals. Railhead altered to GROVETOWN, dumps at PLATEAU destroyed by fire. Refilling point at MARICOURT BOIS	
	17		Repairs effected to damage done by explosions in Train Headquarter camp.	

2449 Wt. W14957/M90 750,000 1/16 J.B.C. & A. Forms/C.2118/12.

Instructions regarding War Diaries and Intelligence Summaries are contained in F. S. Regs., Part II. and the Staff Manual respectively. Title Pages will be prepared in manuscript.

WAR DIARY
or
INTELLIGENCE SUMMARY
(Erase heading not required.)

Army Form C. 2118.

Place	Date	Hour	Summary of Events and Information	Remarks and references to Appendices
PLATEAU	Feb. 18		Railhead re-instituted at PLATEAU	
	20th		O.C. Train visited Divisional Headquarters	
	21st		O.C. Train visited Companies & new wagon lines	
	22		O.C. Train inspected lines of Headquarter Company at PLATEAU	
	23rd		Inspection of first line Transport, 59th Bde by O.C. Train	
	24th		Cars nos. 14500, and 15904 to D.S.O workshops	
	25th		Inspection of first line Transport, 60th Bde by O.C. Train. Reported state of mobilization equipment at 12 M.N.	
	26th		Motor Car no. 14015 received from Div. Supply Column	

2449 Wt. W14957/M90 750,000 1/16 J.B.C. & A. Forms/C.2118/12.

Instructions regarding War Diaries and Intelligence Summaries are contained in F. S. Regs., Part II. and the Staff Manual respectively. Title Pages will be prepared in manuscript.

WAR DIARY
or
INTELLIGENCE SUMMARY
(Erase heading not required.)

Army Form C. 2118.

Place	Date	Hour	Summary of Events and Information	Remarks and references to Appendices
PLATEAU	Feb 27		O.C. Train inspected 61st Brigade 1st line Transport	
			[signature] Lt. Col. Comm'd XX Div. Train	

2449 Wt. W14957/M90 750,000 1/16 J.B.C. & A. Forms/C.2118/12.

Vol 18

WAR DIARY

OF

20th DIVISIONAL TRAIN.

MARCH 1917.

Army Form C. 2118.

Instructions regarding War Diaries and Intelligence Summaries are contained in F. S. Regs., Part II. and the Staff Manual respectively. Title pages will be prepared in manuscript.

WAR DIARY
or
INTELLIGENCE SUMMARY.
(Erase heading not required.)

Place	Date MARCH	Hour	Summary of Events and Information	Remarks and references to Appendices
PLATEAU	2		G.O.C sent for O.C Train + requested information on subject of personnel of Train. O.C Train also saw "Q" Staff.	
	3		Discussion of points in connection with new Railhead between "Q" Staff, O.C Train, and S.S.O. O.C Train visited TRONES WOOD and COMBLES.	
	4		New Railhead at MARICOURT BOIS opened, + supply train unloaded into sheds. Visited by D.A. + Q.M.G. XIV Corps. Divisional Commander inspected experimental improvised pack saddlery.	
	5		Heavy snow-fall. Re-filling commenced at new Railhead. O.C Train visited 53rd Bde Headquarters re pack saddlery.	
	6.		O.C Train visited Brigade Companies at MARICOURT BOIS	

A5834 Wt. W4973/M687 750,000 8/16 D. D. & L. Ltd. Forms/C.2118/13.

Army Form C. 2118.

Instructions regarding War Diaries and Intelligence Summaries are contained in F. S. Regs., Part II. and the Staff Manual respectively. Title pages will be prepared in manuscript.

WAR DIARY
or
INTELLIGENCE SUMMARY.
(Erase heading not required.)

Place	Date	Hour	Summary of Events and Information	Remarks and references to Appendices
PLATEAU	7th		O.C. Train conferred with "Q" branch at Railhead, also re pack saddlery; in p.m. inspected Divisional Laundry and Baths at CORBIE	
	8th		Arrangements made to convey rations & forage to Brigade Companies of the Train by Decauville line. A.A. & Q.M.G. inspected improvised pack saddlery. Conferred with O.C. Guards Div. Train re tramway through Camp.	
	9th		Brigade Companies refill by Decauville.	
	11th		O.C. Train attended Corps "Q" Conference at Railhead, and reported at D.H.Q. in afternoon.	
	12th		All companies report progress in making improvised pack saddles.	

A5834 Wt. W4973/M687 750,000 8/16 D. D. & L. Ltd. Forms/C.2118/13.

Instructions regarding War Diaries and Intelligence Summaries are contained in F. S. Regs., Part II. and the Staff Manual respectively. Title pages will be prepared in manuscript.

WAR DIARY
or
INTELLIGENCE SUMMARY.
(Erase heading not required.)

Army Form C. 2118.

Place	Date	Hour	Summary of Events and Information	Remarks and references to Appendices
PLATEAU	13th		Divisional Commander inspected G.S. and Limbered Wagons at Train Headquarters	
	15th		Explosion at no. 4 camp CARNOY at 6.0 p.m. No casualties in Train	
	16th		Officer Commanding Train visited 1st line Transport forward lines. Received instructions from Divisional Headquarters to take pack saddles to Army Headquarters	
	18th		O.C. Train took three patterns of pack saddles, improvised to PONT NOYELLES to shew to D.D.O.S. IV Army.	
	19th		German retirement from Divisional front. O.C. Train visited forward area, SAILLY-SALLISEL, ROCQUINY, LE TRANSLOY, LES BOEUFS 2nd Lieut. Hutchins joined Div. Train and posted to Trn. Hdqrs. as Requisitioning Officer	

A5834 Wt. W4973/M687 750,000 8/16 D. D. & L. Ltd. Forms/C.2118/13.

Instructions regarding War Diaries and Intelligence Summaries are contained in F. S. Regs., Part II. and the Staff Manual respectively. Title pages will be prepared in manuscript.

WAR DIARY
or
INTELLIGENCE SUMMARY.
(Erase heading not required.)

Army Form C. 2118.

Place	Date	Hour	Summary of Events and Information	Remarks and references to Appendices
PLATEAU	20th		Decauville Railway System not used, supplies drawn by train wagons from Railhead to GINCHY and HAIE WOOD, and taken on from these points by 1st line pack transport.	
	21st		Commanding officer visited 60th Bde 1st line Transport, on occasion of monthly inspection.	
	22nd		O.C. Train visited forward area, in connection with traffic arrangements. Interviewed G.O. commanding Division in p.m. Pack animals being sent up daily carrying reserve rations to LE TRANSLOY.	
	23rd		O.C. Train inspected First Line Transport, 59th Bde	
	24th		Completed transfer of Iron Rations to LE TRANSLOY	
	25th		Capt. A.V.W.C. Bigg proceeded to St POL on transfer to 34th	

A5834 Wt. W4973/M687 750,000 8/16 D. D. & L. Ltd. Forms/C.2118/13.

Instructions regarding War Diaries and Intelligence Summaries are contained in F. S. Regs., Part II. and the Staff Manual respectively. Title pages will be prepared in manuscript.

WAR DIARY
or
INTELLIGENCE SUMMARY.
(Erase heading not required.)

Army Form C. 2118.

Place	Date	Hour	Summary of Events and Information	Remarks and references to Appendices
PLATEAU	25th		Divisional Train. MAJOR J.L.C. SOAMES assumed temporary command of the Div. Train during absence on 10 days leave of Lt Col. R.H.F. STANDEN. – Visited LE MESNIL + ROCQUIGNY to find routes + refilling points for pack transport in the event of the Division moving forward. –	
	26th		Visited Decauville Railhead at HAIE Wood + traced the track past Scott COPSE as far as portion under construction towards COMBLES near LE TRANSLOY. SAILLY – SAILLISEL Road – considered suitable spot for transference of supplies to pack-animals – 59th Bde advanced to BOIS de VALLULART – 61st Bde occupied YTRES – Temp Sec Lieut C W Perry posted to 158 Coy ASC on joining Train.	
	27th		Supplies for 59th + 61st Bde sent by Decauville Railway to COMBLES + thence by pack-transport of Divisional Train to ROCQUIGNY – 120 animals required – Visited these points + found arrangements working satisfactorily – 159 Coy ASC + 161 Coy ASC moved to Camps near LEUZE Wood Siding at T 20 c 5.3 (Map 57c) 158 Coy ASC to Camp at MARICOURT BOIS (A 16 c 9.8. Map ALBERT Combined)	

A5834 Wt. W4973/M687 750,000 8/16 D. D. & L. Ltd. Forms/C.2118/13.

Instructions regarding War Diaries and Intelligence Summaries are contained in F. S. Regs., Part II. and the Staff Manual respectively. Title pages will be prepared in manuscript.

WAR DIARY
or
INTELLIGENCE SUMMARY.
(*Erase heading not required.*)

Army Form C. 2118.

Place	Date	Hour	Summary of Events and Information	Remarks and references to Appendices
PLATEAU	28th		Supplies for 59th Bde sent by Decauville to COMBLES + thence by pack to LE MESNIL - for 61st Bde to ROCQUIGNY - for 20th Div. Works Batt to O 31 a (Map 57C) - 160 pack animals required - calculated average load for improvised saddles as 50 rations per horse - 5 horses required for 1 day's supply of fuel for a Battalion -	
	29th		Supplies for 91st + 92nd sent by Decauville to LEUZE Wood Siding + thence by 14 Supply wagons to ROCQUIGNY + LE MESNIL - 12 limbers from 3 Brigades sent to supplement pack transport. + horsed by 158 Coy A.S.C - Capt Hattaway parked above horses + transport at a camp W. of ROCQUIGNY. (O 27 a 5.3) Supplies for 60th Bde by their own transport from COMBLES to LE TRANSLOY - 59th + 61st Bdes as a previous day. - 160 Coy ASC moved to T 20 c 5.3 (Map 57c) - 61st Bde occupied NEUVILLE.	

A5834 Wt. W4973/M687 750,000 8/16 D. D. & L. Ltd. Forms/C.2118/13.

Army Form C. 2118.

WAR DIARY
or
INTELLIGENCE SUMMARY.
(Erase heading not required.)

Instructions regarding War Diaries and Intelligence Summaries are contained in F. S. Regs., Part II. and the Staff Manual respectively. Title pages will be prepared in manuscript.

Place	Date	Hour	Summary of Events and Information	Remarks and references to Appendices
PLATEAU	30th		Supplies sent forward to ROCQUIGNY + LE MESNIL by limber and 30 pack-horses - 91st + 92nd Bdes supplies passed FRICOURT after control removed at 5-20 pm - Visited Advance Section 1st Coy A.S.C at ROCQUIGNY - and went to BUS to arrange refilling point for 31st Div - Lieut. Corker sent to G.H.Q.	
	31st		Supplies for Works Batt. sent to their camp at O 31 a by limbers from 2 Brigade Coys. afterwards parked at Camp at ROCQUIGNY - Train H.Qs moved to MARICOURT Bois (A 16 c 9.7 Ref Map ALBERT Combined) -	
			J. G. Ll. Soames Major A.S.C a/ O.C. 20th Div Train	

War Diary Vol 19

20th Divisional Train

April 1917

Instructions regarding War Diaries and Intelligence Summaries are contained in F. S. Regs., Part II. and the Staff Manual respectively. Title pages will be prepared in manuscript.

WAR DIARY
or
INTELLIGENCE SUMMARY.
(Erase heading not required.)

Army Form C. 2118.

Place	Date	Hour	Summary of Events and Information	Remarks and references to Appendices
MARICOURT BOIS A 16 c 9.7	APRIL 1st		To COMBLES Railhead – and to ROCQUIGNY with O.C. 158 Coy to inspect Capt Hathaway's camp + to BUS to arrange for transferring point for 60 Bde – RUYALCOURT taken by 59th Bde – 61st Bde relieved by 60th Bde.	
	2nd		Arranged for building sheds at COMBLES Railhead – inspected lines of 3 Bde Coys at LEUZE Wood – 61st Bde supplies sent forward by their own transport – 60th Bde's supplies to BUS on Brigade limbers with 158 Coy's horses – D.H.Q. moved to ROCQUIGNY	
	3rd		24 horses drawing limbers for 2 Brigades relieved by horses from 159 + 161 Coys A.S.C. – went to see AA + QMG at ROCQUIGNY with reference to giving horses of Divisional Train a rest – inspected Train horses at ROCQUIGNY with A.D.V.S., who considered their condition good	
	4th		158 Coy moved to BUS – supply waggons of Field Ambulances attached to 158 Coy ASC – provided to COMBLES Railhead + D.H.Q. – Reserve ration dump at Bullet Cross roads transferred to ROCQUIGNY – Reserve dump at HALE Wood withdrawn to MARICOURT BOIS – 59th Bde captured METZ-EN-COUTURE + S. fringe of Bois d'Havrincourt	

A5834 Wt. W4973/M687 750,000 8/16 D. D. & L. Ltd. Forms/C.2118/13.

Instructions regarding War Diaries and Intelligence Summaries are contained in F. S. Regs., Part II. and the Staff Manual respectively. Title pages will be prepared in manuscript.

WAR DIARY
or
INTELLIGENCE SUMMARY.
(Erase heading not required.)

Army Form C. 2118.

Place	Date	Hour	Summary of Events and Information	Remarks and references to Appendices
MARICOURT BOIS	5th		Supplies for BUS + ROCQUIGNY sent forward by G.S. wagons for first time – visited Railhead + D.H.Q. to arrange for transference of Reserve rations from LE TRANSLOY to ROCQUIGNY + to form a Divisional Dump there – visited 158 Coy at BUS to arrange transport for supplies on 6th inst – Lt Col. R.H.F. Standen returned off leave + resumed command of Divisional Train.	
	6th.		Brigade Companies moved forward: No. 159 Co LE TRANSLOY. No. 160 to BUS and 161 Co. to ROCQUIGNY. O.C. Train visited all four companies and reported at Divn! Headquarters. Reserve Supplies sent by lorries from MARICOURT BOIS to FINS.	

Army Form C. 2118.

Instructions regarding War Diaries and Intelligence Summaries are contained in F. S. Regs., Part II. and the Staff Manual respectively. Title pages will be prepared in manuscript.

WAR DIARY
or
INTELLIGENCE SUMMARY.

(Erase heading not required.)

Place	Date	Hour	Summary of Events and Information	Remarks and references to Appendices
MARICOURT BOIS	7th		O.C. Train visited Reserve Ration dump at FINS with S.S.O.; also Companies. Called at Divisional Head-quarters	
	8th		Rations for 59th Brigade Group delivered by Decauville at ~~Sail~~ SAILLISEL and issued from there. O.C. Train visited XV Corps Headquarters, and received instructions from D.A. & Q.M.Genl.	
	9th		Rations for two Brigade Groups delivered by Decauville at ~~SAILLY~~ SAILLISEL Railhead. O.C. Train visited the Brigade & Headquarter Companies, also D.H.Q.	
	10th		Divisional Troops refilling point advanced to COMBLES	

A5834 Wt. W4973/M687 750,000 8/16 D. D. & L. Ltd. Forms/C.2118/13.

Instructions regarding War Diaries and Intelligence Summaries are contained in F. S. Regs., Part II. and the Staff Manual respectively. Title pages will be prepared in manuscript.

WAR DIARY
or
INTELLIGENCE SUMMARY.
(Erase heading not required.)

Army Form C. 2118.

Place	Date	Hour	Summary of Events and Information	Remarks and references to Appendices
MARICOURT BOIS	11th		O.C. Train visited Divisional Headquarters, and Headquarter Company. Visited NEUVILLE and METZ-EN-COUTURE	
	12		Nothing of importance	
	13th		Lt Smith 3/ Coldstream Guards reported for attachment under instruction in Staff "Q" duties	
	14th		O.C. Train visited D.H.Q., also LE MESNIL and LECHELLE, with a view to selection of site for Camp of Train Headquarters.	
	15th		O.C. Train attended at Divisional Headquarters, and inspected No. 2 Company at LE TRANSLOY	

A5834 Wt. W4973/M687 750,000 8/16 D. D. & L. Ltd. Forms/C.2118/13.

Army Form C. 2118.

Instructions regarding War Diaries and Intelligence Summaries are contained in F. S. Regs., Part II. and the Staff Manual respectively. Title pages will be prepared in manuscript.

WAR DIARY
or
INTELLIGENCE SUMMARY.
(Erase heading not required.)

Place	Date	Hour	Summary of Events and Information	Remarks and references to Appendices
MARICOURT BOIS	16th		COMBLES — BUS road, via FREGICOURT — BULLET CROSS-ROADS and ROCQUIGNY opened for lorry traffic.	
	17th		Decauville Railway broke down, necessitating removal of railhead to COMBLES, and forwarding supplies by horse transport.	
	18th		Refilling at COMBLES	
	19th		~~CAPT~~ Captain M. M. PAKENHAM proceeded to FOUCAURT for duty with IV Army ~~A~~.T. Supply Column	
	20th		Lieut. J. H. SMITH, 2/ Coldstream Guards, returned to D.H.Q.	

A5834 Wt. W4973/M687 750,000 8/16 D. D. & L. Ltd. Forms/C.2118/13.

Instructions regarding War Diaries and Intelligence Summaries are contained in F. S. Regs., Part II. and the Staff Manual respectively. Title pages will be prepared in manuscript.

WAR DIARY
or
INTELLIGENCE SUMMARY.
(Erase heading not required.)

Army Form C. 2118.

Place	Date	Hour	Summary of Events and Information	Remarks and references to Appendices
MARICOURT BOIS	21st		O.C. Train visited Headquarter Company and D.H.Q.	
	22nd		Decauville Railway repaired; refilling at BAPAUME Rd.	
			Major N. CLEGG returned from leave.	
	23rd		Capt. & Adj. C.L EVANS evacuated to hospital	
			Lieut. J.H EVANS, from 160 Coy. joined Train Headquarters as Acting Adjutant	
	24th		Commenced move of Train Headquarters.	
	25th		Train Headquarters moved to LECHELLE.	
			Three supply reinforcements arrived for Train	
LECHELLE	26th		No. 2 Company under Captain OPENSHAW warned to move to LECHELLE at an early date	
	28th		No. 2 Company moved from LE TRANSLOY to LECHELLE	
			O.C. Train inspected 1st Line Transport of 60th Bde.	

A5834 Wt. W4973/M687 750,000 8/16 D. D. & L. Ltd. Forms/C.2118/13.

Army Form C. 2118.

WAR DIARY
or
INTELLIGENCE SUMMARY.
(Erase heading not required.)

Instructions regarding War Diaries and Intelligence Summaries are contained in F. S. Regs., Part II. and the Staff Manual respectively. Title pages will be prepared in manuscript.

Place	Date	Hour	Summary of Events and Information	Remarks and references to Appendices
LECHELLE	28th		O.C. Train inspected First Line Transport of 60th Brigade	
	29th		Two days rations drawn at Decauville railhead –	
	30th		O.C. Train inspected First Line Transport of 59th + 61st Brigades Last day of using Decauville Railway for Supplies	
			R Standen Lt Col. Comm^d Div. Train XX Divn.	

A5834 Wt. W4973/M687 750,000 8/16 D. D. & L. Ltd. Forms/C.2118/13.

WAR DIARY

Vol 20

20th Divisional Train.

May 1917

Instructions regarding War Diaries and Intelligence Summaries are contained in F. S. Regs., Part II. and the Staff Manual respectively. Title pages will be prepared in manuscript.

WAR DIARY
or
INTELLIGENCE SUMMARY.
(*Erase heading not required.*)

Army Form C. 2118.

Place	Date	Hour	Summary of Events and Information	Remarks and references to Appendices
LECHELLE	1st		New Railhead opened between ROCQUIGNY and LE MESNIL. Supplies drawn in bulk by Train wagons, and subsequently issued to units from Companies wagon lines.	
			Capt. G.O. Openshaw proceed on 10 days leave to U.K.	
	2nd		Lt C.W. PERRY attached to 161 Coy. for instruction in Supply duties.	
	3rd		Gas alarm at 10.0 pm found to be a false alarm, & cancelled at 11.0 pm.	
	4th		Gas alarm at 9.45 pm. "dismiss" sounded at 10.15 pm	
	5th		Unusually warm day. Heavy bombardment on our right front at 11.0 pm	

A5834 Wt. W4973/M687 750,000 8/16 D. D. & L. Ltd. Forms/C.2118/13.

Instructions regarding War Diaries and Intelligence Summaries are contained in F. S. Regs., Part II. and the Staff Manual respectively. Title pages will be prepared in manuscript.

WAR DIARY
or
INTELLIGENCE SUMMARY.
(Erase heading not required.)

Army Form C. 2118.

Place	Date	Hour	Summary of Events and Information	Remarks and references to Appendices
LECHELLE	6th		Notification received of posting of MAJOR N.B. CLEGG as S.S.O. to 5th Cav. Divl. A.S.C., and of CAPT. C.B. MASCHMEYER to the 21st Div. Train	
	7th		COLONEL WILSON, DDST, IV Army visited Train Headquarters 158, & 160 Companies. O.C. Train inspected ground for camping ground in vicinity of BARASTRE, in event of moving there. CAPT. C.W. WALKER, RA.M.C, thrown from horse, fracturing arm. Evacuated in pm., relieved by CAPT. TURNBULL, R.A.M.C.	
	8th		MAJOR N.B. CLEGG transferred to 5th Cav. Divl. A.S.C, as S.S.O. Capt. R.A.K. MEADE took over duties of S.O. Artillery Group. Captain C.B. MASCHMEYER reported for duty from 8th Divl. Train, and posted to 161 Co. for as S.O. 62nd Brigade. CAPT. TURNBULL R.A.M.C joined 158 Co. in relief of CAPTAIN WALKER	

A5834 Wt. W4973/M687 750,000 8/16 D. D. & L. Ltd. Forms/C.2118/13.

Army Form C. 2118.

Instructions regarding War Diaries and Intelligence Summaries are contained in F. S. Regs., Part II. and the Staff Manual respectively. Title pages will be prepared in manuscript.

WAR DIARY
or
INTELLIGENCE SUMMARY.
(Erase heading not required.)

Place	Date	Hour	Summary of Events and Information	Remarks and references to Appendices
LECHELLE	10th		Notification received of return of CAPT. C.S. EVANS from 4 Corps Officers Rest Station on 13th inst.	
	11th		CAPT. BROADMEAD 12th/K.R.R. left Train Headquarters for duty with Hdqrs. 91st Bde. R.F.A.	
	12th		S.O.C. Division inspected lines of Train Headquarters, 158, 159 & 160 Coys. O.C. Train inspected 161 Company.	
	13th		Capt. & Adjt. C.S. EVANS returned to duty from Corps Officers rest station ABBEVILLE. Supplies drawn jointly from DROMORE railhead and FINS, thus completing issue of the 3 days reserve rations stored at latter place.	

A5834 Wt. W4973/M687 750,000 8/16 D. D. & L. Ltd. Forms/C.2118/13.

Instructions regarding War Diaries and Intelligence Summaries are contained in F. S. Regs., Part II. and the Staff Manual respectively. Title pages will be prepared in manuscript.

WAR DIARY
or
INTELLIGENCE SUMMARY.
(Erase heading not required.)

Army Form C. 2118.

Place	Date	Hour	Summary of Events and Information	Remarks and references to Appendices
LECHELLE	14th		O.C. 42nd Div. Train called re taking over camp –	
	15th		Lt J. H. EVANS returned to 160 Co., after handing over duties of acting Adjt.	
			O.C. went to TINCOURT to confer with O.C. 42nd Div. Train	
	16th		O.C. Train went to Army Hdqrs. re railheads in new area. O.C. 42nd Div. Train & S.S.O. called.	
	17th		O.C. & S.S.O. to 48th Divnl. Train & 5th Australian Div. Train with reference to taking over new areas.	
	18th		O.C. Train again visited 5th Australian Div. Train area.	
	19th		O.C. Train visited A.H.Q., to confer with D.D.R. re remounts.	
	20th		No. 161 Co. moved with 61st Bde to BEAULENCOURT.	
	21st		C.O. inspected 59th Bde first line transport in p.m. Arranged to take over camp of Headquarters Co. 1st Australian Divnl. Train	

A5834 Wt. W4973/M687 750,000 8/16 D. D. & L. Ltd. Forms/C.2118/13.

Instructions regarding War Diaries and Intelligence Summaries are contained in F. S. Regs., Part II. and the Staff Manual respectively. Title pages will be prepared in manuscript.

WAR DIARY
or
INTELLIGENCE SUMMARY.
(Erase heading not required.)

Army Form C. 2118.

Place	Date	Hour	Summary of Events and Information	Remarks and references to Appendices
LECHELLE	21st (cont)		Driver PEACHEY returned from D.S.C with WOLSELEY Car. C.O. inspected First Line Transport of 60th Dde in pm.	
	22nd		No. 159 Company marched into new area.	
	23rd		Train Headquarters and No. 160 Coy. marched into new area.	
BAPAUME	25th		No. 158 Co. moved to new area at cross roads on BAPAUME – FREMICOURT and HAPLINCOURT – BEUGNATRE roads.	
	26th		Train Headquarters established in camp on S. of BAPAUME – MONUMENT Road.	
	27th		Rations delivered from Decauville Railhead to Transport lines of units by Supply Wagons of Train. O.C Train to D.H.Q. in am.	
	28th		Refilling at railhead, BAPAUME at 4.0 am.	

A5834 Wt. W4973 M687 750,000 8/16 D. D. & L. Ltd. Forms/C.2118/13.

Instructions regarding War Diaries and Intelligence Summaries are contained in F. S. Regs., Part II. and the Staff Manual respectively. Title pages will be prepared in manuscript.

WAR DIARY
or
INTELLIGENCE SUMMARY.
(Erase heading not required.)

Army Form C. 2118.

Place	Date	Hour	Summary of Events and Information	Remarks and references to Appendices
BAPAUME	29th		Refilling at Railhead at 7.0 am - 2 HD from No 2 Sec DAC lost by 15th Coy - RA Group refill at H 26.	
	30th		R.A Group refill with Bde Coys by Decauville at EARLS COURT	
	31st		Capt. Pakenham returned from duty with Fourth A.T Supply Column. Lieut Miles 161 Coy ASC admitted to 61st Field Ambulance - Refilling delayed owing to lack of Baldwin Engines.	
			J. f. H. Symmes Major ASC for O.C. 20th Div Train	

A5834 Wt. W4973/M687 750,000 8/16 D. D. & L. Ltd. Forms/C.2118/13.

War Diary

of

20th Divnl Train

JUNE 1917

Vol 21

Instructions regarding War Diaries and Intelligence Summaries are contained in F. S. Regs., Part II. and the Staff Manual respectively. Title pages will be prepared in manuscript.

WAR DIARY
or
INTELLIGENCE SUMMARY.
(Erase heading not required.)

Army Form C. 2118.

Place	Date	Hour	Summary of Events and Information	Remarks and references to Appendices
BAPAUME	JUNE 1st		Decanville railway destroyed by shell fire in early morning. Refilling in bulk from Railhead by Train Supply wagons Rations split up near company lines.	
			Lt NORMAN attached to Train Headquarters for instruction in Supply duties, under S.S.O.	
			Nos. 159 and 160 moved further from Ammunition Dump.	
	2nd		Bulk refilling by Train wagons at Railhead at 4 0 am RA. group by Decanville.	
			28 H.D. horses drawn for 1st Line transport of Division	
			S.S.O. to DOULLENS.	
	3rd		2nd Lieut. PERRY to 160 Co. for duty	
	4th		Refilling as on previous day	

A5834 Wt. W4973/M687 750,000 8/16 D. D. & L. Ltd. Forms/C.2118/13.

Instructions regarding War Diaries and Intelligence Summaries are contained in F. S. Regs., Part II. and the Staff Manual respectively. Title pages will be prepared in manuscript.

WAR DIARY
or
INTELLIGENCE SUMMARY.
(Erase heading not required.)

Army Form C. 2118.

Place	Date	Hour	Summary of Events and Information	Remarks and references to Appendices
	4th		D.A.Q.M.G. proposed competition for horses of Divisional Train O.C. Train to ALBERT in p.m. to see D.D.O.S.	
	5th		O.C. Train arranged for all ranks to use miniature rifle range at FAVREUIL Proceeded to A.H.Q. in p.m. to see D.D.S. & T.	
	6th		O.C. Train visited firing party on miniature rifle range, and saw S.M.T.O. IV Corps in p.m.	
	7th		Horse Show, under arrangements made by D.A.Q.M.G. No. 1 Coy. shewed best horses, No. 3 Coy. the best turn-out, No. 4 Coy. the best individual pair, No. 2 Co. shewing the second best individual pair.	
	8.		O.C. went to Divisional Supply Column re repairs to motor car	

A5834 Wt. W4973/M687 750,000 8/16 D. D. & L. Ltd. Forms/C.2118/13.

Instructions regarding War Diaries and Intelligence Summaries are contained in F. S. Regs., Part II. and the Staff Manual respectively. Title pages will be prepared in manuscript.

WAR DIARY
or
INTELLIGENCE SUMMARY.
(Erase heading not required.)

Army Form C. 2118.

Place	Date	Hour	Summary of Events and Information	Remarks and references to Appendices
BAPAUME	9th		O.C. called at 59th Bde Headquarters.	
	10th		O.C. Train reported at Divisional Headquarters with reference to inspection of Front Line Transport.	
	11th		Heavy rain in early morning. C.O. to EARL'S COURT Siding.	
			60th Bde Horse Show in afternoon. No. 160 Company won first prize for water cart, and also for pair of Heavy Draught horses.	
	12th		Pte Peachey returned from D.S.C with Wolseley car	
	13th		Capt. & Adj. C.S. EVANS proceeded on leave. Capt M.M. PAKENHAM took over duties temporarily	
			C.O. inspected Brigade Camps	

Instructions regarding War Diaries and Intelligence Summaries are contained in F. S. Regs., Part II. and the Staff Manual respectively. Title pages will be prepared in manuscript.

WAR DIARY
or
INTELLIGENCE SUMMARY.
(Erase heading not required.)

Army Form C. 2118.

Place	Date	Hour	Summary of Events and Information	Remarks and references to Appendices
BAPAUME	14th		C.O. inspected camp & lines of Headquarter Company	
	15th		Preliminary arrangements made with O.C. 14th Reserve Park to hold a combined sports meeting at an early date	
	17th		Date of sports fixed for 23rd June, circumstances permitting.	
	18th		Companies busy running off heats, & semi finals.	
	19th		O.C. Train reported at office of D.D.S.&T. III Army ALBERT, and also saw D.D.R. re officers chargers.	
	20		Order received for move of artillery; Headquarter Company withdrawn from Sports.	
	21st		Party sent to FREVENT to draw Remounts, under charge of 2Lt ANDERSON, and 2Lt HUTCHINS (for Headqr. Co.)	

A5834 Wt. W4973/M687 750,000 8/16 D. D. & L. Ltd. Forms/C.2118/13.

Instructions regarding War Diaries and Intelligence Summaries are contained in F. S. Regs., Part II. and the Staff Manual respectively. Title pages will be prepared in manuscript.

WAR DIARY
or
INTELLIGENCE SUMMARY.
(Erase heading not required.)

Army Form C. 2118.

Place	Date	Hour	Summary of Events and Information	Remarks and references to Appendices
BAPAUME	22nd		Refilled from Railhead. 7.30 am. Artillery Railhead ALBERT. Headquarters Company marched to MAMETZ, and re-filled at FRICOURT CIRCUS.	
			O.C. 62nd Divnl Train visited Camp	
	23rd		Drew Remounts, for Division; 20 H.D., 24 L.D. 17 Heavy Draught allotted to Divisional Train. 8 to No. 2 Co., and 9 to No. 4 Co:	
	24th		Orders received for move. CAPT. EVANS returns from leave.	
	25th		Selected refilling points in new area –	
	26th		3rd Sec. D.A.C. joins Artillery, refill at FRICOURT CIRCUS Capt. PAKENHAM rejoins Headquarters Co. from Train Headquarters.	

A5834 Wt. W4973/M687 750,000 8/16 D. D. & L. Ltd. Forms/C.2118/13.

Army Form C. 2118.

Instructions regarding War Diaries and Intelligence Summaries are contained in F. S. Regs., Part II. and the Staff Manual respectively. Title pages will be prepared in manuscript.

WAR DIARY
or
INTELLIGENCE SUMMARY.
(Erase heading not required.)

Place	Date	Hour	Summary of Events and Information	Remarks and references to Appendices
BAPAUME	27th		C.O. visited ~~no~~ Headquarters Company at MAMETZ.	
	28th		Train Headquarters and no. 2 Company moved to ACHEUX. en route for new area. C.O. proceeded to BERNAVILLE to arrange billets.	
BERNAVILLE	29th		Train Headquarters opened here. No. 2 Company arrived at EPERCAMPS	
			No. 3 Company marched to ACHEUX.	
"	30th		No. 3 Company arrived at CANAPLES.	
			No. 4 Company to ACHEUX.	

R. Launders Lt. Col.
Comm^d 20th Div. Train

A5834 Wt. W4973 M687 750,000 8/16 D. D. & L. Ltd. Forms/C.2118/13.

Vol 22

War Diary

20th Divisional

Train

July 1917

Instructions regarding War Diaries and Intelligence Summaries are contained in F. S. Regs., Part II. and the Staff Manual respectively. Title pages will be prepared in manuscript.

WAR DIARY
or
INTELLIGENCE SUMMARY.
(Erase heading not required.)

Army Form C. 2118.

Place	Date	Hour	Summary of Events and Information	Remarks and references to Appendices
BERNAVILLE	1st July		161 Coy ASC marched from ACHEUX to FIENVILLERS - 61st Bde Group refilled at FIENVILLERS at end of march - Adjutant visited 1st Coy ASC at FRICOURT to arrange loaning of waggons for the move. O.C. Train left for England on leave.	
	2nd "		Went to CANDAS to purchase vegetables & arranged for an issue twice weekly - arranged for supplies of R.A. Group during move	
	3rd		Capt. Parry 11th R.B arrived at Train HQrs for instruction - RA Group & 1st Coy ASC marched to ENGLEBELMER - Visited ALBERT Railhead & DDS.T to arrange drawing from Dump at Railhead - also RA. HQrs & 1st Coy to make necessary arrangements.	
	4th		Visited 3 Brigade Coys to inspect lines & mens billets - Arranged to draw wood from Area Commandant & straw from Army Purchase Board at DOULLENS - Capt. Whitty joined HQrs Coy as S.O. for R.A. Group - Lieut Norman to No 2 Coy during absence of S.O. 61st Bde - Adjutant visited HQrs Coy at SARTON.	

A5834 Wt. W4973 M687 750,000 8/16 D. D. & L. Ltd. Forms/C.2118/13.

Army Form C. 2118.

Instructions regarding War Diaries and Intelligence Summaries are contained in F. S. Regs., Part II. and the Staff Manual respectively. Title pages will be prepared in manuscript.

WAR DIARY
or
INTELLIGENCE SUMMARY.
(Erase heading not required.)

Place	Date	Hour	Summary of Events and Information	Remarks and references to Appendices
BERNAVILLE	5th July		Visited Railhead & 161 Coy ASC — G.O.C. Division inspected No 2 Coy at 2.30 pm. No 4 Coy at 4 pm & No 3 Coy at 5 pm.	
	6th "		Arranged at 10th Bde HQrs for billets for 160 Coy ASC & for a new dump for 58th Bde Group	
	7th "		No 3 Coy loaded up at ROSEL Railhead & dumped at new waggon lines at BONNEVILLE — Arranged to issue large proportion of wood so that field ovens might be substituted for travelling kitchens	
	8th "		60th Bde Group refilled at BONNEVILLE — DHQ Group & 58th Bde Group at BERNEUIL — visited DHQ to arrange for substitution of loaders by men from Employment Coy	
	9th "		R.E. Coys went to LA CHAUSSEE. TIRANCOURT — arranged for their rations to be sent there by lorry. 158 Coy ASC to 1st Army —	
	10th		Visited 161 Coy ASC & 160 Coy ASC to arrange leave & to see S.O.S — to Q Office with reference to move Capt. Parry reported to D.HQ.	

A5834 Wt. W4973/M687 750,000 8/16 D. D. & L. Ltd. Forms/C.2118/13.

Army Form C. 2118.

Instructions regarding War Diaries and Intelligence Summaries are contained in F. S. Regs., Part II. and the Staff Manual respectively. Title pages will be prepared in manuscript.

WAR DIARY
or
INTELLIGENCE SUMMARY.
(Erase heading not required.)

Place	Date	Hour	Summary of Events and Information	Remarks and references to Appendices
BERNAVILLE	11th	July	Visited D.H.Q. + 161 Coy A.S.C. + worked out scheme for move North.	
	12th	July	Major J. SOAMES, D.S.O., proceeded on leave of absence	
			O.C. Train returned from leave	
	13th		Divisional Horse Show took place at PERNOIS. No. 1 Coy Arrived at HERZEELE.	
	14th		O.C. Train to Divnl. Hdqrs. re move to northern area –	
	15th		Inspection of Brigade Coys. by C.O., also search for missing motor cycle	
			T/Capt. F.M. MAY reported from B.H.T. Depôt, HAVRE, and posted to No 4 Co.	
			O.C. Train to Advd. M.T. Depôt ABBEVILLE	
	16th		O.C. Train to D.H.Q	
			10 H.D. horses arrived from ABBEVILLE	

A5834 Wt. W4973/M687 750,000 8/16 D. D. & L. Ltd. Forms/C.2118/13.

Instructions regarding War Diaries and Intelligence Summaries are contained in F. S. Regs., Part II. and the Staff Manual respectively. Title pages will be prepared in manuscript.

WAR DIARY
or
INTELLIGENCE SUMMARY.
(Erase heading not required.)

Army Form C. 2118.

Place	Date	Hour	Summary of Events and Information	Remarks and references to Appendices
BERNAVILLE	17th		O.C. Train proceeded to PROVEN area, and visited Headquarters Co. at BAMBECQUE	
	18th		Lt C.W. MILES, no 4 Cos. struck off strength of Train	
			Sergt POWELL, Headqrs. Co., killed and 5 men wounded, near INTERNATIONAL CORNER, when attached to ~~to~~ 29th Divnl. Train. Also 2 horses killed.	
	19th		C.O. to DOULLENS, to see arrangements for entraining.	
	20th		No. 3 Company marched from BONNEVILLE to DOULLENS, to entrain there	
			Headquarters of Train marched from BERNAVILLE,	
	21st		Nos. 2 and 4 Companies marched from EPERCAMPS & FIENVILLERS, entrained, and arrived at new area at midnight	
PROVEN			Headquarters Train arrived at PROVEN	

A5834 Wt. W4973 M687 750,000 8/16 D. D. & L. Ltd. Forms/C.2118/13.

Instructions regarding War Diaries and Intelligence Summaries are contained in F. S. Regs., Part II. and the Staff Manual respectively. Title pages will be prepared in manuscript.

WAR DIARY
or
INTELLIGENCE SUMMARY.
(Erase heading not required.)

Army Form C. 2118.

Place	Date	Hour	Summary of Events and Information	Remarks and references to Appendices
PROVEN	22nd		Headquarters Train established with No. 3 Co. Co to DS column, & No. 4 Co.	
	23rd		Railhead changed to GRUBBEM. Major SOAMES, S.S.O. returned from leave.	
	24th		Lt ANDERSON to BAILLEUL for interview with officer of R.F.C.	
	25th		O.C. Train conferred with O.C. 38th Divnl. Train reference move of No. 1 Co. Lecture by Divisional Gas Officer to Nos 1 and 4 Company in evening.	
	26th		O.C. Train to D.A.Q. in a.m. Gas Officer lectured to Nos. 2 & 3 Companies in p.m.	
	27		with S.S.O to HAZEBROUCK to purchase supplies. Lt COL WILSON, Adviser in Horsemastership, XIV Corps, visited	

A5834 Wt. W4973/M687 750,000 8/16 D. D. & L. Ltd. Forms/C.2118/13.

Instructions regarding War Diaries and Intelligence Summaries are contained in F. S. Regs., Part II. and the Staff Manual respectively. Title pages will be prepared in manuscript.

WAR DIARY
or
INTELLIGENCE SUMMARY.
(Erase heading not required.)

Army Form C. 2118.

Place	Date	Hour	Summary of Events and Information	Remarks and references to Appendices
PROVEN	27/7		Nos. 2 and 3 companies, also Train Headquarters.	
			C.O. had interview with D.D.S.&T. V Army.	
	28th		O.C. Train visited Office of D.A.D.T., with reference to return of car to Purchasing Board. Also visited Headquarters Company, informing Company Commander that he would receive orders to move from O.C. 38th Train.	
	29th		O.C. Train inspected GRUBBEM Railhead arrangements in am.	
			Headquarters Co. moved to INTERNATIONAL CORNER.	
	30th		No. 2 Company marched into camp near INTERNATIONAL CORNER.	
	31st		O.C. Train conferred with O.C. 38th Div. Train with reference to possible move of Division. XIX attached at 7.50 am.	

R.H. Launder Lt Col
Comm'd Train XX Div.

Vol 23

War Diary

20th Divisional Train

Instructions regarding War Diaries and Intelligence Summaries are contained in F. S. Regs., Part II. and the Staff Manual respectively. Title pages will be prepared in manuscript.

WAR DIARY
or
INTELLIGENCE SUMMARY.
(Erase heading not required.)

Army Form C. 2118.

Place	Date	Hour	Summary of Events and Information	Remarks and references to Appendices
PROVEN	AUGUST 1st		C.O. went to D.H.Q. in a.m., & to Corps Headquarters in p.m. to see S.M.T.O.	
	2nd		O.C. Train visited Headquarters Company at INTERNATIONAL CORNER in a.m., also Hdqrs. R.A.	
			Captain MASCHMEYER returned from leave	
	3rd		Arrangements made with O.C. 38th Div. Train reference move of Brigade Companies & Train Headquarters to new area.	
	4th		No. 4 Company moved to INTERNATIONAL CORNER	
	5th		No. 3 Company moved to INTERNATIONAL CORNER	
			O.C. Train to R.A. Hdqrs. re location of Train Headquarters at A. 14. a. 5. 2.	
PESELHOEK	6th		Train Headquarters moved to A. 14. a. 6.5. 1. Refilling at INTERNATIONAL CORNER	

A5834 Wt. W4973/M687 750,000 8/16 D. D. & L. Ltd. Forms/C.2118/13.

Army Form C. 2118.

Instructions regarding War Diaries and Intelligence Summaries are contained in F. S. Regs., Part II. and the Staff Manual respectively. Title pages will be prepared in manuscript.

WAR DIARY
or
INTELLIGENCE SUMMARY.
(Erase heading not required.)

Place	Date	Hour	Summary of Events and Information	Remarks and references to Appendices
PESELHOEK	7th		Headquarters Co. 38th Divisional Train taken over for administration.	
			Lt ROBERTSON reported from B.H.T.D. HAVRE.	
	8th		2nd Lieut. ANDERSON left for R.F.C Headquarters, HESDIN.	
			38 tons of coal cleared by Train wagons.	
	9th		O.C. Train visited Headquarters Company.	
	10th		Headquarters, Nos. 2 and 3 companies moved to	
			VOX VRIE farm, A.15 central.	
	11.		O.C. Train inspected companies in new location	
	12		26 Remounts (H.D) drawn from PROVEN Railhead.	
	13		O.C. Train to Railhead and D.H.Q.	
	14		O.C. Train to DAWSON'S CORNER in p.m.	
			Lt Col. Wilson from XIV Corps inspected horses	

A5834 Wt. W4973/M687 750,000 8/16 D. D. & L. Ltd. Forms/C2118/13.

Instructions regarding War Diaries and Intelligence Summaries are contained in F. S. Regs., Part II. and the Staff Manual respectively. Title pages will be prepared in manuscript.

WAR DIARY
or
INTELLIGENCE SUMMARY.
(Erase heading not required.)

Army Form C. 2118.

Place	Date	Hour	Summary of Events and Information	Remarks and references to Appendices
PESELHOEK			of Headquarters Company.	
	17th		C.O. and S.S.O. to Army Headquarters and 38th Divnl. Train Headquarters, with reference to move of Brigade Companies into PROVEN area.	
	18th		C.O. to DUNKIRK re purchase of bran. No. 2 Co. moved to PASTURE CAMP, at F.14 a.5.4. No. 3 Company to SOUTHEND CAMP at X.29. c.9.2. No. 4 Company to PARDO CAMP at F.14. c.8.6.	
	19th		Train Headquarters moved to PARDO Camp near PROVEN.	
PROVEN	20th		O.C. Train visited Headquarters Cos. also area Commandant, "G" Camp.	
	21st		All groups drawing from GRUBBEM Railhead.	
	22nd		C.O. dined with Divisional General.	
	23rd		7 reinforcements received from BASE.	

A5834 Wt. W4973/M687 750,000 8/16 D. D. & L. Ltd. Forms/C.2118/13.

Instructions regarding War Diaries and Intelligence Summaries are contained in F. S. Regs., Part II. and the Staff Manual respectively. Title pages will be prepared in manuscript.

WAR DIARY
or
INTELLIGENCE SUMMARY.
(Erase heading not required.)

Army Form C. 2118.

Place	Date	Hour	Summary of Events and Information	Remarks and references to Appendices
PROVEN	24th		O.C. Train visited Headquarters Company.–	
			7th D.C.L.I., 84th & 76th Field Co. R.E. & 6/Ox & Bucks L.I. proceeded to forward area, rationed by S.O. No 1 Co.	
	26th		D.D.A.S. visited Train Headquarters re withdrawal of Category "A" men. Drew 10 tons of Coal from GROBBEM railhead Army Reserve.	
	27th		Captain LOWE proceeded on leave, and Capt. MAY returned	
			6th K.S.L.I. proceeded to forward area in relief of 6/Ox & Bucks rationed by S.O. No 1 Co.	
	28th		Major CHAPLIN went on leave. H.Qrs. and 2 Battalions, 61st Brigade moved to HERZEELE, rationed by lorries. Refilling at HOUDTKERQUE ——	
	29th		Supplied Y.M.C.A., ELVERDINGHE with 2500 lbs biscuits under orders from D.D.S.T., V Army.	

A5834 Wt. W4973/M687 750,000 8/16 D. D. & L. Ltd. Forms/C.2118/13.

Instructions regarding War Diaries and Intelligence Summaries are contained in F. S. Regs., Part II. and the Staff Manual respectively. Title pages will be prepared in manuscript.

WAR DIARY
or
INTELLIGENCE SUMMARY.

(Erase heading not required.)

Army Form C. 2118.

Place	Date	Hour	Summary of Events and Information	Remarks and references to Appendices
PROVEN	August 29th		Supply wagons dump rations for 61st Brigade.	
	30th		O.C. Train visited all companies in area leaving in view expected visit by Divisional Commander.	
			S.Sergts. WARRINER and JOHNS interviewed by Brigadier 59th Bde re application for commission	
			Iron ration issue completed for Division	
	31st		2/Lieut. C.W. PERRY to England on leave prior to joining No. 2 Infantry School at BEDFORD.	
			CAPT. MASCHMEYER assumed duties of Divisional claims officer.	
			83rd Field Company relieved 96th Fd.Co. in forward area.	

R. Saunders Lt Col.
Comd 20th Divn Train

A5834 Wt. W4973/M687 750,000 8/16 D. D. & L. Ltd. Forms/C.2118/13.

Vol 24

War Diary

Divisional Train

Instructions regarding War Diaries and Intelligence Summaries are contained in F. S. Regs., Part II. and the Staff Manual respectively. Title pages will be prepared in manuscript.

WAR DIARY
or
INTELLIGENCE SUMMARY.
(Erase heading not required.)

Army Form C. 2118.

Place	Date SEPT.	Hour	Summary of Events and Information	Remarks and references to Appendices
PROVEN	1st		OC Train visited Army School of Cookery	
	2nd		Inspection of nos. 4 and 2 Companies by OC Train, dis mounted parade 35th Bde. headquarters and 4 battalions moved to HERZEELE and supplies taken to HOUDKERQUE by Supply Column. OC Train to HOUSKERQUE in am. supplies to latter by horse transport.	
	3rd		Inspection of nos. 3 and 1 Companies in pm. dismounted, by OC Train	
	4		OC Train to 38th DHQ at WELSH FARM to see Area Com mandant. One CSM and one CQMS arrived from B.D. Havre, and posted to nos 4 and 2 Company. Divisional Commander visited Train Headquarters and inspected nos. 4 and 2 Companies	
	5th		Co. to railhead in am. S.S.O. to DUNKIRK in pm.	

A5834 Wt. W4973/M687 750,000 8/16 D. D. & L. Ltd. Forms/C.2118/13.

Instructions regarding War Diaries and Intelligence Summaries are contained in F. S. Regs., Part II. and the Staff Manual respectively. Title pages will be prepared in manuscript.

WAR DIARY
or
INTELLIGENCE SUMMARY.
(Erase heading not required.)

Army Form C. 2118.

Place	Date	Hour	Summary of Events and Information	Remarks and references to Appendices
PROVEN	7th		O.C. Train saw all four companies of the Train on mounted parade, accompanied by Lt Col. [illegible], advisor in Horsemastership, XIV Corps.	
	8th		Supply section, No. 4 Company left in afternoon for G. Camp, Co. CORNISH CROSS.	
	9th		Headquarters of No. 4 Co. moved to G. Camp. also supply section of No. 3 Company.	
	10th		Headquarters of No. 3 Company and supply section of No. 2 Company moved to G. Camp.	
	11th		Train Headquarters moved to DRAGON CAMP, and Headquarters of No. 2 Company to G. Camp.	
DRAGON CAMP.	12th		O.C. Train to D.H.Q. in car. Visit of Commander BICK-FORD, R.N., and other naval officers from DUNKIRK	

A5834 Wt. W4973/M687 750,000 8/16 D. D. & L. Ltd. Forms/C.2118/13.

Army Form C. 2118.

Instructions regarding War Diaries and Intelligence Summaries are contained in F. S. Regs., Part II. and the Staff Manual respectively. Title pages will be prepared in manuscript.

WAR DIARY
or
INTELLIGENCE SUMMARY.
(Erase heading not required.)

Place	Date	Hour	Summary of Events and Information	Remarks and references to Appendices
DRAGON CAMP	13th		O.C. Train to Army Headquarters. Major EDWARDS, S.S.O. 4th Division reported, and stayed the night.	
	14th		5 H.D. horses drawn from INTERNATIONAL CORNER railhead. 4th Div R.A. drawn from I.C. by lorry.	
	15th		O.C. Train visited G camp & inspected lines of Brigade Companies. Also made arrangements for accommodation of No. 1 Co. 4th Divisional Train.	
	16th		Lt Col F STANTON. O.C. TRAIN proceeded on special leave to PARIS. Supply wagons of 93rd Bde A.F.A. detached from No 1 Coy on leaving for XVIII Corps area – arranged with D.D.S.&T for adjustment of park –	

A5834 Wt. W4973/M687 750,000 8/16 D. D. & L. Ltd. Forms/C.2118/13.

Instructions regarding War Diaries and Intelligence Summaries are contained in F. S. Regs., Part II. and the Staff Manual respectively. Title pages will be prepared in manuscript.

WAR DIARY
or
INTELLIGENCE SUMMARY.
(Erase heading not required.)

Army Form C. 2118.

Place	Date	Hour	Summary of Events and Information	Remarks and references to Appendices
DRAGON CAMP	17th		93rd + 65th Bdes A.F.A. refill at International Corner Rhead for last time by lorry before being transferred to 58th Division – 59th + 60th Bdes draw 2 days rations for Infantry personnel – Visited Brigade Coys + D.H.Q.	
	18th		11th D.L.I. draw 2 days rations – visited Railhead + H.Q. Coy.	
	19th		40 tons coal drawn from International Corner Railhead. Sent up 400 lbs Solidified Alcohol to 59th Bde for men in isolated posts.	
	20th		Visited Railhead to check oats, as quantities sent from Base inaccurate – + DHQ with reference to two hand-wagons shown as surplus to establishment. Lt. Colonel R Standen returned from leave.	
	21		O.C. Train visited D.D. of S. & T. V Army with reference to motor cars for the Train in the event of a move. Also to see A.D. of S. re shortage of oats.	
	22nd		Seven riding horses handed over to the Camp Commandant D.H.Q.	

Instructions regarding War Diaries and Intelligence Summaries are contained in F. S. Regs., Part II. and the Staff Manual respectively. Title pages will be prepared in manuscript.

WAR DIARY
or
INTELLIGENCE SUMMARY.
(Erase heading not required.)

Army Form C. 2118.

Place	Date	Hour	Summary of Events and Information	Remarks and references to Appendices
DRAGON CAMP	23rd		76th A.F.A. Brigade transferred for supplies to 3rd Division. 59th & 60th Bdes. relieved by 61st Bde.	
	24th		O.C. Train visited all companies of the Train, & called at D.H.Q. in p.m.	
	25th		O.C. 4th Divisional Train visited Train headquarters, and walked round the companies lines & billets. Steps taken to separate horses on lines with a view to minimising casualties from bombs & shells.	
	26th		G.O.C inspected all four companies of the Train. In evening Supply Section of No 3. Co. moved to Staging area.	
	27th		Headquarters of No 3 Co. moved to S. area; Supply Section of No. 2 Company to PASTURE CAMP.	
	28th		Headquarters of No. 2 Company to PARDO CAMP. Supply Section, No. 4 Company to PARDO CAMP.	
	29th		Train H'qrs. and H'qrs. No 4 Co. to PARDO CAMP. Railhead changed to PROVEN.	
PROVEN	30th		SSO to new area to arrange re filling for 1st & 2nd October.	

[illegible] Lt Col
Commdg 20th Div. Train

A5834 Wt. W4973/M687 750,000 8/16 D. D. & L. Ltd. Forms/C.2118/13.

Instructions regarding War Diaries and Intelligence Summaries are contained in F. S. Regs., Part II. and the Staff Manual respectively. Title pages will be prepared in manuscript.

WAR DIARY
or
INTELLIGENCE SUMMARY.
(Erase heading not required.)

Army Form C. 2118.

20 D Train
Vol 25

Place	Date	Hour	Summary of Events and Information	Remarks and references to Appendices
PROVEN	Oct. 1st		Train Headquarters and Nos. 2. 3. and 4 Companies moved to new area, III Army.	
ROCQUIGNY	2nd		Train Hdqrs. & Brigade Companies arrived in new area. Took over accommodation from 55th Divl. Train	
-do-	3rd		O.C. Train to D.H.Q. in pm. S.S.O. to see S.S.O. 40th Division with reference to transfer.	
-do-	4th		O.C. Train to NURLU to see O.C. 40th Divl. Train with reference to accommodation. No. 3 Co. moved to SOREL area. No 4 Co. to HAUT ALLAINES area.	
	5th		Train Headquarters moved to NURLU. O.C. Train reported to D.D. of S.&T. III Army.	
NURLU	6th		No. 2 Co. arrived in new area, NURLU	

A5834 Wt. W4973/M687 750,000 8/16 D. D. & L. Ltd. Forms/C.2118/13.

Instructions regarding War Diaries and Intelligence Summaries are contained in F. S. Regs., Part II. and the Staff Manual respectively. Title pages will be prepared in manuscript.

WAR DIARY
or
INTELLIGENCE SUMMARY.
(Erase heading not required.)

Army Form C. 2118.

Place	Date	Hour	Summary of Events and Information	Remarks and references to Appendices
NURLU	8th		No 4 Company moved into the NURLU area.	
	9th		O.C. Train went to LIERAMONT with reference to transport work, Rl services. Also to D.H.Q.	
	10th		O.C. Train inspected accommodation, horse standings and camps of the three Brigade Companies. 40th Divisional Train Headquarters & last Brigade Company marched out.	
	11th		All supplies loaded on Decauville at FINS Railhead including 40th D.A.	
	12th		O.C. Train arranged for planting vegetables by Brigade Coys.	
	13th		O.C. Train examined the feasibility of charcoal-burning. S.S.O. to AMIENS to purchase tousing-knives & to arrange for a supply of beer & vegetables to the Division	

A5834 Wt. W4973/M687 750,000 8/16 D. D. & L. Ltd. Forms/C.2118/13.

Instructions regarding War Diaries and Intelligence Summaries are contained in F. S. Regs., Part II. and the Staff Manual respectively. Title pages will be prepared in manuscript.

WAR DIARY
or
INTELLIGENCE SUMMARY.
(Erase heading not required.)

Army Form C. 2118.

Place	Date	Hour	Summary of Events and Information	Remarks and references to Appendices
NURLU	14th		Lieut-Colonel R. H. F. Standen proceeded to England on leave. S.S.O. assumed temporary command of the Train.	
	15th		DDS & T Third Army inspected lines of 3 Brigade Coys, & expressed his approval of the condition of horses, harness & waggons.	
	16th		Visited Town Major NURLU with reference to requisition of bricks & to arrange baths for the personnel of the Train.	
	17th		S.S.O. purchased vegetables at CAMON.	
	18th		- Loaded supplies for R.E. units 40th Division on lorries for dumping at PERONNE. . VII Corps relieved III Corps.	
	19th		- C.R.E. Pioneers & 2 Field Coys R.E. 40th Div. transferred for rations to their own Division. - Adjutant returned from leave, & Captain May assumed temporary command of No 3 Coy.	
	20th		- Lieut. R. G. White joined from B.H.T.D HAVRE & was posted temporarily to No 2. Coy. Arranged supplies for D.A. on arrival.	

A5834 Wt. W4973/M687 750,000 8/16 D. D. & L. Ltd. Forms/C.2118/13.

Instructions regarding War Diaries and Intelligence Summaries are contained in F. S. Regs., Part II. and the Staff Manual respectively. Title pages will be prepared in manuscript.

WAR DIARY
or
INTELLIGENCE SUMMARY.
(Erase heading not required.)

Army Form C. 2118.

Place	Date	Hour	Summary of Events and Information	Remarks and references to Appendices
NURLU	21st		Visited DHQ with reference to seeds & bricks for Coy lines – No 1 Coy arrived at NURLU.	
	22nd		To AMIENS with S.S.O. to arrange for further supply of beer & vegetables –	
	23rd		Coal-train cleared at ROISEL –	
	24th		Visited DHQ with a view to reducing amount of H.T. required for fatigues.	
	25th		HQ 40th DA & ATM B. moved to PERONNE –	
	26th		Visited Bde Coys & D.H.Q. – SSO to PERONNE Railhead to obtain details	
	27th		40th D.A. left Divisional area. No 1 Coy 40th D.W.T. moved out at midnight. Summary taken in cases of Capt. Hattaway.	
	28th		To III rd Corps for conference on Decauville system & the construction of new sidings – No 1 Coy moved into Camp at NURLU.	
	29th		Arrangements made to start ploughing 10 acre plots with 4 ploughs. Adjutant selected ground.	
	30th		Arranged to reduce numbers of Decauville trucks by adjustment of loads.	

A5834 Wt. W4973/M687 750,000 8/16 D. D. & L. Ltd. Forms/C.2118/13.

Instructions regarding War Diaries and Intelligence Summaries are contained in F. S. Regs., Part II. and the Staff Manual respectively. Title pages will be prepared in manuscript.

WAR DIARY
or
INTELLIGENCE SUMMARY.
(Erase heading not required.)

Army Form C. 2118.

Place	Date	Hour	Summary of Events and Information	Remarks and references to Appendices
NURLU.	31st		To [illegible] at AMIENS [illegible] to [illegible] vegetables at CAMON with S.S.O. Rationed Field Coys R.E. of 29th, 12th & 6th Divisions –	
			J. [illegible] Soames Major A.S.C. of O.C. 29th Div Train	
			31/10/17	

A5834 Wt. W4973 M687 750,000 8/16 D. D. & L. Ltd. Forms/C.2118/13.

~~20th Division G~~

Herewith War Diary for month of November 1917

HEADQUARTERS
Date 1-12-17
No HT/XX/1542
20th DIVISIONAL TRAIN A.S.C.

1/12/17

R Standen Lieut Colonel
Comdg 20th Divl Train ASC

Instructions regarding War Diaries and Intelligence Summaries are contained in F. S. Regs., Part II. and the Staff Manual respectively. Title pages will be prepared in manuscript.

WAR DIARY
or
INTELLIGENCE SUMMARY.
(Erase heading not required.)

Army Form C. 2118.

20 D Train
Vol 26

Place	Date	Hour	Summary of Events and Information	Remarks and references to Appendices
NURLU	Nov. 1st		Inspected ploughing of 3 Bde Companies -	
	2nd		Capt Carpenter to U.K to report at Infantry School, Bedford. Capt May assumed command of No 3 Coy in his place -	
			To DHQ to arrange rationing of additional units.	
	3rd		To DHQ & to choose a new refilling point on NURLU - MANANCOURT Road - & to obtain trench boards from DADOS.	
	4th		Kiln built for obtaining solder from P.M. tins.	
	5th		To see AA & QMG with reference to necessity of moving camps -	
			To LIERAMONT HEUDICOURT & GOUZEAUCOURT to choose sidings for refilling.	
	6th		91st, 92nd Bdes R.H. refill at W8a3.3 - no supply wagons used for them -	
	7th		To a conference at DHQ to arrange for new dumps & Railhead on Decauville system.	
	8th		To see Commandant III Corps & III C.T.S.C. with reference to transfer of Labour units	

A5834 Wt. W4973 M687 750,000 8/16 D. D. & L. Ltd. Forms/C.2118/13.

Army Form C. 2118.

Instructions regarding War Diaries and Intelligence Summaries are contained in F. S. Regs., Part II. and the Staff Manual respectively. Title pages will be prepared in manuscript.

WAR DIARY
or
INTELLIGENCE SUMMARY.
(Erase heading not required.)

Place	Date	Hour	Summary of Events and Information	Remarks and references to Appendices
NURLU	Nov	9th	Arrangement made to carry petrol tins in crates on pack saddles.	
		10th	To D.D.S.T Third Army to arrange for adjustments of Divisional Pack & to obtain an extra supply of candles.	
		11th	S.S.O. to CORBIE to procure vegetables & to AMIENS for beer. Labour Coys returned by III Corps Troops S.C.	
		12th	Visited officers in charge of Light Railway Controls at FINS & YTRES to arrange for carriage of rations from ROCQUIGNY.	
		13th	To conference at D.H.Q. with Staff Captains. S.S.O to GOUZEAUCOURT to arrange with D.G.O for forward fuel dump. To DHQ to arrange Refilling Points & accomodation for Train Coys. Adjutant to No 1 Sect DAC to see ammunition available. To DHQ to make further arrangements	
		14th	To D.D.S.T Third Army to arrange for transference of Div. Park to ROCQUIGNY. 100 crates for petrol tins made by each Bde Coy & issued to Brigades for water. S.S.O. to ETRICOURT to arrange with III Corps T.S.C for transference of Corps Troops to their park.	

A5834 Wt. W4973/M687 750,000 8/16 D. D. & L. Ltd. Forms/C.2118/13.

Instructions regarding War Diaries and Intelligence Summaries are contained in F. S. Regs., Part II. and the Staff Manual respectively. Title pages will be prepared in manuscript.

WAR DIARY
or
INTELLIGENCE SUMMARY.
(Erase heading not required.)

Army Form C. 2118.

Place	Date	Hour	Summary of Events and Information	Remarks and references to Appendices
NURLU	Nov	15th	To D.H.Q. to arrange for special issues of solidified alcohol, chewing gum & P.M. & Biscuit – To 20th DAC to arrange for use of Lorries from 19th inst.	
			Lieutenant Colonel R. Standen returned from leave.	
		16th	O.C. Train inspected camp of D.A.C. on the road to MANANCOURT, and went to D.H.Q. to discuss arrangements for future accommodation –	
		17th	O.C. Train attended conference in a.m. at D.H.Q.	
			Nos. 3 & 4 Companies moved into camp vacated by DAC.	
			S.S.O. 29th Division visited Train H.Qrs. with reference to accommodation of 29th Train	
		18th	O.C. 29th Train visited Train Headquarters, and arrangements made to share accommodation between the two Trains	
			Lt. WOODFORD, 6/Ox. & Bucks. L.I. acted as judge at the ploughing competition between the Companies and awarded prizes as follows:–	

A5834 Wt. W4973/M687 750,000 8/16 D. D. & L. Ltd. Forms/C.2118/13.

Army Form C. 2118.

Instructions regarding War Diaries and Intelligence Summaries are contained in F. S. Regs., Part II. and the Staff Manual respectively. Title pages will be prepared in manuscript.

WAR DIARY
or
INTELLIGENCE SUMMARY.
(Erase heading not required.)

Place	Date	Hour	Summary of Events and Information	Remarks and references to Appendices
NURLU	~~19~~th		1st Prize — No. 2 Company 2nd Prize — Nos. 1 and 3 Companies 3rd Prize — No. 4 Company–	
	19th		O.C. Train went to Army Headquarters to see D.D. of S. & T. S.S.O. to GOUZEAUCOURT to arrange about new refilling points	
	20th		Date of the attack– O.C. Train inspected roads in forward area, and went to Corps Headquarters in p.m. New railhead fixed at HEUDICOURT. The supply sections, R.A. & Brigade Companies proceeded to W.14.15.b.	
	21st		New railhead at HEUDICOURT opened–	
	22nd		No. 2 Company moved into camp vacated by No. 2	

A5834 Wt. W4973/M687 750,000 8/16 D. D. & L. Ltd. Forms/C.2118/13.

Army Form C. 2118.

Instructions regarding War Diaries and Intelligence Summaries are contained in F. S. Regs., Part II. and the Staff Manual respectively. Title pages will be prepared in manuscript.

WAR DIARY
or
INTELLIGENCE SUMMARY.
(Erase heading not required.)

Place	Date	Hour	Summary of Events and Information	Remarks and references to Appendices
NURLU	22		Section D.A.C. in NURLU.	
	23rd		O.C. Train visited advanced supply sections of the Companies –	
	24th		Visited forward area of division to inspect roads & tracks for transport.	
	26th		Captain HATHAWAY proceeded to England, to join the Infantry School at ~~BEDFORD~~ on the 1st Prox.	
	27th		Train headquarters vacated camp at NURLU, and moved into lines of No. 1 Co. at V.29 central, just outside village. No. 2 Company moved into Camp of No. 1 Company. Supply Sections of the Companies rejoined their headquarters	

A5834 Wt. W4973/M687 750,000 8/16 D. D. & L. Ltd. Forms/C.2118/13.

Instructions regarding War Diaries and Intelligence Summaries are contained in F. S. Regs., Part II. and the Staff Manual respectively. Title pages will be prepared in manuscript.

WAR DIARY
or
INTELLIGENCE SUMMARY.
(*Erase heading not required.*)

Army Form C. 2118.

Place	Date	Hour	Summary of Events and Information	Remarks and references to Appendices
NURLU	29th		O.C. Train visited advance section of the Company at REVELON FARM, accompanied by Major CHAPLIN, O.C. No. 1 Coy.	
	30th		Enemy attack on right flank of Division at 6.0 a.m. Four Companies of the Train ordered to retire to MANANCOURT. Marched at 1.0 p.m. Train Headquarters remained in Camp at V.29 Central.	
			Nov. 30th R. Slanden Lt Col. Comm'd 20th Div. Train	

A5834 Wt. W4973/M687 750,000 8/16 D. D. & L. Ltd. Forms/C.2118/13.

H.Q. "G"
20th Div.

Herewith War Diary for the month of December 1917.

R. Saunders Lt Col
Comm^d Train

1/1/18.

Instructions regarding War Diaries and Intelligence Summaries are contained in F. S. Regs., Part II. and the Staff Manual respectively. Title pages will be prepared in manuscript.

WAR DIARY
or
INTELLIGENCE SUMMARY.
(*Erase heading not required.*)

20 D Train
Vol 27

Army Form C. 2118.

Place	Date	Hour	Summary of Events and Information	Remarks and references to Appendices
NURLU	DEC. 1		Rations brought from ROCQUIGNY Railhead to V.27.d by lorry, refilling by supply wagons. Four Companies returned from MANANCOURT to their previous locations. S.S.O. went to 3rd C.T.S.C. re transfer of rations.	
	2.		O.C. Train to Div. Headquarters with reference to move of Division. Arranged with Town Major, NURLU, for accommodation of 1st line Transport. O.C. 61st Train called re taking over accommodation.	
	3.		Arrangements for accommodation of 1st line transport cancelled. O.C. Train to Corps Hdqrs. in fun	
	4th		Division relieved – Division (less artillery) moved out of the line. 59th Brigade to BUIRE, 60th to BOUZINCOURT and 61st ACHEUX; Div. Hdqrs. to BAIZIEUX. Transport to MEAULTE. S.S.O. to ALBERT.	

A5834 Wt. W4973/M687 750,000 8/16 D. D. & L. Ltd. Forms/C.2118/13.

Army Form C. 2118.

Instructions regarding War Diaries and Intelligence Summaries are contained in F. S. Regs., Part II. and the Staff Manual respectively. Title pages will be prepared in manuscript.

WAR DIARY
or
INTELLIGENCE SUMMARY.
(Erase heading not required.)

Place	Date	Hour	Summary of Events and Information	Remarks and references to Appendices
NURLU	5th		Train Headquarters moved to ALBERT. Railhead there. Transport to AMPLIER	
ALBERT	6th		Railheads: ALBERT for personnel, FREVENT for transport. 59th Brigade moved to TORCY, 60th to MARESQUIER, 61st to CREQUY. Divisional Headquarters to HUCQUELIERS. Transport to CONCHY. Train Headquarters moved to FRUGES.	
FRUGES	7th		Railhead at HESDIN. 60th Bde. to VERCHOCQ. Transport to St VAAST. Refilling VIEIL HESDIN.	
	8th		Transport to Brigade areas and HUCQUELIERS. Railhead HESDIN.	
	9th		O.C. Train to BLARINGHEM to arrange for accommodation.	
	10th		O.C. Train to Divnl. Hdqrs. also via FRUGES to new area along	

A5834 Wt. W4973/M687 750,000 8/16 D. D. & L. Ltd. Forms/C.2118/13.

Army Form C. 2118.

Instructions regarding War Diaries and Intelligence Summaries are contained in F. S. Regs., Part II. and the Staff Manual respectively. Title pages will be prepared in manuscript.

WAR DIARY
or
INTELLIGENCE SUMMARY.
(Erase heading not required.)

Place	Date	Hour	Summary of Events and Information	Remarks and references to Appendices
FRUGES			Route suitable for horse transport via DELETTES.	
	11th		Railhead AUCHY-LES-HESDIN. 59th Bde to RACQUING-	
			-HEM. No 2 Company marched to THIEMBRONNE.	
			O.C. Train called to see Lt Col. BEADON.	
	12th		Divisional & Train Headquarters moved to BLARINGHEM	
			No 2 Company arrived at CAMPAGNE. Lt ARONSON	
			attached to Train Headquarters. Railhead EBBLINGHEM.	
			~~59~~ 61st Bde to SERCUS.	
1 BLARINGHEM	13th		No 3 Company marched from RUMILLY to billets near	
			BLARINGHEM. 60th Brigade to LYNDE	
	14th		No 4 Company reached new area at WALLON CAPPEL	
			59th Brigade rations cleared from Railhead by Supply	
			wagons. Units re-filled with First Line Transport. 60th &	
			61st Brigade drew from Railhead by lorry. All forage	

A5834 Wt. W4973/M687 750,000 8/16 D. D. & L. Ltd. Forms/C.2118/13.

Instructions regarding War Diaries and Intelligence Summaries are contained in F. S. Regs., Part II. and the Staff Manual respectively. Title pages will be prepared in manuscript.

WAR DIARY
or
INTELLIGENCE SUMMARY.
(Erase heading not required.)

Army Form C. 2118.

Place	Date	Hour	Summary of Events and Information	Remarks and references to Appendices
			brought by lorry from HAZEBROUCK.	
			Baggage wagons returned to train.	
BLARINGHEM	15th		Rations for three brigades drawn from Railhead by supply wagons. CAPT. MASCHMEYER returned from leave. Supply & baggage wagons of 11th D.L.I., 6th K.S.L.I., 7th K.O.Y.L.I., 83rd and 84th Field Companies proceeded to forward area with 1st line transport.	
	18th		O.C. Train and R.O. to STRAZEELE to purchase vegetables	
	19th		Major J. SOAMES S.S.O. proceeded on leave. O.C. Train visited nos. 3 and 4 companies in a.m., and no. 2 Co. in p.m.	
	20th		O.C. Train inspected Transport of the 6/Ox. & Bucks. L.I., 12/R.B., 12/K.R.R. and 60th Bde Hdqrs. in morning. That of the 60th M.G.C. and 61st Field Ambulance in afternoon	
	21st		To A.D.T. (Northern) with reference to spare parts for Car no. 14500	

A5834 Wt. W4973/M687 750,000 8/16 D. D. & L. Ltd. Forms/C.2118/13.

Army Form C. 2118.

WAR DIARY
or
INTELLIGENCE SUMMARY.

(Erase heading not required.)

Instructions regarding War Diaries and Intelligence Summaries are contained in F. S. Regs., Part II. and the Staff Manual respectively. Title pages will be prepared in manuscript.

Place	Date	Hour	Summary of Events and Information	Remarks and references to Appendices
BLARINGHEM	22nd		O.C. Train went to new Area to see accommodation of S.S.M. INGRAM arrived from the Base for No 4 Company. Xmas puddings arrived.	
	23rd		Pudding issued to Brigade groups. Informed that No. 1 Company arrives today at ROBECQ.	
	24th		Acting S.S.O proceeded to AMIENS to settle accounts for beer.	
	25th		Supply wagons went to railhead at 8.0 8.10, & 8.20.	
	26th		Captain WHITTY proceeded to No. 1 Company to take over duties of S.O. 20th RA. vice Capt. MEADE going on leave.	
	27th		Lieut. ARONSON to No. 3 Company as S.O. 60th Bde. Lieut. ROBERTSON to No. 2 Company as S.O. 59th Bde.	
	29th		No. 1 Company marched to STRAZEELE area.	
	31			

A5834 Wt. W4973/M687 750,000 8/16 D. D. & L. Ltd. Forms/C.2118/13.

Army Form C. 2118.

Instructions regarding War Diaries and Intelligence Summaries are contained in F. S. Regs., Part II. and the Staff Manual respectively. Title pages will be prepared in manuscript.

WAR DIARY
or
INTELLIGENCE SUMMARY.

(Erase heading not required.)

Place	Date	Hour	Summary of Events and Information	Remarks and references to Appendices
BLARINGHEM	30/12		No. 1 Company reached destination at R 17 b. 6. 4, map 27-C.	
	31		Divisional Commander inspected 61st Brigade. O.C. Train inspected the whole of the 1st line Transport. S.S.O. proceeded to AIRE to buy vegetables. 5 reinforcements (drivers) from H.T. Base.	

R. Saunders Lt. Col.
Commd 20th Div. Train.

A5834 Wt. W4973/M687 750,000 8/16 D. D. & L. Ltd. Forms/C.2118/13.

Instructions regarding War Diaries and Intelligence Summaries are contained in F. S. Regs., Part II. and the Staff Manual respectively. Title pages will be prepared in manuscript.

WAR DIARY
or
INTELLIGENCE SUMMARY.

(Erase heading not required.)

Army Form C. 2118.

Place	Date	Hour	Summary of Events and Information	Remarks and references to Appendices
BLARINGHEM	Jan. 1st 1918		S.S.O. to forward area to see S.S.O., 37th Division & make arrangements for taking over. O.C. Train called upon D.D.S.T. Northern	
	2nd		60th Brigade inspected by Divisional Commander. O.C. Train inspected First Line Transport, and submitted report. 7 Remounts arrived to complete establishment	
	3rd		Major Soames S.S.O. returned from leave.	
	4th		59th Brigade inspected by Divisional Commander. O.C. Train inspected First Line Transport, & submitted report. Nos. 3 and 4 Companies moved to GODE area.	
	5th		S.S.O. to new area to see S.S.O. 30th Division, also railhead & refilling points. O.C. 37th Train visited Train Headquarters with reference to accommodation, &c.	

A5834 Wt. W4973/M687 750,000 8/16 D. D. & L. Ltd. Forms/C.2118/13.

Army Form C. 2118.

Instructions regarding War Diaries and Intelligence Summaries are contained in F. S. Regs., Part II. and the Staff Manual respectively. Title pages will be prepared in manuscript.

WAR DIARY
or
INTELLIGENCE SUMMARY.

(Erase heading not required.)

Place	Date	Hour	Summary of Events and Information	Remarks and references to Appendices
	6th		O.C. Train moved to new area. No 2 Company and Train Headquarters to GODE area	
HEKSKEN	7th		No. 2 Company reached camp near ZEVECOTEN, & Train Headquarters at HEKSKEN. Capt. MASCHMEYER relinquished duties of Claims Officer	
	8th		S.S.O. went round dumps in a.m. with AA & QMG. Lt A.W. WALMSLEY left for U.K. to report to Infantry School, BEDFORD.	
	9th		Very cold with heavy snow.	
	10th		O.C. Train visited No. 1 Company at WOLFHOEK	
	11th		2nd Lieut. LEGROVE returned from leave. Heavy thaw.	
	12th		Thaw precautions in force from 11.0 a.m.	

A5834 Wt. W4973/M687 750,000 8/16 D. D. & L. Ltd. Forms/C.2118/13.

Instructions regarding War Diaries and Intelligence Summaries are contained in F. S. Regs., Part II. and the Staff Manual respectively. Title pages will be prepared in manuscript.

WAR DIARY
or
INTELLIGENCE SUMMARY.
(Erase heading not required.)

Army Form C. 2118.

Place	Date	Hour	Summary of Events and Information	Remarks and references to Appendices
	6th		O.C. Train moved to new area. No 2 Company and Train Headquarters to GODE area.	
HEKSKEN	7th		No. 2 Company reached camp near ZEVECOTEN, & Train Headquarters at HEKSKEN. Capt. MASCHMEYER relinquished duties of Claims Officer	
	8th		S.S.O. went round dumps in a.m with AA & QMG. 2nd A.W. WALMSLEY left for U.K. to report to Infantry School, BEDFORD.	
	9th		Very cold with heavy snow.	
	10th		O.C. Train visited No. 1 Company at WOLFHOEK	
	11th		2nd Lieut. LEGROVE returned from leave. Heavy thaw.	
	12th		Thaw precautions in force from 11.0 a.m	

Instructions regarding War Diaries and Intelligence Summaries are contained in F. S. Regs., Part II. and the Staff Manual respectively. Title pages will be prepared in manuscript.

WAR DIARY
or
INTELLIGENCE SUMMARY.
(Erase heading not required.)

Army Form C. 2118.

Place	Date	Hour	Summary of Events and Information	Remarks and references to Appendices
	13th		No hay drawn from railhead.	
			9 reinforcements arrived from Base.	
	14th		No forage drawn from railhead. OC Train and Major CHAPLIN to Corps Headquarters, to see SMTO, Lt Col. BLAMEY.	
			Thaw precautions suspended. Heavy snow, followed by rain	
	15th		Very strong S.W gale + rain. railway beds washed away Railhead changed to OUDERDOM. To lecture on 'NAVY' in afternoon	
	16th		OC 37th Train visited Train Headquarters. Still no forage from Railhead.	
	17th		Full forage ration. CO to lecture at Corps School on "Censorship"	

A5834 Wt. W4973/M687 750,000 8/16 D. D. & L. Ltd. Forms/C.2118/13.

Instructions regarding War Diaries and Intelligence Summaries are contained in F. S. Regs., Part II. and the Staff Manual respectively. Title pages will be prepared in manuscript.

WAR DIARY
or
INTELLIGENCE SUMMARY.
(Erase heading not required.)

Army Form C. 2118.

Place	Date	Hour	Summary of Events and Information	Remarks and references to Appendices
	18th		SSO to 365 Forestry Co. at EDWARDSHOEK.	
	19th		Capt MEADE returned off leave. O.C. Train at S.S.O. to railhead to conduct officers from French G.Q.G. round. Then to o/ADofS.&T. and Corps Headquarters. Major Chaplin and QMS. BOYD temporarily attached to o/A.D.S.&T., Lt Col. BLAMEY.	
	20th		O.C. Train interviewed 2/Lieut. GOODWORTH R.F.A.	
	21st		Fire occurred at Train Headquarters, 11.0 pm., starting in S.S.O.'s office; offices + some Officers quarters burnt out.	
	22nd		O.C. Train to Divisional Headquarters, to report occurrence of fire. Then to Corps Headquarters. Afterwards to see D.D.S.&T. II Army.	

A5834 Wt. W4973/M687 750,000 8/16 D. D. & L. Ltd. Forms/C.2118/13.

Instructions regarding War Diaries and Intelligence Summaries are contained in F. S. Regs., Part II. and the Staff Manual respectively. Title pages will be prepared in manuscript.

WAR DIARY
or
INTELLIGENCE SUMMARY.
(Erase heading not required.)

Army Form C. 2118.

Place	Date	Hour	Summary of Events and Information	Remarks and references to Appendices
HEKSKEN	23rd		O.C. Train to Headquarters 112th Bde. to get material for re-construction of Train Headquarters, also to Divisional Headquarters.	
			T/Major BELL reported for duty from Base H.T. Depôt, HAVRE, and was posted to No. 1 Co.	
	24th		To No. 1 Co. Camp, also to see of A.D.S.T., IX Corps. of A.A. & Q.M.G. visited scene of fire.	
	25th		To Railhead in am. Capt. MASCHMEYER on short leave to PARIS. Major CHAPLIN relinquished temporary duty at IX Corps Headquarters & handed over command of No. 1 Company to MAJOR BELL	
	26th		Major CHAPLIN left to take over command of No.	

A5834 Wt. W4973/M687 750,000 8/16 D. D. & L. Ltd. Forms/C.2118/13.

17

Instructions regarding War Diaries and Intelligence Summaries are contained in F. S. Regs., Part II. and the Staff Manual respectively. Title pages will be prepared in manuscript.

WAR DIARY
or
INTELLIGENCE SUMMARY.
(*Erase heading not required.*)

Div. Train
Vol 28

Army Form C. 2118.

Place	Date	Hour	Summary of Events and Information	Remarks and references to Appendices
			4 Cavalry Reserve Park. Court of Enquiry held at D.H.Q. to enquire into fire which occurred on 21st inst.	
	27th		Court of Enquiry re-assembled at 2.30 p.m.	
	28th		O.C. Train went round Brigade Companies in a.m. & to Corps Headquarters in p.m.	
	29th		O.C. Train visited all companies in conjunction with Area Commandant and A/A.A. & Q.M.G. To Div. H.Qrs. in p.m.	
	30th		Divisional Commander inspected all Companies of Train, also Railhead and Refilling Points, supply dumps, etc., & visited Train H.Qrs.	
	31st		O.C. Train saw all Company Officers, reference G.O.C.'s inspection.	

R. Slaudey[?] Lt. Col.
Comm. 20th Divn. Train

A5834 Wt. W4973/M687 750,000 8/16 D. D. & L. Ltd. Forms/C.2118/13.

Instructions regarding War Diaries and Intelligence Summaries are contained in F. S. Regs., Part II. and the Staff Manual respectively. Title pages will be prepared in manuscript.

HEADQUARTERS, 20TH DIVISIONAL TRAIN.
No. H.T./XX/73
Date 28-2-18

WAR DIARY or INTELLIGENCE SUMMARY. 20th Divisional Train A.S.C.

(Erase heading not required.)

Army Form C. 2118.

Vol 29

Place	Date	Hour	Summary of Events and Information	Remarks and references to Appendices
HEKSKEN	FEB. 1		O.C. Train inspected First Line Transport of 61st Bde. in conjunction with D.A.D.V.S	
	2nd		Inspection of First Line Transport 59th Bde., with D.A.D.V.S S.S.O. went to Army Hdqrs., to interview D.D.S.T.	
	3rd		Captain EVANS proceeded on leave. a/Adjutancy taken over by Capt. MASCHMEYER. Capt. MEADE admitted to Field Ambulance.	
	4		O.C. Train inspected First Line Transport of 60th Bde., in conjunction with D.A.D.V.S. Capt. WHITTY relieved Capt. MEADE as S.O. Divisional Artillery; latter evacuated to No. 2. C.C.S.	
	5th		S.S.O. went to A.H.Q. to see D.D. of S.&T. arrival of 80 tons of coal & 25 tons of wood.	

A5834 Wt. W4973/M687 750,000 8/16 D. D. & L. Ltd. Forms/C.2118/13.

Instructions regarding War Diaries and Intelligence Summaries are contained in F. S. Regs., Part II. and the Staff Manual respectively. Title pages will be prepared in manuscript.

WAR DIARY
or
INTELLIGENCE SUMMARY.
(Erase heading not required.)

Army Form C. 2118.

Place	Date	Hour	Summary of Events and Information	Remarks and references to Appendices
HERZEELE	6th		Horses from no. 4 Company dipped in the Sulphur bath at St JANS CAPPEL	
	7th		Remaining horses of nos. 2 & 4 Company dipped. of A.D.S.T. IX Corps visited Train Headquarters.	
	8th		O.C. Train went to 55th Bde. headquarters in am. 140 tons of coal arrived. Lt R WHITE reported sick.	
	9		O.C. Train visited new area with reference to billets for Train Hdqrs. & Companies. Lt WHITE handed command of no. 2 Company to Lt SYKES.	
	10.		O.C. Train went to PROVEN to confer with O.C. 66 Train re office, etc., at ARQUES	

Army Form C. 2118.

Instructions regarding War Diaries and Intelligence Summaries are contained in F. S. Regs., Part II. and the Staff Manual respectively. Title pages will be prepared in manuscript.

WAR DIARY
or
INTELLIGENCE SUMMARY.
(Erase heading not required.)

Place	Date	Hour	Summary of Events and Information	Remarks and references to Appendices
HERSKEN	11		O.C. Train called at office of A.D.S.T. XV Corps in am. Inspected First Line Transport of 60th Bde. in p.m.	
			Horses of Nos. 1 and 3 Company dipped.	
	12th		142 tons of coal arrived. Inspected Field Coy. R.E. Transport in p.m. Also 7/Scottish Rifles.	
	13th		O.C. Train to BLARINGHEM re change of location	
			No. 2 Company marched to STRAZEELE	
	14th		59th Bde moved to BLARINGHEM area – No 2 Coy to WALLON CAPPEL.	
			S.S.O. to DOST Fourth Army with reference to change of parks –	
	15th		O.C. Train inspected 60th Field Ambulance. No 4 Coy marched to STRAZEELE –	
	16th		Train HQ moved to BLARINGHEM. No 4 Coy to BLARINGHEM. 61st Bde to WARDRECQUES area.	
BLARINGHEM	17th		37th Division relieved 20th Division in the line – D.H.Q. to BLARINGHEM. No 3 Coy to STRAZEELE. 61st Bde Group refilled at BELLE CROIX – 59th Bde Group at SERCUS	

A5834 Wt. W4973/M687 750,000 8/16 D. D. & L. Ltd. Forms/C.2118/13.

Instructions regarding War Diaries and Intelligence Summaries are contained in F. S. Regs., Part II. and the Staff Manual respectively. Title pages will be prepared in manuscript.

WAR DIARY
or
INTELLIGENCE SUMMARY.
(Erase heading not required.)

Army Form C. 2118.

Place	Date	Hour	Summary of Events and Information	Remarks and references to Appendices
BLARINGHEM	18th		No 3 Coy to EBBLINGHEM – No 1 Coy to MONT NOIR – S.S.O. to DUS.T with reference to move to Fifth Army – O.C. Train visited DHQT with reference to evacuation of Wolseley car. G.O.C. Division dined at Train H.Qs.	
	19th		O.C. Train inspected transport of 58th Bde – & left on leave for England in the afternoon. No 1 Coy to MORBECQUE.	
	20th		Division started to entrain for Fifth Army at STEENBECQUE. A second days rations for units entraining early dumped at the Station – No 2 Coy entrained – Captain C.S. Marchmayer proceeded to NESLE.	
	21st		No 3 Coy entrained at 4 pm.	
	22nd		No 4 Coy entrained at 7 pm – Captain C.S. Evans. Adjutant admitted to C.C.S. DHQ closed at BLARINGHEM – R.A. Group drew two days rations – 2 Bdes rationed from NESLE Railhead – remainder from STEENBECQUE. 105 tons Coal handed over to New Zealand Division –	
	23rd		Proceeded to new area – DHQ & HQ Train at ERCHEU. No 2 Coy at BEAULIEU. No 3 Coy at ERCHEU – No 4 Coy at FRENICHES – No 1 Coy entrained at STEENBECQUE.	

A5834 Wt. W4973/M687 750,000 8/16 D. D. & L. Ltd. Forms/C.2118/13.

Instructions regarding War Diaries and Intelligence Summaries are contained in F. S. Regs., Part II. and the Staff Manual respectively. Title pages will be prepared in manuscript.

WAR DIARY
or
INTELLIGENCE SUMMARY.
(Erase heading not required.)

Army Form C. 2118.

Place	Date	Hour	Summary of Events and Information	Remarks and references to Appendices
ERCHEU	24th		No 1 Coy to VOYENNES – Refilling at ERCHEU for Div Troops & 60th Bde – at BEAULIEU for 59th Bde – at FRENICHES for 61st Bde – Visited No 3 & No 4 Coy: Railhead for whole Division at NESLE –	
	25th		R.A Group refilled on NESLE-VOYENNES Road – Supplies for 61st Bde delivered by lorry – No 4 Coy to ROUVROY – Arranged with DDS&T for rationing of attached Artillery Brigades – Inspected No 2 Coy lines at BEAULIEU – Capt. Maschmeyer to CANNY to purchase vegetables – detailed an Officer from each company to superintend ploughing of 3 acre plots by each unit –	
	26th		Inspected No 1 Coy lines – To refilling points, Railhead & DDS&T. Inspected lines of No 4 Coy in the afternoon – 60th Bde Refilling Point moved to ~~a better~~ site – 7/2nd Lieut C F Barnes joined & was posted to No 2 Coy –	
	27th		Ammunition visited ~~No 2~~ Coy & No 4 Coy – visited attached Artillery Brigades & No 1 Coy – Capt MASCHMEYER arranged details of ploughing –	
	28th		No 4 Coy drew supplies for 61st Bde from HAM Railhead – visited 60th & 61st Bde HQs – All baggage wagons returned to units	

J. G. H. Soames
Major ASC
A/- O.C. 20th Divisional Train

28/2/18

A5834 Wt. W4973/M687 750,000 8/16 D. D. & L. Ltd. Forms/C.2118/13.

1

20th Division Q.

—

Herewith War Diary for the month of March.

[signature] Lieut Colonel

1/4/18.

Comndg 20th Div Train

Army Form C. 2118.

20 D Train
Vol 30

WAR DIARY
or
INTELLIGENCE SUMMARY.
(Erase heading not required.)

Instructions regarding War Diaries and Intelligence Summaries are contained in F. S. Regs., Part II. and the Staff Manual respectively. Title pages will be prepared in manuscript.

Place	Date	Hour	Summary of Events and Information	Remarks and references to Appendices
ERCHEU	March 1st		To XVIII Corps Q to make arrangements for A.F.A. Bdes – inspected No 4 Coy lines in the afternoon – DHQ refill by lorry from NESLE – Issued an extra P.M. + Biscuit ration to Infantry in case of emergency – T/2nd Lieut. Dowling joined Train + was posted to No 4 Coy.	
	2nd		To conference at Corps Q with AA&QMG – visited No 1 Coy to arrange for detachments of supply wagons in case of a forward move – inspected wagons of No. 2 + No 3 Coy returning from Railhead –	
	3rd		14th Bde AFA transferred to 61st Division – 83rd + 84th Field Coys move up to HAM Area + rationed with 61st Bde group – 2nd S.R. to CHAULNES. 7th DCLI to CURCHY	
	4th		To conference at Q Office on supplies – 96th Field Coy to III Corps Area – inspected work done in preparing racecourse – Adjutant to 3 Bdes to arrange for cultivation of 3-acre plots.	
	5th		To DDS&T to arrange for transfer of 60th Bde to HAM – To No 2 Coy – 60th Bde HQs to arrange refilling – Adjutant to 4 Coys to obtain reports on Agricultural progress.	

A5834 Wt. W4973/M687 750,000 8/16 D. D. & L. Ltd. Forms/C.2118/13.

Instructions regarding War Diaries and Intelligence Summaries are contained in F. S. Regs., Part II. and the Staff Manual respectively. Title pages will be prepared in manuscript.

WAR DIARY
or
INTELLIGENCE SUMMARY.
(Erase heading not required.)

Army Form C. 2118.

Place	Date	Hour	Summary of Events and Information	Remarks and references to Appendices
ERCHEU	March 6th		60th Bde moved to HAM. No 3 Coy to ST SULPICE. Inspected billets & arranged Refilling Point there. To RA Dump to inspect transport. Adjutant to 3 Brigade Coys to obtain particulars of employment of personnel.	
	7th		To No 2 Coy & No 4 Coy with Adjutant. 60th Bde Group refill at St Sulpice by Supply wagons. Lieutenant Colonel R Standen returns from leave & resumes command of the Train.	
	8th		O.C. Train inspected lines & wagon park of No. 2 Company.	
	9th		Divisional race meeting at ERCHEU. Four M.G. Companies to LIBERMONT forming M.G. Battalion.	
	10th		O.C. Train reported to D.D.S.T. V Army, also saw SMTO, Corps re evacuation of Wolseley car no. 14,500. S.S.O. to FALLOUEL re purchase of wood.	

A5834 Wt. W4973/M687 750,000 8/16 D. D. & L. Ltd. Forms/C.2118/13.

Army Form C. 2118.

Instructions regarding War Diaries and Intelligence Summaries are contained in F. S. Regs., Part II. and the Staff Manual respectively. Title pages will be prepared in manuscript.

WAR DIARY
or
INTELLIGENCE SUMMARY.
(Erase heading not required.)

Place	Date	Hour	Summary of Events and Information	Remarks and references to Appendices
ERCHEU	11th		O.C. Train visits Nos. 1 and 4 Company. No. 96 Field Co. RE rejoins division.	
	12th		O.C. Train visited lines & billets of No. 3 Company. 7/Somerset L.I. relieved 7/D.C.L.I. at CHAULNES.	
	13th		O.C. Train inspected first Line Transport of the Field Ambulances, also Signals Headquarters, with D.A.D.V.S. Lieut. Norman joined Train Headquarters as Requisitioning Officer. Lieut BARNES to No. 4 Company as S.O. 61st Brigade	
	14th		Inspection of No. 2 Company on parade –	
	15th		Petrol Cases issued to Brigade Companies for con-	

A5834 Wt. W4973/M687 750,000 8/16 D. D. & L. Ltd. Forms/C.2118/13.

Instructions regarding War Diaries and Intelligence Summaries are contained in F. S. Regs., Part II. and the Staff Manual respectively. Title pages will be prepared in manuscript.

WAR DIARY
or
INTELLIGENCE SUMMARY.
(Erase heading not required.)

Army Form C. 2118.

Place	Date	Hour	Summary of Events and Information	Remarks and references to Appendices
	15th		conversion into water carriers, for pack animals	
	16th		96th Field Co. R.E. to CHAUNY.	
	17th		Two days rations issued to Batteries R.F.A. proceeding to Army School.	
			One N.C.O. from each company detailed to attend Hotchkiss gun course at ESTOUILLY. 60th Bde Horse Show –	
	18th		O.C. Train inspected transport at R.A. Ration Dump, afterwards visited No. 1 Company's lines –	
	19th		O.C. Train inspected No. 4 company on parade; a very good turn-out	
	20th		Capt. and Adjt. MASCHMEYER went on leave; Lieut. NORMAN took over duties of acting adjutant	

Instructions regarding War Diaries and Intelligence Summaries are contained in F. S. Regs., Part II. and the Staff Manual respectively. Title pages will be prepared in manuscript.

WAR DIARY
or
INTELLIGENCE SUMMARY.
(Erase heading not required.)

Army Form C. 2118.

Place	Date	Hour	Summary of Events and Information	Remarks and references to Appendices
ERCHEU	March 21st		After an intense bombardment, enemy attacked on a wide front. O.C. Train visited all four companies in connection with move to Battle Quarters. Also called at Divisional Headquarters at HAM. In p.m. selected dump for R.A. with S.S.O. Nos 2 & 3 Companies moved to VILLERS – St CHRISTOPHE, No. 4 Company to TUGNY.	
	22nd		O.C. Train visited Divnl. Headquarters at HAM in a.m. In p.m. arranged for accommodation at BEAULIEU. for Train Headquarters, and moved there at 5.0 p.m.	
BEAULIEU	23rd		Train Headquarters moved at 11.0 a.m. to ROYE, halting at ROIGLISE.	
ROYE		3.0 p.m.	No. 1 Company moved to RETHONVILLERS	

A5834 Wt. W4973/M687 750,000 8/16 D. D. & L. Ltd. Forms/C.2118/13.

Instructions regarding War Diaries and Intelligence Summaries are contained in F. S. Regs., Part II. and the Staff Manual respectively. Title pages will be prepared in manuscript.

WAR DIARY
or
INTELLIGENCE SUMMARY.
(Erase heading not required.)

Army Form C. 2118.

Place	Date	Hour	Summary of Events and Information	Remarks and references to Appendices
ROYE	23rd	7.0 pm	No. 2 Company to RETHONVILLERS No 3 Company to CHAMPIEN No. 4 Company attached to 36th Division at W.9.a.4.4. Sheet 66 a. Divisional Headquarters at ~~ROYE~~ NESLE	
—do—	24th		O.C. Train visited Corps & Divisional Headquarters; also saw S.M.T.O. re petrol dump. No 1 Company moved to CARREPUITS.	
		6 pm	Orders received to move with No. 1 Co. to GOUYENCOURT. 4 G.S. wagons detailed to return to CARREPUITS to report ~~to D.A.Q.~~ for duty. No. 2 Co. to CREMERY and on to FRESNOY No. 13 Co. to SOLENTE. No. 4 to GUISCARD.	
GOUYEN-COURT	25th		Division refilled at GOUYENCOURT, Rations drawn from Reserve Ration Store at ROYE	

(A7092). Wt. W12839/M1293. 750,000. 1/17. D. D & L., Ltd. Forms/C2118/12.

Army Form C. 2118.

Instructions regarding War Diaries and Intelligence Summaries are contained in F. S. Regs., Part II. and the Staff Manual respectively. Title pages will be prepared in manuscript.

WAR DIARY
or
INTELLIGENCE SUMMARY.
(*Erase heading not required.*)

Place	Date	Hour	Summary of Events and Information	Remarks and references to Appendices
GOUYEN-COURT	25th		No. 2 Company moved into GOUYENCOURT, also No. 4 Company, rejoining train	
		9.30 p.	Orders received to move at once to LE QUESNEL	
LE QUESNEL	26th		The whole division concentrated during forenoon.	
		2.0 p.	Received orders to march at once to MEZIERES	
			O.C. Train returned to Div. H.Qrs. at LE QUESNEL to arrange about re-filling.	
MEZIERES	27th		Orders received at 7.0 a.m. from D.A.A.G. in person to take command of all surplus Divisional Transport, & to march with Train via MOREUIL JUMEL and St SAUFLIEU to FOSSEMANENT area; arrived 5.30 p.m. S.S.O. remained behind with Supply Officers and details.	

A7092). Wt. W12839/M1293 750,000. 1/17. D. D & L., Ltd. Forms/C2118/14.

Instructions regarding War Diaries and Intelligence Summaries are contained in F. S. Regs., Part II. and the Staff Manual respectively. Title pages will be prepared in manuscript.

WAR DIARY
or
INTELLIGENCE SUMMARY.
(Erase heading not required.)

Army Form C. 2118.

Place	Date	Hour	Summary of Events and Information	Remarks and references to Appendices
FOSSEMANENT	28th		Marched at 8.0 p.m. to MOLLIENS-VIDAME area; arrived 2.20 p.m	
MOLLIENS-VIDAME	29th		Marched at 8.0 a.m. to HUCHENNEVILLE; arrived 3.30 p.m. Supply wagons refilled at LONGPRÉ.	
HUCHENNEVILLE	30		All surplus First Line Transport paraded on main ROUEN – ABBEVILLE road; O.C. Train saw D.D.T. and O.C. A.H.T. Depôt. Handed in First Line Battn Transport of K.O.Y.L.I., Ox. & Bucks L.I. and 10th Rifle Brigade. Train and remainder of Transport moved to CAHON – GOUY area.	

A7092). Wt. W12839/M1297. 750,000. 1/17. D. D & L., Ltd. Forms/C2118/14.

Instructions regarding War Diaries and Intelligence Summaries are contained in F. S. Regs., Part II. and the Staff Manual respectively. Title pages will be prepared in manuscript.

WAR DIARY
or
INTELLIGENCE SUMMARY.
(Erase heading not required.)

Army Form C. 2118.

Place	Date	Hour	Summary of Events and Information	Remarks and references to Appendices
CAHON	31st		O.C. Train reported to D.D.T., also to Area Commandant, St VALERY Sub-area. Further surplus transport from 59th and 61st Brigades arrived.	
			R Standen Lt Colonel Comm'g. 20th Divl. Train	

A7092). Wt. W12839/M1293. 750,000. 1/17. D. D & L., Ltd. Forms/C2118/14.

20th Divn "G"

Herewith War Diary for month of April 1918

T 6/1/18

[signature] Lieut-Colonel
Cmdg 20th Div. Train ASC

Instructions regarding War Diaries and Intelligence Summaries are contained in F. S. Regs., Part II. and the Staff Manual respectively. Title pages will be prepared in manuscript.

WAR DIARY
or
INTELLIGENCE SUMMARY.
(Erase heading not required.)

Army Form C. 2118.

20 D Train

Vol 31

Place	Date	Hour	Summary of Events and Information	Remarks and references to Appendices
CAHON	APRIL 1		O.C. Train reported to D.D.T. Southern at ABBEVILLE and saw O.C. A.H.T.D. with reference to return of surplus transport.	
	2nd		Additional surplus transport from 60th Brigade reported. A.D. of T., Southern called with reference to supply of transport for ammunition convoy.	
	3rd		Seventy wagons under Captain MAY reported at MARTAINNEVILLE at 2.0 p.m. loaded with ammunition and remained the night there.	
	4th		Convoy under Capt. MAY returned, after unloading ammunition at SAIGNEVILLE O.C. Train to Div. Hdqrs. at MOYENVILLE	
	5th		O.C. Train to A.H.T. Depot in a.m. In p.m. to ABBEVILLE to obtain map of new area.	

A7092). Wt. W12839/M1293 750,000. 1/17. D. D & L., Ltd. Forms/C2118/14.

Instructions regarding War Diaries and Intelligence Summaries are contained in F. S. Regs., Part II. and the Staff Manual respectively. Title pages will be prepared in manuscript.

WAR DIARY
or
INTELLIGENCE SUMMARY.

(Erase heading not required.)

Army Form C. 2118.

Place	Date	Hour	Summary of Events and Information	Remarks and references to Appendices
CAHON	5th	6 pm	Heard over phone that orders had been issued for the Divisional Train to rejoin Division. These orders were never received. Fresh instructions received at 11 pm for march at 8 o a.m. 6th	
	6th		Moved off at 8 a.m. to ALLERY. O.C. Train reported to O.C. ABBEVILLE area en route [illegible] pm. O.C. Train reported at Divnl H.Q. DAQMG visited Train at ALLERY with reference to missing Officers kits.	
ALLERY	7th		O.C. Train rode to CAMPS to see about billets, finding no accommodation notified Division & received instructions to stay at ALLERY. Supplies First Line Transport, also baggage wagons, rejoined units.	

A7092). Wt. W12839/M1293. 750,000. 1/17. D. D & L., Ltd. Forms/C2118/14.

Instructions regarding War Diaries and Intelligence Summaries are contained in F. S. Regs., Part II. and the Staff Manual respectively. Title pages will be prepared in manuscript.

WAR DIARY
or
INTELLIGENCE SUMMARY.
(Erase heading not required.)

Army Form C. 2118.

Place	Date	Hour	Summary of Events and Information	Remarks and references to Appendices
ALLERY	8th		O.C. Train to Divnl. Headquarters. Sent to ABBEVILLE in p.m. for remounts. No. 1 Company marched in p.m. to SENARPONT, with instructions to report to Staff Captain RA.	
			2nd Lieut ARCHER relieved Lieut BARNES as Supply Officer 61st Bde.	
	9th		O.C. Train to Divnl. Headquarters. Supply wagons rejoined units. In p.m. O.C. Train visited new area. Received orders to move to HUPPY.	
	10th		Train Headquarters moved to GREBAULT—MESNIL. Brigade Companies rejoined their Brigade areas. O.C. Train to Divisional Headquarters at HUPPY	

A7092). Wt. W12839/M1293. 750,000. 1/17. D. D & L., Ltd. Forms/C2118/14.

Instructions regarding War Diaries and Intelligence Summaries are contained in F. S. Regs., Part II. and the Staff Manual respectively. Title pages will be prepared in manuscript.

WAR DIARY
or
INTELLIGENCE SUMMARY.
(*Erase heading not required.*)

Army Form C. 2118.

Place	Date	Hour	Summary of Events and Information	Remarks and references to Appendices
GREBAULT MESNIL	11th		Train Headquarters moved at 10.30 am to GAMACHES	
			No. 2 Company to BOUVAINCOURT	
			No. 3 " " HOCQUELUS	
			No 4 " " St QUENTIN	
GAMACHES	12th		No 1 Company moved to CAUBERT, near ABBEVILLE	
	13th		Surplus 2nd Line Transport of 1/Ox & Bucks L.I., 10th R.B.s and 7/K.O.Y.L.I. ordered to report to No 2 Section D.A.C., en route for A.H.T.D. ABBEVILLE.	
	14th		O.C. Train visited Brigade Companies	
	16th		Major SOAMES, S.S.O., evacuated sick to HAVRE	

A7092). Wt. W12839/M1293. 750,000. 1/17. D. D & L., Ltd. Forms/C2118/14.

Instructions regarding War Diaries and Intelligence Summaries are contained in F. S. Regs., Part II. and the Staff Manual respectively. Title pages will be prepared in manuscript.

WAR DIARY
or
INTELLIGENCE SUMMARY.
(Erase heading not required.)

Army Form C. 2118.

Place	Date	Hour	Summary of Events and Information	Remarks and references to Appendices
GAMACHES	17th		O.C. Train to No. 1 Co. at ABBEVILLE in a.m. In p.m. orders received for move of Divisional Train. Brigade Companies concentrated at GAMACHES and moved off at midnight under CAPT. LOVE	
FROHEN-LE GRAND	18th		A long march, arrived at 6.0 p.m.	
	19th		Rested horses in a.m., in p.m. marched to HERLIN-LE-SEC area	
HERLIN-LE SEC	20th		Train Headquarters rejoined Division and located at MINGOVAL No. 2 & 4 Companies at TINQUETTE No. 3 Company at CAUCOURT	

A7092). Wt. W12839/M1293. 750,000. 1/17. D. D & L., Ltd. Forms/C2118/14.

Instructions regarding War Diaries and Intelligence Summaries are contained in F. S. Regs., Part II. and the Staff Manual respectively. Title pages will be prepared in manuscript.

WAR DIARY
or
INTELLIGENCE SUMMARY.
(Erase heading not required.)

Army Form C. 2118.

Place	Date	Hour	Summary of Events and Information	Remarks and references to Appendices
MINGOVAL	21st		O.C. train to Div. H.Qrs. in am and to Army Headquarters in pm. Also visited No 3 Company's lines	
	22nd		O.C. Train to Divl. Headquarters and Railhead	
	23rd		A.A. & Q.M.G. visited Brigade Companies and Dumps.	
	24th		12 G.S. Wagons detailed for moving road making material from LIGNY- St FLOCHEL Station.	
			1 N.C.O. and 3 men sent to attend M.G. Course at CARENCY	
	25th		Inspection of First Line Transport of 57th Brigade in conjunction with D.A.D.V.S	

A7092). Wt. W12839/M1292. 750,000. 1/17. D. D & L., Ltd. Forms/C2118/14.

Instructions regarding War Diaries and Intelligence Summaries are contained in F. S. Regs., Part II. and the Staff Manual respectively. Title pages will be prepared in manuscript.

WAR DIARY
or
INTELLIGENCE SUMMARY.
(Erase heading not required.)

Army Form C. 2118.

Place	Date	Hour	Summary of Events and Information	Remarks and references to Appendices
MINGOVAL	26th		Inspected Transport of 61st Field Ambulance in am and of the 60th Brigade in pm	
			Lt FINLAY, A.I.F., joined Train Headquarters for Course of instruction	
	27th		Inspected 62nd Field Ambulance Transport in am and 61st Brigade First Line Transport in pm	
	28th		Capt (W.) C.S. EVANS rejoined Train Headquarters	
			Lieut BARNES admitted to Hospital	
	29th		Inspected Transport of M.G. Battalion (A.C.D. Coy) in am Interview with Divisional Commander reference Transport of Division –	
			In pm inspected Transport of Durham L.I.	

A7092). Wt. W12839/M1293. 750,000. 1/17. D. D & L., Ltd. Forms/C2118/14.

Instructions regarding War Diaries and Intelligence Summaries are contained in F. S. Regs., Part II. and the Staff Manual respectively. Title pages will be prepared in manuscript.

WAR DIARY
or
INTELLIGENCE SUMMARY.
(Erase heading not required.)

Army Form C. 2118.

Place	Date	Hour	Summary of Events and Information	Remarks and references to Appendices
MINGOVAL	30th		61st Brigade moved forward to new area. No. 4 Company to CAMBLAIN – L'ABBE. S.S.O. to forward area with D.A.Q.M.G. Inspected Transport of Divisional Headquarters and 60th Field Ambulance	
			R Standen Lt Col. Commd 20th Divl Train	

(A7092). Wt. W12839/M1293. 750,000. 1/17. D. D. & L., Ltd. Forms/C.2118/14.

Instructions regarding War Diaries and Intelligence Summaries are contained in F. S. Regs., Part II. and the Staff Manual respectively. Title pages will be prepared in manuscript.

Dvl Train

Army Form C. 2118.

WAR DIARY
or
INTELLIGENCE SUMMARY.

(Erase heading not required.)

Vol 32

Place	Date	Hour	Summary of Events and Information	Remarks and references to Appendices
CHATEAU DE LA HAIE	30	pm	Divisional Commander visited Farm and inspected Nos. 2 and 4 Companies at CARENCY	
	31st		O.C. Train visited railhead in am	

[signature] Lt Col.
Comm^g 20th
Divisl Train

(A7092). Wt. W12839/M1293. 750,000. 1/17. D. D. & L., Ltd. Forms/C.2118/14.

Instructions regarding War Diaries and Intelligence Summaries are contained in F. S. Regs., Part II. and the Staff Manual respectively. Title pages will be prepared in manuscript.

WAR DIARY
or
INTELLIGENCE SUMMARY.
(Erase heading not required.)

Army Form C. 2118.

Place	Date	Hour	Summary of Events and Information	Remarks and references to Appendices
	MAY			
MINGOVAL	1st		O.C. Train went to D.H.Q. in a.m. with reference to move of Train Headquarters. Nos. 3 & 4 Company moved forward to CARENCY. S.S.O. went with A.A. & Q.M.G. to see Canadian Railway Company in p.m. O.C. Train went to new area in p.m. to see about billets.	
	2nd		O.C. Train to Divnl Hdqrs. & forward area in a.m. No. 2 Company moved to forward area. Train Headquarters moved in p.m. to VILLERS-AU BOIS. No 1 Co. arrived at MAIZIERES.	
VILLERS AU BOIS	3rd		O.C. Train went to MAIZIERES to see O.C. No. 1 Coy. In p.m. saw O.C. No. 1 Co. 4th Canadian Divisional Train re accommodation for No. 1 Co.	
	4th		O.C. Train visited Companies. In p.m. to Army Headquarters to see D.D. of S. & T. re car. No. 1 Co. moved to ABLAIN St NAZAIRE	

(A7092). Wt. W12839/M1293. 750,000. 1/17. D. D. & L., Ltd. Forms/C.2118/14.

Instructions regarding War Diaries and Intelligence Summaries are contained in F. S. Regs., Part II. and the Staff Manual respectively. Title pages will be prepared in manuscript.

WAR DIARY
or
INTELLIGENCE SUMMARY.
(Erase heading not required.)

Army Form C. 2118.

Place	Date	Hour	Summary of Events and Information	Remarks and references to Appendices
VILLERS-AU-BOIS	5		Went with Capt. LOWE to see about land taken over from 4th Canadian Division for Divisional Farm. In afternoon inspected Light Railway through LIEVIN & VIMY RIDGE	
	6th		O.C. Train visited companies with reference to painting of Divisional sign.	
	7		Train Headquarters moved to CHATEAU de la HAIE. O.C. Train to Army Headquarters in afternoon	
CHATEAU DE LA HAIE	8th		O.C. Train to D.A.D.O.S. and mining area re supply of coal.	
	9th		Visited A.D. of S. at Army Headquarters with reference to coal supplies. Capt. R.E. FORBES, A.S.C. reported for duty, & posted to No. 4 Company.	

(A7092). Wt. W12839/M1293. 750,000. 1/17. D. D. & L., Ltd. Forms/C.2118/14

Instructions regarding War Diaries and Intelligence Summaries are contained in F. S. Regs., Part II. and the Staff Manual respectively. Title pages will be prepared in manuscript.

WAR DIARY
or
INTELLIGENCE SUMMARY.
(Erase heading not required.)

Army Form C. 2118.

Place	Date	Hour	Summary of Events and Information	Remarks and references to Appendices
CHATEAU DE LA HAIE	10th		O.C. Train saw "Q" General at Corps Headquarters with reference to coal supply. Also visited Army Headquarters & Canadian Light Railways. Inspected Transport at WEBB SIDING. Inspn	
	11th		visited Corps Headquarters & fuel dumps with the Corps Fuel Officer.	
	12th		O.C. Train visited LIEVIN with AA & QMG, also 2/Lieut. DOWLING & completed arrangements for salving fuel.	
	13th		2/Lieut. BARNES rejoined for duty from No. 12 Stationary Hospital	
	14th		O.C. Train went on special leave for 3 days to UK. 2Lt ARONSON posted for duty to No. 1 Company	

(A7092). Wt. W12839/M1293. 750,000. 1/17. D. D. & L., Ltd. Forms/C.2118/14.

Army Form C. 2118.

Instructions regarding War Diaries and Intelligence Summaries are contained in F. S. Regs., Part II. and the Staff Manual respectively. Title pages will be prepared in manuscript.

WAR DIARY
or
INTELLIGENCE SUMMARY.
(Erase heading not required.)

Place	Date	Hour	Summary of Events and Information	Remarks and references to Appendices
CHATEAU DE LA HAIE	15th		AA & QMG inspected turn-outs of No. 3 Company 55th & 60th Bde. refilled a second time in pm	
	16th		AA & QMG went to WEDD SIDING in am. and with S.S.O. inspected turn-outs of No. 4 & 1 Co. also saw 2/Lt DOWLING at LIEVIN re coal. To TINCQUES railhead in pm	
	17th		S.S.O. went with AA & QMG with reference to re placement of open Wolseley car	
	18th		2nd Lieut. T.E. Train returned from special leave. MERO reported from hospital	
	19th		O.C. Train visited C. Lt Rly officer with a view to arranging for coal to be brought back from forward area by Decauville. To BARLIN in pm. to see Corps	

(A7092). Wt. W12839/M1293. 750,000. 1/17. D. D. & L., Ltd. Forms/C.2118/14.

Instructions regarding War Diaries and Intelligence Summaries are contained in F. S. Regs., Part II. and the Staff Manual respectively. Title pages will be prepared in manuscript.

WAR DIARY
or
INTELLIGENCE SUMMARY.
(Erase heading not required.)

Army Form C. 2118.

Place	Date	Hour	Summary of Events and Information	Remarks and references to Appendices
			Coal Officer and D.D. of S.&T. at A.H.Q.	
			2/Lieut MEAD transferred from No 1 to No 3 Coy	
			AA & QMG judged turnout of No 3 Company in am	
CHATEAU DE LA HAIE	20th		O.C. Train called at Office of D.D. of S&T with reference to cars for the Train.	
	21st		O.C. Train went with adjutant to LIEVIN where 2/Lieut DOWLING from No 4 company was killed while supervising loading of coal	
	22nd		Inspection of the First Line Transport of 57th Bde	
	23rd		Inspection of Transport of 60th Field Ambulance	
	24		A wet morning. Inspection of First Line Transport of 60th Brigade in afn.	

(A7092) Wt. W12839/M1293. 750,000. 1/17. D. D. & L., Ltd. Forms/C.2118/14.

Instructions regarding War Diaries and Intelligence Summaries are contained in F. S. Regs., Part II. and the Staff Manual respectively. Title pages will be prepared in manuscript.

WAR DIARY
or
INTELLIGENCE SUMMARY.

(Erase heading not required.)

Army Form C. 2118.

Place	Date	Hour	Summary of Events and Information	Remarks and references to Appendices
CHATEAU de la HAIE	25		O.C. Train inspected First Line Transport of 61st Fd. Amb-ulance in am and judged at parade of No. 2 Company.	
	26th		Inspection of 61st Bde First Line Tpt. in am. O.C. Train visited Divisional Farm in pm	
	27th		O.C. Train inspected Transport of 62nd Field Ambulance and 7/ D.L.I. in am and accompanied Brig Genl PARKER to coal dump at CALONNE in pm. 2nd Lt BARNES proceeded on special leave to UK.	
	28th		O.C. Train inspected Transport of Machine Gun Battalion	
	29th		O.C. Train to dump in am. & to office of A.D. of S. with S.S.O. in pm.	
	30th		O.C. Train visited No 1 Co. in am.	

Instructions regarding War Diaries and Intelligence Summaries are contained in F. S. Regs., Part II. and the Staff Manual respectively. Title pages will be prepared in manuscript.

WAR DIARY
or
INTELLIGENCE SUMMARY.
(Erase heading not required.)

20 D Train

Vol 33

Army Form C. 2118.

Place	Date	Hour	Summary of Events and Information	Remarks and references to Appendices
CHATEAU DE LA HAIE	June 1st		O.C. Train saw D.D.S.T. in am reference brigading, and in p.m. to BARLIN to see the Corps Fuel Officer.	
	3.		Train Headquarter mess destroyed by fire. S.O. to new railhead at SAVY-BERLETTE. O.C. Train to Army Headquarters in p.m.	
	4.		Court of Enquiry held on cause of fire.	
	5.		Major ARNOLD accompanied the O.C. Train with A.A. & Q.M.G. on his visit to the Corps Fuel Dump.	
	6		2nd Lt J. J. DOWLING returned to his company from CALONNE. O.C. Train to see Corps Fuel Officer.	
	7		2nd Lt W. MEAD left to report to O.C. 40th Div. Train	
	8.		O.C. Train delivered a lecture to Company Commanders & Supply Officers on economy.	
	9.		O.C. Train to WEBB SIDING in the morning –	

(A7092). Wt. W12839/M1293. 750,000. 1/17. D. D. & L., Ltd. Forms/C.2118/14.

Army Form C. 2118.

Instructions regarding War Diaries and Intelligence Summaries are contained in F. S. Regs., Part II. and the Staff Manual respectively. Title pages will be prepared in manuscript.

WAR DIARY
or
INTELLIGENCE SUMMARY.

(Erase heading not required.)

Place	Date	Hour	Summary of Events and Information	Remarks and references to Appendices
CHATEAU de la HAIE	10th		O.C. Train saw DA & QMG XVIII Corps & shewed him a briquette made by No. 2 Company –	
	12th		S.S.O. went to PARIS on two days special leave. No. 1 Company inspected in pk and prizes awarded.	
	13th		O.C. Train to Rail Head, also workshops of Divnl. M.T. Company	
	14th		61st Brigade Horse Show. O.C. Train acted as one of the judges	
	15th		O.C. Train visited Divisional Farm & also saw Nos. 1 & 3 companies regarding briquette making	
	16th		O.C. Train met A.Q.M.G., XVIII Corps at No. 3 Com.	

(A7092). Wt. W12839/M1293. 750,000. 1/17. D. D. & L., Ltd. Forms/C.2118/14.

Instructions regarding War Diaries and Intelligence Summaries are contained in F. S. Regs., Part II. and the Staff Manual respectively. Title pages will be prepared in manuscript.

WAR DIARY
or
INTELLIGENCE SUMMARY.
(Erase heading not required.)

Army Form C. 2118.

Place	Date	Hour	Summary of Events and Information	Remarks and references to Appendices
			-pany lines, the Staff Officer to the C.E. of the Corps was also present; looked at briquetting experiments	
	17th		Saw Divisional Commander with regard to an application by MAJOR ARNOLD for a transfer. Heavy rain 1 in [illegible]	
	18th		O.C. Train to Corps Q in am, to obtain scythes + rakes for cutting hay. G.O.C. inspected No. 1 + 3 Company on parade in evening	
	19th		Adjt to Nos. 2 + 4 Companies re making of coalcakes from salved small coal + clay. Lettuce from Div. Farm issued to units	
	20th		O.C. Train to Corps H.Q. re making of Coalcakes—	
	21st		O.C. Train went with Capt. MAY to Corps Hdqrs.—	

(A7092). Wt. W12839/M1293. 750,000. 1/17. D. D. & L., Ltd. Forms/C.2118-14.

WAR DIARY
or
INTELLIGENCE SUMMARY.
(Erase heading not required.)

Army Form C. 2118.

Instructions regarding War Diaries and Intelligence Summaries are contained in F. S. Regs., Part II. and the Staff Manual respectively. Title pages will be prepared in manuscript.

Place	Date	Hour	Summary of Events and Information	Remarks and references to Appendices
CHATEAU de la HAIE	22nd		O.C. Train accompanied by A.A. & Q.M.G. in his visit to No. 2 Co. at ARLAIN, to see demonstration of Coal cakes. "Q" Corps Staff present. Inspection of D.H.Q. transport in p.m. S.S.O. to Corps Troops Dump to arrange for special issue of rum.	
	23rd		O.C. Train to Corps Headquarters with reference to manufactory of Coal cakes.	
	24th		O.C. Train inspected First Line Transport of 61st Bde. in a.m. Visited Companies later. Conference of Supply Officers under S.S.O. re economies and underdrawals	
	25th		O.C. Train inspected 1st line Tpt. of 60th Bde. then to 7th A. & S. Highlanders to see progress made in use of Coal cakes.	

(A7092). Wt. W12839/M1293. 750,000. 1/17. D. D. & L., Ltd. Forms/C.2118/14.

Instructions regarding War Diaries and Intelligence Summaries are contained in F. S. Regs., Part II. and the Staff Manual respectively. Title pages will be prepared in manuscript.

WAR DIARY
or
INTELLIGENCE SUMMARY.
(Erase heading not required.)

Army Form C. 2118.

Place	Date	Hour	Summary of Events and Information	Remarks and references to Appendices
CHATEAU DE LA HAIE	26th		O.C. Train inspected 57th R.F.A.? in am. Afterwards to coal cake factory at no. 3 Company. Met Corps Fuel Officer & O.C. 1st Corps M.T. Column. 2nd Lieut D C W THOMAS, ASC reported from Base H.T. Depot & posted to no. 4 Co.	
	27th		O.C. Train inspected 1st Line Transport of the Mach. Gun Battalion and 1/1 Durham Light Infantry. Later, visited all four companies of the Train with reference to coal cake —	
	28		O.C. Train proceeded to CAEN on leave	
	29 30		S.S.O. to Corps H.Q. re special tin for carrying complete Iron Ration. Specimen moulds for making coal cakes applied for & sent to H.Q. 24th Div Train	

C. Evans? Capt & Adjt
for O.C. 20th Div Train

(A7092). Wt. W12839/M1293. 750,000. 1/17. D. D. & L., Ltd. Forms/C.2118/14

Instructions regarding War Diaries and Intelligence Summaries are contained in F. S. Regs., Part II. and the Staff Manual respectively. Title pages will be prepared in manuscript.

WAR DIARY
or
INTELLIGENCE SUMMARY.
(Erase heading not required.)

Army Form C. 2118.

20 D Train
Vol 34

Place	Date	Hour	Summary of Events and Information	Remarks and references to Appendices
Chateau de la Haie	July 1st		S.S.O. went to Rail head to arrange for supply of Chloride of Lime for Divnl. Gas Officer.	
	2nd		Divisional Race meeting	
	3rd		Arrangements made for two refillings on 4th for whole Division (less Artillery)	
	4th		Refilling for Divn. at 3.0 p.m. O.C. Train returned from PARIS leave	
	5th		O.C. Train visited D.D. of S.T. and Army Headquarters	
	6th		O.C. Train accompanied Corps Fuel Officer on visit to see deposit of pitch. S.M.T.O. 1st Corps called to see Coal Cake factory. Capt. NORMAN, Claims Officer, went on leave to U.K.	
	7th		O.C. Train visited companies in a.m. Also called at Headquarters 12th Division re Coal Cakes.	

(A7092). Wt. W12839/M1293. 750,000. 1/17. D. D. & L., Ltd. Forms/C.2118/14.

Instructions regarding War Diaries and Intelligence Summaries are contained in F. S. Regs., Part II. and the Staff Manual respectively. Title pages will be prepared in manuscript.

WAR DIARY
or
INTELLIGENCE SUMMARY.
(Erase heading not required.)

Army Form C. 2118.

Place	Date	Hour	Summary of Events and Information	Remarks and references to Appendices
CHATEAU DE LA HAIE	8th		S.S.O. made arrangements for taking part of the Pack, i.e., Preserved meat, Biscuit & Salt, from No. 1 G.H.Q. Reserve Depot.	
			Arrangements made for a War Savings Certificate Lottery in the Train. O.C. Train to WEKE Siding to select site for Coal Cake Factory.	
	9th		Capt. MAY joined Train Headquarters temporarily while managing Coal Cake Factory. 2nd Lieut. DOWLING put in charge.	
	10th		Arrangements made to turn over Secret reserve rations.	
			O.C. 24th Divisional Train called, to inspect Coal Cake Factory.	

(A7092). Wt. W12839/M1293. 750,000. 1/17. D. D. & L., Ltd. Forms/C.2118/14.

Instructions regarding War Diaries and Intelligence Summaries are contained in F. S. Regs., Part II. and the Staff Manual respectively. Title pages will be prepared in manuscript.

WAR DIARY
or
INTELLIGENCE SUMMARY.
(*Erase heading not required.*)

Army Form C. 2118.

Place	Date	Hour	Summary of Events and Information	Remarks and references to Appendices
CHATEAU DE LA HAIE	11th		60 N.C.O.s and men from the M.T. Companies in the Corps attached to the Train for instruction in coal cake making.	
			O.C. Train accompanied D.A.Q.M.G. to ADANCOURT	
	12th		2nd Lieut. LE GROVE admitted to 61st Field Ambulance.	
			O.C. Train to Dump.	
	13th		O.C. Train made arrangements to salve pitch from forward area near BETHUNE.	
			Detachment at refilling point.	
	14th		C.O. visited Coal cake factory in [illegible] 2nd Lieut. G.C. COOKE returned from leave, and attached to No. 2 Company.	
	15th		Coal Cake in lieu of $\frac{3}{4}$ of the fuel ration to men out of trenches issued from today.	
			O.C. Train & S.S.O. fetched pitch from ROUVRY	

(A7092). Wt. W12839/M1293. 750,000. 1/17. D. D. & L., Ltd. Forms/C.2118/14.

Instructions regarding War Diaries and Intelligence Summaries are contained in F. S. Regs., Part II. and the Staff Manual respectively. Title pages will be prepared in manuscript.

WAR DIARY
or
INTELLIGENCE SUMMARY.
(Erase heading not required.)

Army Form C. 2118.

Place	Date	Hour	Summary of Events and Information	Remarks and references to Appendices
CHATEAU DE LA HAIE	16th		O.C. Train went to Army Headquarters with Sample of Coal Cakes.	
			No refilling for Infantry & Divisional Troops.	
	17th		Refilling for the whole division at 9.0 am	
			O.C. Train met D.A.Q.M.G returning off leave.	
	18th		Lt ARONSON took over duties of Supply Officer 60th Bde.	
	19th		O.C. Train visited Nos 1 and 2 company in am and Dump & Coal cake factory in pm	
	20th		To Dump in am. Inspected Coal Cake Factory	
	21st		Hay ration from railhead reduced to 8 lbs.	

(A7092). Wt. W12839/M1293. 750,000. 1/17. D. D. & L., Ltd. Forms/C.2118/14.

Instructions regarding War Diaries and Intelligence Summaries are contained in F. S. Regs., Part II. and the Staff Manual respectively. Title pages will be prepared in manuscript.

WAR DIARY
or
INTELLIGENCE SUMMARY.

(Erase heading not required.)

Army Form C. 2118.

Place	Date	Hour	Summary of Events and Information	Remarks and references to Appendices
CHATEAU de la HAIE	22nd		O.C. [illegible] visited Corps Headquarters to obtain authority to draw trench boards for the Coal-cake factory. Capt. NORMAN returned from leave to U.K. 1 N.C.O. and 15 O.R. attached from 5th M.T. Co. for Coal cake making	
	23rd		S.S.O. drew 5 lbs. of charcoal from D.A.D.S., Army and visited Corps Fuel Office re wood.	
	24th		Capt. WHITTY, S.O. R.A., went on leave, duties taken over by Capt. NORMAN. S.D. of S.&T. visited Coal-cake factory in [illegible]. 2/Lt DOWLING returned to Company duty, and relieved at Coal-cake factory by S.S.M. SEABORNE	

(A7092). Wt. W12839/M1293. 750,000. 1/17. D. D. & L., Ltd. Forms/C.2118/14.

Instructions regarding War Diaries and Intelligence Summaries are contained in F. S. Regs., Part II. and the Staff Manual respectively. Title pages will be prepared in manuscript.

WAR DIARY
or
INTELLIGENCE SUMMARY.
(Erase heading not required.)

Army Form C. 2118.

Place	Date	Hour	Summary of Events and Information	Remarks and references to Appendices
CHATEAU de la HAIE	25th		O.C. Train visited Brickmaking plant with a view to finding a mechanical mixer. DA & QMG Corps visited Coal cake factory – 1 Sergt and 15 OR from VIII Divisional M.T. Co. reported at Coal cake factory.	
	26th		100 heads of lettuce issued as green vegetables	
	27th		O.C. Train inspected First Line Transport of 59th Bde, also 60th Field Ambulance – Arrival of first consignment of Green Vegetables from Base.	
	28th		Conference of Supply Officers in a.m. 2 p.m. inspection of Coal cake factory by Corps Commander	
	29th		18,000 Iron Rations drawn from PERNES. CAPT. MAY crossed to England on special leave	

(A7092). Wt. W12839/M1293. 750,000. 1/17. D. D. & L., Ltd. Forms/C.2118/14.

Instructions regarding War Diaries and Intelligence Summaries are contained in F. S. Regs., Part II. and the Staff Manual respectively. Title pages will be prepared in manuscript.

WAR DIARY
or
INTELLIGENCE SUMMARY.
(Erase heading not required.)

Army Form C. 2118.

Place	Date	Hour	Summary of Events and Information	Remarks and references to Appendices
CHATEAU de la HAIE	29th		O.C. Train inspected transport of 60th Bde. and 61st Field Ambulance –	
"	30th		O.C. Train inspected First Line Transport of 61st Bde. + 62nd Field Ambulance –	
			Turnips drawn from Divisional farm –	
	31st		13 tons of Carrots arrived on pack train	
			O.C. Train presided over a Board on 250,000 Iron Rations at PERNES –	

R Standing Col.
Commd 20th Div. Train

(A7092). Wt. W12839/M1293. 750,000. 1/17. D. D. & L., Ltd. Forms/C.2118/14.

Instructions regarding War Diaries and Intelligence Summaries are contained in F. S. Regs., Part II. and the Staff Manual respectively. Title pages will be prepared in manuscript.

WAR DIARY
or
INTELLIGENCE SUMMARY.
(Erase heading not required.)

20th DIVISIONAL TRAIN

Army Form C. 2118.

VR 35

Place	Date	Hour	Summary of Events and Information	Remarks and references to Appendices
CHATEAU DE LA HAIE	1st		O.C. Train inspected first Line Transport of Machine Gun Battalion & D.L.I. Capt Norman went to U.K. on 5 days special leave, and 2Lt WEBB on 14 days ordinary leave	
	2nd		S.S.O. proceeded to PARIS on duty	
	3rd		O.C. Train to PERNES to sit as President of a Court of Enquiry on Iron Rations at the Field Supply Depot.	
	5th		Meat arrived from Base damaged & dirty owing to enemy action at Base.	
	6th		O.C. Train visited Headquarters of 8th & 24th Trains reference Gymkhana meeting	

(A7092). Wt. W12839/M1293. 750,000. 1/17. D. D. & L., Ltd. Forms/C.2118/14.

Army Form C. 2118.

Instructions regarding War Diaries and Intelligence Summaries are contained in F. S. Regs., Part II. and the Staff Manual respectively. Title pages will be prepared in manuscript.

WAR DIARY
or
INTELLIGENCE SUMMARY.
(Erase heading not required.)

Place	Date	Hour	Summary of Events and Information	Remarks and references to Appendices
✓	7th		Divisional Commander congratulates all concerned upon excellent return of A.S.C. returnable stores during month of July	
	8th		Divisional Train inspected by His Majesty the King at 2.30 pm	
	9th		O.C. Train proceeded to BOULOGNE with reference to printing for Divisional Gymkhana	
	10th		Gymkhana meeting under auspices of the Divisional Train	
	11th		Lt SYKES returned off leave. 2 bombs dropped in lines of No. 2 Co. and 2 casualties therefrom.	

Instructions regarding War Diaries and Intelligence Summaries are contained in F. S. Regs., Part II. and the Staff Manual respectively. Title pages will be prepared in manuscript.

WAR DIARY
or
INTELLIGENCE SUMMARY.
(Erase heading not required.)

Army Form C. 2118.

Place	Date	Hour	Summary of Events and Information	Remarks and references to Appendices
✓	12th		O.C. Train to No. 2 Company's lines to inspect damage done by bombs.	
	13th		Arrangements made for supply of fresh vegetables from Divisional Farm	
	14th		S.S.O. to PARIS on duty, relieved by Capt. NORMAN	
	15th		3 bombs dropped on No. 1 Coy. Camp. Five casualties to N.C.O.s, & one to a horse. Sergt. MATTHEWS died of wounds.	
			O.C. Train to No. 1 Coy. Camp, afterwards to Salvage Dump.	
	16th		O.C. Train to No. 7 Fosse, also to CALONNE re Slag for Coal Cakes.	

(A7092). Wt. W12839/M1293. 750,000. 1/17. D. D. & L., Ltd. Forms/C.2118/14.

Army Form C. 2118.

WAR DIARY
or
INTELLIGENCE SUMMARY.
(Erase heading not required.)

Instructions regarding War Diaries and Intelligence Summaries are contained in F. S. Regs., Part II. and the Staff Manual respectively. Title pages will be prepared in manuscript.

Place	Date	Hour	Summary of Events and Information	Remarks and references to Appendices
✓	17th		O.C. Train to Nos. 2 & 4 Coy. Camps, for inspection by Corps Commander.	
			Major RASHLEIGH, 8th Train inspected & judged H.D. horses, shipped, of Train & Field Ambulances for the Corps Horse Show	
			Lt. WEBB returned from leave.	
	18th		Visit of neighbouring Coal mine managers to Coal Cake factory.	
	19th		O.C. Train went to No. 16 M.A.C. to fetch Dr. Bracey.	
	20th		1st Corps Horse Show at La BUISSIERE	
	21st		Railhead changed to AUBIGNY. Very hot weather 92° in shade. Artillery dump changed to WEBB	

(A7092). Wt. W12839/M1293. 750,000. 1/17. D. D. & L., Ltd. Forms/C.2118/14.

Instructions regarding War Diaries and Intelligence Summaries are contained in F. S. Regs., Part II. and the Staff Manual respectively. Title pages will be prepared in manuscript.

WAR DIARY
or
INTELLIGENCE SUMMARY.
(Erase heading not required.)

Army Form C. 2118.

Place	Date	Hour	Summary of Events and Information	Remarks and references to Appendices
✓	21		SIDING as metre gauge railway does not touch	
			Govt Division finds 9 men for Coal Cake	
			factory in place of M.T. men withdrawn	
	22nd		94° in shade. Corps Commander lectures in	
			Theatre. Divisional Standard Pack commenced	
			Dr Main presided over a Board to interview Coal-	
	23rd		miners. with Major D. WATTS-MORGAN.	
			Corps Horse Show. No. 2 Company second in	
	24th		the G.S. wagon turn-out.	
	25th		To Coal Cake factory.	
	26th		Shortage of fresh meat & bread, owing to R.S.O. using	
			Section 10 3	

(A7092). Wt. W12839/M1293. 750,000. 1/17. D. D. & L., Ltd. Forms/C.2118/14.

Instructions regarding War Diaries and Intelligence Summaries are contained in F. S. Regs., Part II. and the Staff Manual respectively. Title pages will be prepared in manuscript.

WAR DIARY
or
INTELLIGENCE SUMMARY.
(Erase heading not required.)

Army Form C. 2118.

Place	Date	Hour	Summary of Events and Information	Remarks and references to Appendices
✓	27th		O.C. Train ~~too~~ called upon Corps Commander, & presented him with an Aflame Coal-cake model.	
	28th		O.C. Train despatched several parcels of small size Coal cakes to U.K.	
	30th		O.C. Train went to A.H.Q. in am.	
	31st		Conference of Supply Officers. O.C. Train to No. 3 Company.	
			R. Flanders Lt. Col. Comm'd 20th Div'l Train	

(A7092). Wt. W12839/M1293. 750,000. 1/17. D. D. & L., Ltd. Forms/C.2118/14.

Instructions regarding War Diaries and Intelligence Summaries are contained in F. S. Regs., Part II. and the Staff Manual respectively. Title pages will be prepared in manuscript.

WAR DIARY
or
INTELLIGENCE SUMMARY.
(Erase heading not required.)

20 Div Train

Vol 36

Army Form C. 2118.

Place	Date SEPT	Hour	Summary of Events and Information	Remarks and references to Appendices
CHATEAU DE LA HAIE	1st		Capt. NORMAN attached to Corps Troops for temporary duty as S.O.	
	2.		Capt. A.F. WILSON reported for duty from BASE H.T. Depot & posted to no. 1 Co.	
	3		Revised forage ration notified.	
	4		S.S.O. visited Divisional farm with reference to supply of fresh vegetables.	
	5		A quantity of hay & oats at the R.A. dump found unfit for issue, destroyed and replaced by R.S.O. AUBIGNY	
	6		S.S.O. visited Army Headquarters with reference to shortage of oats.	

(A7092). Wt. W12839/M1293. 750,000. 1/17. D. D. & L., Ltd. Forms/C.2118/14.

Instructions regarding War Diaries and Intelligence Summaries are contained in F. S. Regs., Part II. and the Staff Manual respectively. Title pages will be prepared in manuscript.

WAR DIARY
or
INTELLIGENCE SUMMARY.
(Erase heading not required.)

Army Form C. 2118.

Place	Date	Hour	Summary of Events and Information	Remarks and references to Appendices
	7th		O.C. Train visited Coal Cake Factory	
	8th		Sports at Divisional Headquarters	
			30,000 Soda tablets to be issued from WAVRANS	
	9th		Lieut. ROBERTSON proceeded on 14 days leave	
			Bad bacon received on pack train	
	10th		Lt. ARONSON returned from leave & relieved	
			Capt. NORMAN as S.O. Corps Troops. 10 Drivers	
			2 Saddlers & 2 Sergeants reported from	
			R.H.T. Depot.	
	11th		S.S.O. to ~~BARLIN~~ to see Corps Fuel Officer re	
			Coal shortage	
	12th		S.S.O. to ~~BOULOGNE~~ on divisional duty	
	13th		Capt. MASCHMEYER to ~~PARIS~~ with Major BELL	

(A7092). Wt. W12839/M1293. 750,000. 1/17. D. D. & L., Ltd. Forms/C.2118-14

Instructions regarding War Diaries and Intelligence Summaries are contained in F. S. Regs., Part II. and the Staff Manual respectively. Title pages will be prepared in manuscript.

WAR DIARY
or
INTELLIGENCE SUMMARY.
(Erase heading not required.)

Army Form C. 2118.

Place	Date	Hour	Summary of Events and Information	Remarks and references to Appendices
	14th		Capt. EVANS accompanied D.A.Q.M.G. to adjoining area to select billets & standings in case of a move	
	15th		O.C. Train returned from leave in France	
	16		Capt. WILSON took over Divisional Train from Capt. SYKES	
	17		Capt. HOTCHINS proceeded on 14 days leave	
	18		Colonel HUTCHINS and a Staff Officer from the War Office visited Train Headquarters & Coal Cake factory	
	19		Lecture on Transport inspection at lines of 11th K.R.R. Transport Lines.	

(A7092). Wt. W12839/M1293. 750,000. 1/17. D. D. & L., Ltd. Forms/C.2118/14

Army Form C. 2118.

WAR DIARY
or
INTELLIGENCE SUMMARY.
(*Erase heading not required.*)

Instructions regarding War Diaries and Intelligence Summaries are contained in F. S. Regs., Part II. and the Staff Manual respectively. Title pages will be prepared in manuscript.

Place	Date	Hour	Summary of Events and Information	Remarks and references to Appendices
	20th		Lieut. ARCHER met with an accident, and transferred to 62nd Field Ambulance.	
	21st		The Adjutant proceeded on 14 days leave of absence to U.K. Duties taken over by Capt. NORMAN.	
			Refilling at 11.0 am for all groups.	
	22nd		Divisional Sports.	
	23rd		Lt ARONSON resumed Train & duties of S.O. 61st Bde	
	24th		Instructions received re administration of 2nd Line Transport of No. 242 Army Field Artillery Brigade.	
	25th		O.C. Train called upon D.D. of S. & T. at Army H.Qrs.	

(A7092). Wt. W12839/M1293. 750,000. 1/17. D. D. & L., Ltd. Forms/C.2118/14

Instructions regarding War Diaries and Intelligence Summaries are contained in F. S. Regs., Part II. and the Staff Manual respectively. Title pages will be prepared in manuscript.

WAR DIARY
or
INTELLIGENCE SUMMARY.
(Erase heading not required.)

Army Form C. 2118.

Place	Date	Hour	Summary of Events and Information	Remarks and references to Appendices
	26th		O.C. Train to Coal Cake factory. S.S.O. to Divisional Farm.	
	27th		O.C. Train to Corps Headquarters with reference to the continuance of work at Coal Cake factory.	
	28th		Lt. WILSON left for 14 days "Special" leave to United Kingdom. Capt. SYKES took over Divisional Farm.	
	29th		O.C. Train & Lt. DOWLING left for BOULOGNE on 14 days leave to U.K.	
	30th		Major J.L. [illegible] D.S.O. took over duties of acting O.C. Train. Capt Forbes returned off leave	

[signature] Major
a/O.C. 20 Div Train

(A7092). Wt. W12839/M1293. 750,000. 1/17. D. D. & L., Ltd. Forms/C.2118/14.

Instructions regarding War Diaries and Intelligence Summaries are contained in F. S. Regs., Part II. and the Staff Manual respectively. Title pages will be prepared in manuscript.

WAR DIARY
or
INTELLIGENCE SUMMARY.
(Erase heading not required.)

Army Form C. 2118.

20 D Train

Vol 37

Place	Date	Hour	Summary of Events and Information	Remarks and references to Appendices
CHATEAU de la HAIE	Oct 1st		O.C. Train attended Conference at Div. Hqrs discussing enemy's retirement.	
	2nd		O.C. Train to M.T. Company re Coal cake and attended Conference at "Q".	
	3		O.C. rode to VILLERS CHATEL to see 12th Division re move.	
	4		O.C. to MINGOVAL to see O.C. 12th Div Train. Supply Officers inspect rations in supplying points.	
	5th		Conference of Supply Officers re move to MONCHY BRETON area. S.S.O. to see DD of S.T.	
	6th		Move of Division to VILLERS CHATEL area. Train Hdqrs. to MINGOVAL. No. 2 Co. to SAVY, No. 3 to ROCOURT, no. 4 to TINQUETTE	

Instructions regarding War Diaries and Intelligence Summaries are contained in F. S. Regs., Part II. and the Staff Manual respectively. Title pages will be prepared in manuscript.

WAR DIARY
or
INTELLIGENCE SUMMARY.
(Erase heading not required.)

Army Form C. 2118.

Place	Date	Hour	Summary of Events and Information	Remarks and references to Appendices
MINGOVAL	7th		No 1 Co. moved to ACHICOURT under XVII Corps. Capt. & Adj. EVANS returned from leave.	
	8th		S.S.O. saw Corps Agricultural Officer re supply of green vegetables. To BARLIN in p.m. re Coal	
	9th		S.S.O. proceeds to PARIS on leave. duties assumed by Capt J. NORMAN	
	10.		Visit from O.C. 63rd Divnl. Train re taking over billets	
	11th		Arranged to draw 10 tons of coal from 52nd Divisional pack.	
	12th		Pack altered to 13,000 and 1850 horses.	

(A7092). Wt. W12839/M1293. 750,000. 1/17. D. D. & L., Ltd. Forms/C.2118/14.

Instructions regarding War Diaries and Intelligence Summaries are contained in F. S. Regs., Part II. and the Staff Manual respectively. Title pages will be prepared in manuscript.

WAR DIARY
or
INTELLIGENCE SUMMARY.
(Erase heading not required.)

Army Form C. 2118.

Place	Date	Hour	Summary of Events and Information	Remarks and references to Appendices
MINGOVAL	13th		S.S.O. arranged for 21 tons of coal from ARRAS	
	14th		Adjutant to see No. 1 Co. at CHERISY. ~~Capt~~ Lieut	
			A.F. WILSON returned from special leave to U.K.	
	15th		O.C. Train rejoined from 14 days leave in ENGLAND	
	16th		R.A. railhead changed to QUEANT	
	17th		C.O. to Corps HdQrs. in am. & CHATEAU de la HAIE in pm.	
	18th		O.C. Train visited No. 2 Company at TINQUETTE	
	19th		O.C. Train visited coal cake factory at CARENCY and railhead, TINCQUES	
	20th		O.C. Train commenced periodical inspection of first line transport, with 59th Bde.	

(A7092). Wt. W12839/M1293. 750,000. 1/17. D. D. & L., Ltd. Forms/C.2118/14.

Instructions regarding War Diaries and Intelligence Summaries are contained in F. S. Regs., Part II. and the Staff Manual respectively. Title pages will be prepared in manuscript.

WAR DIARY
or
INTELLIGENCE SUMMARY.

(*Erase heading not required.*)

Army Form C. 2118.

Place	Date	Hour	Summary of Events and Information	Remarks and references to Appendices
MINGOVAL	22nd		O.C. Train inspected First Line Trpt of 60th Bde	
	23rd		O.C. Train inspected Divisional Headquarters Transport.	
	24th		O.C. Train inspected First Line transport of 61st Bde. S.S.O. returned from leave.	
	25th		Inspection of 62nd Field Ambce, 7/D.C.L.I. and M.G. Battn.	
	26th		Inspection of 60th Fld. Ambulance & "Durham L.I. Transport.	
	27th		Inspection of First Line transport completed with 61st Field Ambulance.	
	28th		O.C. Train to No. 3 Co. in [illegible]	

(A7092). Wt. W12839/M1293. 750,000. 1/17. D. D. & L., Ltd. Forms/C.2118/14.

Army Form C. 2118.

WAR DIARY
or
INTELLIGENCE SUMMARY.
(Erase heading not required.)

Instructions regarding War Diaries and Intelligence Summaries are contained in F. S. Regs., Part II. and the Staff Manual respectively. Title pages will be prepared in manuscript.

Place	Date	Hour	Summary of Events and Information	Remarks and references to Appendices
MINGOVAL	28th		O.C. Train & S.S.O. visited No. 3 Co. with reference to experimental Coal cakes	
	29th		Warning order received for Division to move to Third Army.	
	30th		S.S.O. & Capt NORMAN proceeded to new rail head and MARCOING	
	31st		Train Hdqrs. + 3 companies entrained for BAPAUME, en route for CAMBRAI.	
			R [illegible] Lt Col. Comd 22nd Divl. Train	

(A7092). Wt. W12839/M1293. 750,000. 1/17. D. D. & L., Ltd. Forms/C.2118/14.

Instructions regarding War Diaries and Intelligence Summaries are contained in F. S. Regs., Part II. and the Staff Manual respectively. Title pages will be prepared in manuscript.

WAR DIARY
or
INTELLIGENCE SUMMARY.
(Erase heading not required.)

20 D Train

Army Form C. 2118.

48 38

Place	Date	Hour	Summary of Events and Information	Remarks and references to Appendices
Cambrai	1.		Train H.Q^s & Bde Coy of the Train arrived at CAMBRAI Railhead changed to MARCOING	
	2.		1 Coy of the Train moved with RA to SAULZOIR Movement orders received during night S.S.O to M.T. Coy & to see Supply Officers re supply arrangements during the move	
AVESNES-LEZ-AUBERT	3.		Train H.Q^s moved to AVESNES-LEZ-AUBERT, 2 Coy to CAUROIR 3 Coy to RIEUX & 4 Coy to CAGNONCLES	
	4		Commanding Officer to CAMBRAI R'head in a.m. & to 1 Coy in p.m. No^s 2 & 4 Coy moved to ST AUBERT & 3 Coy to VENDIGIES S.S.O. to M.T. Coy re dumping of supplies on 5th inst.	
	5.		C.O & S.S.O to Army H.Q^s in p.m.	
VENDIGIES	6		Train H.Q^s moved to VENDIGIES. 1 Coy to JENLAIN. 3 Coy to SEMPERIES & 4 Coy to VENDIGIES	
	7.		No 2 Coy moved to VENDIGIES, 3 Coy to JENLAIN, & 4 Coy to SEMPERIES	

(A7092). Wt. W12839/M1293. 750,000. 1/17. D. D. & L., Ltd. Forms/C.2118/14.

Instructions regarding War Diaries and Intelligence Summaries are contained in F. S. Regs., Part II. and the Staff Manual respectively. Title pages will be prepared in manuscript.

WAR DIARY
or
INTELLIGENCE SUMMARY.
(Erase heading not required.)

Army Form C. 2118.

Place	Date	Hour	Summary of Events and Information	Remarks and references to Appendices
WARGNIES-LE-GRAND	8		Train H.Q^s moved to WARGNIES-LE-GRAND, 2 Coy to JENLAIN, 3 Coy to ST WAAST. Railhead changed to ST AUBERT	
BAVAI	9		Train HQ^s moved to BAVAI Railhead changed to SOLESMES. Refilling delayed owing to late arrival of lorries. Rum & Solidified Alcohol received from C.T.M.T. Coy	
	10		3 Coy moved to BETTRICHIES & 4 Coy to ST WAAST.	
	11		Hostilities ceased at 11.am No 2 Coy moved to ST WAAST & 4 Coy to FEIGNIES. No pack train arrived at Railhead. Rations drawn from Detail Issue Store. No hay available, but flat rate of 13 lbs oats per animal issued.	
FEIGNIES	12		Train HQ^s moved to FEIGNIES, 2 Coy to LA TASNIERES. O.C. Train & S.S.O left for PARIS.	
	13		Major W.A.J Bell ~~[illegible]~~ returned from leave in UK & 2nd Lt D.C.W. Thomas went on 14 days leave to U.K.	

(A7092). Wt. W12839/M1293. 750,000. 1/17. D. D. & L., Ltd. Forms/C.2118/14.

Army Form C. 2118.

WAR DIARY
or
INTELLIGENCE SUMMARY.
(Erase heading not required.)

Instructions regarding War Diaries and Intelligence Summaries are contained in F. S. Regs., Part II. and the Staff Manual respectively. Title pages will be prepared in manuscript.

Place	Date	Hour	Summary of Events and Information	Remarks and references to Appendices
FEIGNIES	14.		2 pack trains cleared at Railhead	
	15		~~[illegible]~~ O.C. Train & S.S.O. returned from Paris. Divl race meeting in afternoon	
	16.		—	
	17		—	
	18		S.S.O to AHQ to see O/c Accounts Branch (DDS&T).	
	19.		Folly attached troops. rationed for 1st time – 104th, 23rd, 126th & 13th Labour Coys also 181st Tunnelling Coy	
	20		—	
	21		—	
	22.		No 1 Coy moved to WARGNIES-LE-PETIT. S.S.O fixed refilling points for 1st day of move	
JENLAIN	23.		Train HQrs moved to JENLAIN, 1 Coy to VENDIGIES, 2 Coy to WARGNIES-LE-PETIT, 3 Coy to ETH & 4 Coy to ST WAAST	
	24.		1 Coy moved to CAMBRAI, 2 Coy to BERMERAIN, 3 Coy to VENDIGIES, & 4 Coy to WARGNIES-LE-PETIT	

(A7092). Wt. W12839/M1293. 750,000. 1/17. D. D. & L., Ltd. Forms/C.2118/14.

Army Form C. 2118.

WAR DIARY
or
INTELLIGENCE SUMMARY.
(*Erase heading not required.*)

Instructions regarding War Diaries and Intelligence Summaries are contained in F. S. Regs., Part II. and the Staff Manual respectively. Title pages will be prepared in manuscript.

Place	Date	Hour	Summary of Events and Information	Remarks and references to Appendices
BERMERAIN	25th		Train HQs moved to BERMERAIN, 2 Coy to ST AUBERT, 3 Coy to AVESNES-LEZ-AUBERT & 4 Coy to VENDIGIES	
	26th		1 Coy moved to BEUGNATRE S.S.O moved to RIEUX	
RIEUX.	27th		Train HQs moved to RIEUX 2 Coy to CAMBRAI, & 4 Coy to CAGNONCLES, 1 Coy to HUMBERCAMP.	
CAMBRAI	28th		Train HQs & 3 Coy moved to CAMBRAI. Rations cut into 2 parts, (1) for embussing parties (2) for parties going by road	
	29th		Train HQs & 3 Coy marched to BEUGNATRE, 2 Coy to HAPLINCOURT & 4 Coy to CAMBRAI	
	30th		Train HQs & 3 Coy marched to BIENVILLERS. 4 Coy moved to BEUGNATRE.	

[signature]
Capt & Adjt
for O.C. 20th Divl Train
RASC

(A7092). Wt. W12839/M1293. 750,000. 1/17. D. D. & L., Ltd. Forms/C.2118/14.

Instructions regarding War Diaries and Intelligence Summaries are contained in F. S. Regs., Part II. and the Staff Manual respectively. Title pages will be prepared in manuscript.

WAR DIARY
or
INTELLIGENCE SUMMARY.
(Erase heading not required.)

Army Form C. 2118.

Place	Date	Hour	Summary of Events and Information	Remarks and references to Appendices
PAS.	Dec 1st		Train H.Qrs moved to PAS. No 2 Coy moved to ARQUEVES & 3 Coy to AUTHIE ST LEGER Railhead changed to DOULLENS.	
	2nd		Commanding Officer left for U.K on 5 days special leave 2nd Lt D.C.W. Thomas returned off leave in U.K No 4 Coy moved to ACHEUX.	
	3rd		Pack Train cleared by Train Transport 2 refillings for Division	
	4th		Adjt to Railhead with S.S.O. S.S.O to conference at Div! Q	
	5th		—	
	6th		—	
	7th		Following Corps Troops attached to Divn for rations viz: 32nd Bde. R.G.A. 181 Coy R.E. 258 Coy R.E. 232 Coy R.E.	
	8th		Conference at Train H.Qrs of Div! Educational officer with Train Coys Educational Officers	
	9th		Commanding Officer returned from 5 days special leave in U.K. Fresh vegetables drawn from 3rd Army Farm at Val-de-Maison.	

(A7092). Wt. W12839/M1293. 750,000. 1/17. D. D. & L., Ltd. Forms/C.2118/14.

Instructions regarding War Diaries and Intelligence Summaries are contained in F. S. Regs., Part II. and the Staff Manual respectively. Title pages will be prepared in manuscript.

WAR DIARY
or
INTELLIGENCE SUMMARY.
(Erase heading not required.)

Army Form C. 2118.

20 D Train
Vol 39

Place	Date	Hour	Summary of Events and Information	Remarks and references to Appendices
PAS	10th		—	
	11th		Railhead changed to ACHEUX	
	12th		Capt C.S. Evans proceeded to U.K on 14 days special leave Capt Whitty to PARIS on 5 days leave	
	13th		S.S.O to 3rd Army Farm re drawing of vegetables	
	14th		Lt W.S. Robertson came to Train HQrs for temporary duty S.S.O to DHQ re shortage of candles. Saw Bde S.Os later re distribution of same.	
	15th		S.S.O to PARIS to purchase Xmas provisions for Divn Lt Robertson assumed duties of a/S.S.O.	
	16th		—	
	17th		Refilling Point for 61st Bde changed from ACHEUX to VAUCHELLES Supply & baggage wagons of C/91 & D/91 Batteries R.F.A. detached with their batteries & proceeded with them to Artillery School	
	18th		a/S.S.O saw Central Purchase Board Officer with reference to drawing straw to supplement hay ration.	

(A7092). Wt. W12839/M1293. 750,000. 1/17. D. D. & L., Ltd. Forms/C.2118/14.

Instructions regarding War Diaries and Intelligence Summaries are contained in F. S. Regs., Part II. and the Staff Manual respectively. Title pages will be prepared in manuscript.

WAR DIARY
or
INTELLIGENCE SUMMARY.
(Erase heading not required.)

Army Form C. 2118.

Place	Date	Hour	Summary of Events and Information	Remarks and references to Appendices
PAS	19th		Hay ration reduced to 5 lbs per animal Balance of ration drawn in straw from Central Purchase Board Dump	
	20th		12 OR (Cabmen) proceeded to collecting station at CAMBRAI for interview 2nd Lt Chapman proceeded on 14 days leave to U.K	
	21st		—	
	22nd		Commanding Officer to Army H.Q. S.S.O. returned from PARIS	
	23rd		2nd Lt G J Dowling posted to BASE Supply Depot BOULOGNE	
	24th		Commanding Officer proceeded to PARIS on 10 days leave.	
	25th		—	
	26th		—	
	27th		S.S.O to PARIS on duty Lt C.R. Crownson to PARIS on 10 days leave	
	28th		—	
	29th		Capt C.S. Evans returned from 14 days special leave in U.K.	
	30th		—	
	31st		—	

C.S. Evans
Capt & Adjt
for O.C. 20th Div Train. R.A.S.C

(A7092). Wt. W12839/M1293. 750,000. 1/17. D. D. & L., Ltd. Forms/C.2118/14.

Instructions regarding War Diaries and Intelligence Summaries are contained in F. S. Regs., Part II. and the Staff Manual respectively. Title pages will be prepared in manuscript.

WAR DIARY
or
INTELLIGENCE SUMMARY.
(Erase heading not required.)

Army Form C. 2118.

20 D Train

VS 40

Place	Date	Hour	Summary of Events and Information	Remarks and references to Appendices
PAS	JAN 1919			
	1st		S.S.O. returned from PARIS	
	7th		Capt. J.W.D. Norman proceeded on leave to U.K	
			O.C. Train to Army Headquarters	
			Issue of cabbages short weight & unfit for issue	
	8th		S.S.O. took D.A.Q.M.G. to Hospital in DOULLENS	
	9th		O.C. Train to No. 4 Co. to deal with case of S. Saddler McDonald	
	10th		O.C. Train went round the companies of the Train with S.S.O	
	11th		Capt. WHITTY proceeded on leave to U.K	
			Divisional Commander inspected Nos. 1. 2. & 3 Companies	

(A7092). Wt. W12839/M1293. 750,000. 1/17. D. D. & L., Ltd. Forms/C.2118/14.

Instructions regarding War Diaries and Intelligence Summaries are contained in F. S. Regs., Part II. and the Staff Manual respectively. Title pages will be prepared in manuscript.

Army Form C. 2118.

WAR DIARY
or
INTELLIGENCE SUMMARY.

(Erase heading not required.)

Place	Date	Hour	Summary of Events and Information	Remarks and references to Appendices
PAS	16th		SSO to PARIS on duty. OC Train to Army Headquarters	
	18th		Inspection of First Line Transport begins with 59th Bde.	
	19th		SSO returns from PARIS	
	20th		Inspection of 60th Bde. Trpt.	
	21st		Inspection of 61st Bde. Trpt.	
	22nd		SSO to see DD of S&T, also accounts branch	
			OC Train inspected Transport of Machine Gun Battn.	
	23rd		OC Train inspected transport of Field Ambulances	

(A7092). Wt. W12839/M1293. 750,000. 1/17. D. D. & L., Ltd. Forms/C.2118/14.

Army Form C. 2118.

Instructions regarding War Diaries and Intelligence Summaries are contained in F. S. Regs., Part II. and the Staff Manual respectively. Title pages will be prepared in manuscript.

WAR DIARY
or
INTELLIGENCE SUMMARY.
(Erase heading not required.)

Place	Date	Hour	Summary of Events and Information	Remarks and references to Appendices
PAS	27th		5th Army ask for S.O. of the M.T. Co. to relieve R.S.O. ACHEUX	
	29th		Divisional Commander inspects Brigade Companies of Train	
	30th		Orders received to prepare for Thaw Precautions. Capt. WHITTY & 2nd/Lt COOKE returned from leave	
	31st		O.C. Train to PARIS on short leave.	

R. Glanden Lt Col.
Comm'd Train

(A7092). Wt. W12839/M1293. 750,000. 1/17. D. D. & L., Ltd. Forms/C.2118/14.

Instructions regarding War Diaries and Intelligence Summaries are contained in F. S. Regs., Part II. and the Staff Manual respectively. Title pages will be prepared in manuscript.

WAR DIARY
or
INTELLIGENCE SUMMARY.
(Erase heading not required.)

Army Form C. 2118.

20 D Train

VIII 41

Place	Date	Hour	Summary of Events and Information	Remarks and references to Appendices
PAS	Feb. 1st		—	
	2nd		—	
	3rd		—	
	4th		Commanding Officer returned from 3 days special leave in Paris	
	5th		—	
	6th		—	
	7th		Capt J W D Worman & Capt F.B. Sykes returned from leave in U.K. C.O & S.S.O to duchenx to see wood dump	
	8th		—	
	9th		C.O to BOIS DE LALEAU re wood supply Arranged for 3 Coy to take same from there to Refilling Point	
	10th		S.S.O to PARIS on special leave	
	11th		—	
	12th		—	
	13th		—	

D. D. & L., London, E.C.
(A10266) Wt W5300/P713 750,000 2/18 Sch. 52 Forms/C2118/16.

Instructions regarding War Diaries and Intelligence Summaries are contained in F. S. Regs., Part II. and the Staff Manual respectively. Title pages will be prepared in manuscript.

WAR DIARY
or
INTELLIGENCE SUMMARY.
(Erase heading not required.)

Army Form C. 2118.

Place	Date	Hour	Summary of Events and Information	Remarks and references to Appendices
PAS	14th		5000 tons of wood in LUCHEUX forest taken over.	
	15th		Thaw precautions came into force & all supplies drawn by Horse Transport from ACHEUX R'head. 2nd Lt D.C.W. Thomas reposted to 13th (Army) Aux[y] Horse Co[y]	
	16th		Lt A C Webb returned from leave in UK	
	17th		SSO returned from special leave in PARIS. Lt C W Le Grove returned from special leave in UK. CO to Army HQ's in afternoon.	
	18th		SSO arranged refilling & change of R'head	
	19th		R'head changed to DOULLENS	
	20th		Supplies drawn from DOULLENS & ACHEUX R'heads. 1 Co[y] moved to MONDICOURT	
	21st		2 & 4 Co[ys] moved to AUTHIEULE. 59th & 61st Bde grouped together & refilled at SARTON. RA & DHQ groups refilled at MONDICOURT	
	22nd		—	
	23rd		—	
	24th		—	

D. D. & L., London, E.C.
(A10266) Wt W5300/P713 750,000 2/18 Sch. 52 Forms/C2118/16.

Instructions regarding War Diaries and Intelligence Summaries are contained in F. S. Regs., Part II. and the Staff Manual respectively. Title pages will be prepared in manuscript.

WAR DIARY
or
INTELLIGENCE SUMMARY.

(Erase heading not required.)

Army Form C. 2118.

Place	Date	Hour	Summary of Events and Information	Remarks and references to Appendices
PAS	25th		Capt F H Hutchins proceeded on leave in UK	
	26th		—	
	27th		SSO to SARTON to arrange wood dump for 3 Bdes	
	28th		—	
			3/2/19	
			[signature] Lieut Colonel Comdg 20th Divl Train RASC	

D. D. & L., London, E.C. (A10266) Wt W3300/P713 750,000 2/18 Sch. 82 Forms/C2118/16.

Instructions regarding War Diaries and Intelligence Summaries are contained in F. S. Regs., Part II. and the Staff Manual respectively. Title pages will be prepared in manuscript.

WAR DIARY
or
INTELLIGENCE SUMMARY.
(Erase heading not required.)

Army Form C. 2118.

Vol 42

Place	Date	Hour	Summary of Events and Information	Remarks and references to Appendices
PAS-EN-ARTOIS	March 1st		—	
	2nd		Commanding Officer proceeded to United Kingdom on 14 days special leave	
	3rd		—	
	4th		S.S.O to Paris on duty	
	5th		—	
	6th		—	
	7th		S.S.O returned from PARIS. Major W.A.J. Bell (O.C. No 1 Coy) proceeded to Corps Concentration Camp for demobilization	
	8th		Lt C.W. Le Grove proceeded to U.K on 7 days special leave	
	9th		—	
	10th		—	
	11th		—	
	12th		—	
	13th		Capt & Adjt C.S. Evans proceeded to U.K on 14 days special leave. Capt J.W.S. Norman took over duties of a/Adjutant	
	14th		52 ORs proceeded to Corps Concentration Camp for demobilization. Capt F.H. Hutchin returned from 14 days leave in U.K.	

D. D. & L., London, E.C. (A10266) Wt W5300/P713 750,000 2/18 Sch. 52 Forms/C2118/16.

Instructions regarding War Diaries and Intelligence Summaries are contained in F. S. Regs., Part II. and the Staff Manual respectively. Title pages will be prepared in manuscript.

WAR DIARY
or
INTELLIGENCE SUMMARY.
(*Erase heading not required.*)

Army Form C. 2118.

Place	Date	Hour	Summary of Events and Information	Remarks and references to Appendices
	March			
PAS-EN-ARTOIS.	15th		—	
	16th		Lt W.S. Robertson returned from 14 days leave in U.K. Capt F.H. Hutchins took over command of No 1 Coy of the Train	
	17th		—	
	18th		—	
	19th		Lt C.W. Le Grove returned from 7 days special leave in U.K.	
	20th		Lt Col R. Standen returned from 14 days special leave in U.K.	
	21st		Lt V.R. Cronson & 50 ORs proceeded to Corps Concentration Camp for demobilization.	
	22nd		Lt Col R Standen left to report to War Office for demobilization in U.K. Capt C.S. Maschmeyer assumed command of the Train	
	23rd		—	
	24th		—	
	25th		—	
	26th		—	
	27th		S.O. RA & all supply personnel moved to DOULLENS Railhead	

D. D. & L., London, E.C. (A10266) Wt W5300/P713 750,000 2/18 Sch. 52 Forms/C2118/16.

Instructions regarding War Diaries and Intelligence Summaries are contained in F. S. Regs., Part II. and the Staff Manual respectively. Title pages will be prepared in manuscript.

WAR DIARY
or
INTELLIGENCE SUMMARY.
(Erase heading not required.)

Army Form C. 2118.

Place	Date	Hour	Summary of Events and Information	Remarks and references to Appendices
PAS-EN-ARTOIS	March 28th		Capt R.S. Forbes left for Corps Concentration Camp for demobilization	
	29th		—	
	30th		Capt & Adjt C.S. Evans returned from 14 days special leave in U.K. Lt W.S. Robertson & Lt. C.W. le Grove left to report to O.C. 62nd Divl Train	
	31st		Lt. G.C. Cooke left to report to O.C. 41st Divl Train	
			C.S. Evans Capt & Adjt for O.C. 20th Train	

D. D. & L., London, E.C.
(A10266) Wt W3300/P713 750,000 2/18 Sch. 52 Forms/C2118/16.

Instructions regarding War Diaries and Intelligence Summaries are contained in F. S. Regs., Part II. and the Staff Manual respectively. Title pages will be prepared in manuscript.

WAR DIARY
or
INTELLIGENCE SUMMARY.

(Erase heading not required.)

Army Form C. 2118.

20 D Train

98 43

Place	Date	Hour	Summary of Events and Information	Remarks and references to Appendices
PAS-EN-ARTOIS	April 1st		—	
	2nd		Capt J. W. D. Norman & Lt A. C. Webb proceeded en route to report to O.C. 41st & 62nd Divl Train respectively	
	3rd		—	
	4th		Capt C. F. Collinge left for demobilization	
	5th		—	
	6th		—	
	7th		—	
	8th		—	
	9th		—	
	10th		Capt L. A. Hargreaves repatriated from 62nd Divl Train	
	11th		Capt G. H. Colepaw left for demobilization	
	12th		Capts F. H. Hutchins & F. B. Sykes left to report to 62nd Divl Train	
	13th		Lt. A. R. Young repatriated from 62nd Divl Train	
	14th			
	15th/22nd		—	
	23rd		Capt H. V. Ward repatriated from 41st Divl Train	
	24th		—	

D. D. & L., London, E.C.
(A10266) Wt W5300/P713 750,000 2/18 Sch. 52 Forms/C2118/16.

Instructions regarding War Diaries and Intelligence Summaries are contained in F. S. Regs., Part II. and the Staff Manual respectively. Title pages will be prepared in manuscript.

Army Form C. 2118.

WAR DIARY
or
INTELLIGENCE SUMMARY.
(Erase heading not required.)

Place	Date	Hour	Summary of Events and Information	Remarks and references to Appendices
	25th		Capt & Adjt. C.S. Evans to U.K on 8 days special leave. Capt L.A. Hargreaves left for demobilization camp.	
	26th/27th		—	
	25th		Lt W.R. Chapman to DOULLENS Railhead for duty with R.S.O.	
	29th/30th		—	

C.S. Evans
Capt
a/ O.C. 20th Train RASC

D. D. & L., London, E.C.
(A10266) Wt W3300/P713 750,000 2/18 Sch. 52 Forms/C2118/16.

www.ingramcontent.com/pod-product-compliance
Lightning Source LLC
Chambersburg PA
CBHW080807010526
44113CB00013B/2339
* 9 7 8 1 4 7 4 5 1 1 6 9 8 *